Published by Cacti-Knights

ISBN: 978-1-62154-875-1
First edition: 18th April 2012
Copyright ©2012 by Cacti-Knights

Cover artwork by Alex Polanco www.entheogenart.com

The Reemergence of Man
Kailin

There will come a time when you believe everything is finished, that will be the beginning - Louis L'Amour

For Riley, Laine, and Luke.

Extended Prologue – Part 1

Man counted the planets revolutions around the sun as years, and after another wipe-out and reset of man's recorded history and knowledge, man started to re-emerge again around 11,000BC. The trauma of whatever happened before this time was buried deep into the collective unconscious, and this new epoch would slowly dive down to a dense energy substrate, with man becoming extremely separated from one another.

From this time not much was recorded for many millennia, but remnants of great feats of high consciousness and sacred living were evident from lands known as Egypt, Persia, Tibet, India, England, and the America's. And much scattered symbolism linked-up to point towards higher intelligence and a hybridisation of the specie.

The sacred arts of these ancients never fully died though.

Man repopulated and spread to much of the earth, creating many vibrant languages, traditions, nations, and sub cultures, trading and bartering goods and knowledge.

0AD to 1000AD

After many battles and wars before 0AD, man continued to struggle to live in peace. Battles, skirmishes, and small wars ensued, all fuelled by a leader or regimes' quests for power, conquest, or spread of a belief system.

A small populous known as Athenians created what became known as true democracy. Every member of the city regardless of his standing or way of life had a say in every decision via an equal voting system. This city thrived like no other, until corruption and ego-greed reared its head.

Fragmented but sacred core remnants from ancient civilisations became roots for main global religions. Much of the more mystical streams transmuted over time and developed into splintered hidden doctrines passed from mouth to ear; Tantra, Hermetics, Qabala, Vedic, Sufism, Druidism, and Shamanism.

Gold was used for bartering all around the world, paper money was first used in China, and some of the first embryos of banks emerged within the Roman Empire.

The two largest libraries in the world in Alexandria and Pergamon were destroyed, and the books disappeared. Many finding their way to the Vatican.

Mystical teachings continued to thrive in Europe and the Middle East.

1000AD to 1900AD

It was a low time in the evolution of man. Kings took over lands via murder and war, and people were forced to live in growing feudal systems, were they had to work and fight battles in exchange for a little land with no rights. A first administrative authority of its type, The Doomsday book in England, listed all lands, values, and owners.

Laws controlling millions sprung from the benchmark of the Magna Carta which helped remove common law.

Slavery based upon skin colour was rife.

Religions such as Catholicism, Islam, and Darwinism pushed violent doctrines of externalised dogma to control and eventually socially condition billions. The sixth edition of Darwins book in 1872 was changed from, *On the Origin of Species by Means of Natural Selection, or the Preservation of Favoured Races in the Struggle for Life,* to, *The Origin of Species.* This was to stop the general public knowing of the eugenics links.

Witches, hermetics, shaman, and alchemists were hunted down and murdered by the Catholic Church.

The first official banks appeared in twelfth century Italy during the Renaissance period. Aristocratic families loaned money backed by nothing at interest, and by the sixteenth century large Jewish banking family dynasties had sprung up in other parts of Europe and started to control governments, revolutions, and monarchs. In the late nineteenth century America had seen its first central Bank come and go amidst public outcry, whilst commercial bank notes (paper money) were now being used worldwide.

Indigenous sacred tribes in many countries were slaughtered and their countries taken over by sea-faring colonial countries seeking imperialism.

Hiding behind Marxism, a social experiment named communism was created. In which billions were treated like robots by dictators, and the death of millions occurred by starvation and execution.

1900AD to 2000AD

Consciousness jumped in this time, coaxed along its rising curvature by the vast jumps in technology. But where technology could help man it was sold for profit at low efficiency and short durability. It was used to gain control of empires, lands, people, and to further agendas.

Larger central banks were formed and soon gained control over nations via debt. Mega-corporations gobbled up competition and people, whilst polluting the planet in the name of financial profit. Two world wars using the most advanced technology on the planet took place, including biological warfare, mind control, genetic supremacy (eugenics), and genocide, all at the large profit of the central banks. In this, the atomic bombs was invented by the world's *leading* scientists and dropped on cities.

DNA was found, man went into space, and a sheep was cloned.

High speed transport, the internet, mobile communications, and computing all came and grew. Big pharmaceutical corporations took over medical research whilst shutting down much of natural holistic and herbal healing.

Free energy from water and Tesla's zero point energy was hushed, and the large corporations took their grip over nations using the puppet authorities (governments), propaganda from a media monitor device in every home (television), and their tentacles of force (armies). Even modified drinking water was sold for profit, as were houses, food, and energy.

People needed to sign forms and exist in databases to travel, to be born, and to move or do anything in this new technological world. Unknown to the masses this was a scam based upon maritime law, where someone signed or gave permission they then entered into a corporate contract based upon a straw man.

All was scrutinised and authorities and laws increased under the umbrella of a small world elite. An elite that had slowly begun to control food, energy, education, finance, health, entertainment, science, and the media, without hardly three percent of the populous realising this was so – they thought they were free, they thought this system was here forever and that life here in this form was to be experienced *this* way. This duping of minds was linked to the covertness of the elite, hiding behind banks, corporations, governments, think tanks, organisations, and foundations.

Behind most were two family dynasties – the Rockefellers and the Rothschild's. They were not tangible enough to grasp, and nobody really cared. The elder generation in this time was still in trauma from the last world war, and was busy seeking comfort, security, and entertainment via the systems illusory outlets. The younger generations struggled to climb the systems ladder, and sleepily plodded along the narrow road of work, entertainment, debt, and stagnation. They had no say in the world around them, and their reasoning was dumbed down so much their minds did not even register these facts.

Subliminal advertising grew, and people in tick-tock biorhythms started to seek short term happiness spikes and status through material gain and ignorance of the true 'I.'

Corporate led cultures conditioned minds, and the multi-vaccinated young were taken away at ages of five to be indoctrinated into the taxpaying system that sat within a globalised capitalistic system. A system represented by ugly buildings built for cheap practical efficiency, instead of celebration, or devotion to life itself. The consumer was steadily being lobotomised by sugar coated distraction and instant convenience, while the very life blood of humanities respective cultures was dribbling away between the cracks.

Civil obedience and wilful ignorance were the biggest diseases, they were rife, contagious, and spreading. People loved their servitude. People were coded to never think change would come. People acted based on what they thought and what they knew, and as they were trained what to think and drip fed only certain knowledge, they acted as designed to. They looked at their children as items to please, to make happy, to administer fun to, never giving a thought to the world they would inherit.

....it was getting messy, human consciousness was sinking deeper and deeper into matter, like fireflies sinking into the swamp.

2000 to T0

The internet grew in popularity and *necessity*, and soon everything existed a click away in real-time. Information, books, life footage, opinions, events, theories, truths, collaborations, videos, identification, and creativity all increased exponentially, and soon the people were *online* whilst at work, home, and on the move.

The surge of the out-of-control internet and its plethora of information led to some truths being known; The scam of paper money being created out of nothing to be loaned at interest, the scam of oil, the scam of the mainstream news channels, the scam of false flag terror attacks to pre-empt military and corporate invasions, the scam of removing freedoms (and people) under the guise of security, the scam of the pharmaceutical corps, the scam of insurance, the scam of the whole reality and what a human actually was. A small percentage woke up.....but they were ridiculed.

More information came; that of manmade diseases, of genetically modified food, of toxins in the water and foods, of assassinations, of free energy suppression, of eugenics groups, of nations being asset stripped by central banks, of governments paying interest on loans to central banks from the peoples tax and poverty (austerity) laws. Of big brother control, of planned and created economic turmoil, of the stripping of rain forests, of the reality of radiation disasters from corporate nuclear power errors, all whilst the finance sector made more money than any manufacturing or innovative areas.

The controlled finance system was designed to fail as their debt based currencies were loaned into existence on computers. The interest that had to be paid back on the debt was more than the money in circulation; hence debt could only rise and inevitably kill the currency. Within this, the elite controlled the value of money by tinkering with inflation and the amount of money in supply, enabling them to become extremely money-rich, and more importantly in this capitalistic society, powerful.

With this level of control over the masses, they started to group billions of humans under single currencies and single laws, with one army, one bank, and a handful of corporations to control and sustain their needs, desires, and whims. The created debt within the finance system was bailed out by the people's taxes and savings funds under the guise of *helping the economy*, effectively ridding the world of the middle class. In the fake world there was money, but in the real world there were slaves who worked for the psychopathic rulers who lacked in emotion and conscience.

It was a bit late but some people worked out the whole system was run by a few, realising they were living in a world with illusions drummed into them via conditioning. As more people saw parts or most of the control-suppression agenda, disparate large protests started all across the globe. Corporate mind-conditioned police were brutal to the people whilst the mainstream news channels turned a blind eye or lied for corporate gain. The social side of the internet became more important as it spread truths and realities of the uprisings in real time, enabling even more people to wake up. Momentum was gaining, and in many increasingly populated cities, more unrest and protest ensued.

In these times, more young people started travelling and seeking new experiences, more diversity in art was being created, things were becoming more disparate. Some let the system fall away, they saw it was false and crumbling; they didn't wrench themselves from it, just ignored it to live a freer more authentic life. Some looked to self-sustainable communities, to creating cooperatives. Some looked to shamanic and ancient ways, or to look at one's *own* shadow.

Some saw the illusion and knew change was coming. Change was in the air, and it crackled and hissed. Many looked to the ancient prophecies, to specific dates, and some started to move away from the collapsing, unevenly stacked, money system.

It was like a race to an archetypal finish line, more control versus more awareness. An Internet police force was formed to thwart free information and the hackers that attacked the system. Internet passports came about alongside the growing internet filtering, but there were always ways around it. A cat and mouse game ensued with the internet mice often winning. All emails, voice calls, and locations were recorded, monitored, and stored, and the elite were grooming the G20 to be a new world order front with the UN and NATO bruiser wings to enforce the law of the elite. Most of the species wanted a world government to solve the marketed world problems and queued up gleefully to join and obey.

***

In the second decade of the twenty first century there was an agenda moving forward much unknown to the awakening masses, that of Transhumanism.

It morphed from its earlier experiments in the elitist pseudo-science, eugenics, and was launched forward in the World Genome Project, where knowledge of how to decode DNA was gained.

The goal was to transcend the human by merging biology and technology, to create the posthuman with the ability to upgrade and downgrade humans. The economy was the elephant in the living room, the red herring, as the elite knew they had to destroy an old system whenever they wished to roll out a new one.

The elite wanted to use and control the fact that AI and quantum computing were evolving millions of times faster than man's intelligence. Computer science was no more about computers than astronomy was about telescopes, it was really all about intelligence and information.

As a created economy collapse was progressing, trillions of dollars of funding still slipped to the army of labs via the biotech corps, military, and universities.

At the time, this agenda was already taking its slow march into consciousness; genetically modified and genetically created plant and food seeds were invented in labs, then patented and aggressively distributed.

Drone planes killed civilians, vaccines with toxic cocktails and viruses were administered via fear, microchips were inserted under the skin, genetically modified food was worldwide with misleading labels, and wireless and other networks such as 4G invaded brain frequencies. Geoengineering and corporate pollution ensured natural ecologies fell apart, resulting in the planets carbon dioxide levels being at an all time low. Plants died, bees died, birds fell out of the sky, whales beached themselves, farmers committed suicide, sperm counts lowered, and many places experienced a strange white hazy sky. And as solar flare activity increased (creating changes at a cellular level), and ionispheric HAARP technology was experimented with, more *natural* disasters occurred, killing and wrecked lives.

Life was mutating, and man didn't even know it.

The areas of development in the transhumanism agenda were mainly NBIC (nano, biological, information, and cognitive) and GNR (genetic, nano, and robotic) technologies. Merging the bits from computers, the neurons from cellular networks, and the genes from Biotech. But many related areas were being developed at this time, in a whole new language that the main media channels kept relatively hidden:

AI - intelligent sentient life forms created from computers and/or biotech that have the ability to learn, think, perceive, and grow.
Bioinformatics - process of collecting data from a biological system to understand it.
Biomedical – the closing of the gap between medicine and engineering.
Biomimetics - the study of the function of biological systems as models for the design and engineering of materials and machines.
Biotech - genetic, cell, or tissue technological applications that use biological systems and living organisms.
BMI - brain machine interfaces
Cognitive - an information processing view of an individual's or social movements psychological functions and dynamics.
Cryonics - freezing bodies or heads of humans for future use and re-activation.
Cybernetics - understand the capacity and limits of any system, whether technological, biological, or social.
Genomics - a discipline in genetics concerning the study of the genomes of organisms.
Memetics - an approach to evolutionary models of cultural information.
Nanotechnology - the space measured between one atom and about 400 atoms.
Neuroprosthetics- the ability to substitute a motor, sensory, or cognitive modality, such as artificial neural prostheses (limbs).
Neuroengineering - the repair, replace, enhance, or otherwise exploit the properties of neural systems in the brain and tissues.
Transgenisis - the process of introducing a foreign gene, called a transgene, into a living organism so that it will exhibit a new property.

They knew that if the Cognitive Scientists could think it, the Nano people could build it, the Bio people could implement it, and the IT people could monitor and control it, while they could manage and steer it from above.

This agenda had already put strings of DNA together, cloned animals, created robotic blood cells, invented GNA and PNA, kept a human brain alive whilst out of the skull, grown ears, organs, meat, and wings on chickens. Altered baby genes inside the womb, created nano-engines, created self replicating nanobots, grown brain cells, inserted bootable DNA into cells, controlled a network of brain cells, created e-skin, recorded neuron data activity in the brain, interfaced neurochips into the brain, placed microchips into pets, put genes onto nanochips, manipulated individual protein molecules and cellular nanostructures, created exoskeletons for soldiers, and invented AI bots that created profiles upon personal trends. And as always throughout technical history, much more was held back from prying eyes and ears, and the military had the main pick of the fruits.

Transhumanism had a massive PR marketing and subliminal conditioning campaign well underway. Instead of "racial hygiene," they promoted "sociobiology," and instead of "deficient genes" they promoted "superior genes." The techno-progressives peddled that the immune system was not good enough in its natural state, and promoted enhanced happiness, longer life, raised consciousness, telepathy, cures, increased intelligence, and enhanced tools for learning and creativity.

They flounced that they could eventually overcome the weaknesses of a frail biological body by merging with machines, and eventually obtain the ability of exploring the cosmos without the problems of maintaining human bodies. The image was that if you didn't embrace transhumanism you would be left behind. Those that succumbed to the PR embraced this future willingly, and many of those that had not even been privy to the PR were subconsciously willing anyway. Most saw a dreamy utopian landscape.

But the elite had a true agenda far different to that which they spun, an agenda they'd been implementing slowly for decades with the slow bombardment in schools and the media. They made people feel like they were competing and needing to improve externally, issuing a low self esteem in every way they could. In many parts of the world people looked to cosmetic surgery to find happiness as they were so low with what they naturally were. Hundreds of millions brought prescribed drugs daily, and others played computer games or watched TV shows with upgraded men or soldiers. The true agenda was being implemented slowly, just like the frog in boiling water.

Smartphones were aggressively pushed into popularity, and then became tracked by law and used as payment devices as the species marched towards a cashless society. A laboratory created H1N1 virus was unleashed via worldwide marketed fear, and many queued up to pay for mysterious vaccines. Children in schools were forced to have multiple vaccines too, with punishments of fines or even imprisonment for those declining, all whilst hospitals sent organs, embryo's, and placentas to the Biotech labs, and pop artists became virtual. The agenda was moving forward.

The elite wanted ultimately to direct and control evolution and human enhancement, to create a slave race with a hive mind, a Homo Evolutis. To do this the transhumanists created the problems they wanted to solve; the fear of death, depression, and hopelessness. As with eugenics the elite looked at humans as cattle stock, but this time also as useless, jobless, eaters.

But where Eugenics sterilisation and destruction of the weak programmes were found out, Transhumanism hid behind helping the species. One covert goal was to remove sexual desire and free will from man, making it easier to create workers in a beehive controlled by networked brain chips. All within a synthetic reality.

There were two singularities they strived for, one where a technological hive mind would merge with the biological brain, and two, where a human mind could be uploaded to a synthetic organism; be that a computer, cyborg, network, or AI of some kind. Some earth like planets were found in this time, and the elite ultimately wanted to be able to explore as post-human.

Hidden papers and reports from the twisted, atheistic, and wealthy scientists stated that both of these singularities were inevitable, and that the current human would soon become more obsolete than a monkey is to the current human.

As the species entered slowly and unknowingly into the transhumanists age of transition, the narcissistic elite cognative modelled societal behavior to allow easy predictions. They always remained two or three steps ahead of the half-awakened protesters.

The collective subconscious did not know it at the time, but Transhumanism was the new religion, the religion of the elite, a religion of Transhuman fundamentalists that cared not for the thirty thousand children that died each day from starvation.

***

False beliefs were the curse of this time. Like spiritual locusts they swarmed across the open planes of post-rational spirituality and robbed the people of the fruition of cosmic truth; using the individual human being as an unassuming host for their ignorant and self seeking lies and assumptions. If only the people started to think truly they would've been accountable.   Many that had the heart and soul to help fell into the new-age traps, where they only thought positive thoughts, and only placed awareness into the present moment, nullifying them from what was going on.

Reality was hacked, the human mind was hacked, which in turn shut down the soul, resulting in humans' experiencing just a tiny fraction of what they could within their potential blueprints.

There was only so much this whole reality fractal could take, the natural harmonic swung back with force, there was only so much disconnection from what is, *what is* can tolerate. False idols, greed, slavery, externalisation, elitism, toxicity, and sub conscious-conditioned slaves…..who thought they were free.

In times of great stress, when pre-existing environments, whether physical, social, or both, become unsustainable, gradual change is no longer able to maintain equilibrium, and the forces of revolutionary evolution are energised.

Consciousness was left at the door and it could not continue anymore. Not for the earth organism, the collective consciousness, the collective unconscious, the mineral, vegetable, or animal kingdoms, it was all too much, all too toxic.

Something had to give, a gasket, many knew it was coming, and then it came – with perfect harmony, with perfect destruction and devastation.

A total system collapse occurred.

Extended Prologue – Part 2

In the second decade of the twenty first century, the tipping point(s) and event(s) occurred in quick succession. It was like dominos or spinning plates all falling at near the same time. Akin to a snowball tipping off a mountain to become a non stoppable avalanche of beautiful, natural, harmonious, unmerciful, crashing destruction to existing paradigms.

The impeding force of these events rang loudly in the collective consciousness, shattering the minds of many, and shattering emotional body energy systems like a laser through soft cheese. Many souls perished without even a whimper or cry, and many of the remaining were thrown into schizophrenic or numb zombie states due to the trauma of the new reality state. A state with no illusory handrails or safety nets. For some, the trauma blew their minds, it was too much and they still walked around the empty malls in dull madness, with their personalities, stories, and narrow lives blown to bits.

But change was needed objectively, and for whatever chaos was evident in the minds of man at this time, it was as a fractal no different to the chaos shingle shows as an old wave retracts, ready for a new fresh larger wave to come forth at an oceans shore.

In the future this time became known as TRUE ZERO, or simply T0. A new reset of the yearly count based upon these massive changes, but starting on the vernal equinox instead of the meaningless January first..

T0

Chaos ensued, the cash machines were dormant never to return, the wheels of supermarket lorries ceased to roll, and policemen and military were with their families with little hierarchy, organisation, or money to coax them. Each person was in a state of shock thinking of water, food, and warmth.

Looting took place, vigilante groups formed, and fear and paranoia created a layer of icing on the cake of trauma and disbelief. Good men with hungry families soon turned into desperate men, and shootings, murders, robberies, and vengeance was common place, alongside men who stepped up to share and help. Many stayed in their homes with their trust at an all time low.

Early in these times, most said that the world was broke, but it wasn't the world, the planet was perfect, it was human society that had broken (itself), and in this time it was the destabilised human mind that was near breaking. The chaos that reigned in this time was not the world in chaos, it was the chaos within the minds of men. Where were the handrails? Where were the safety nets? Where were the authorities? But these thoughts were to be directed internally, not externally, but this took many more years to work out.

Some places were danger zones, other places were in a state of surprising cohesion and relative harmony, but the feelings of *what to do? What will happen?* Filled the thoughts of man in many walks of life, or limbo. It was fragmented, disparate, and desperate.

From the tipping point(s), the population of man was reduced to around eighty four million souls, the east and southern hemispheres were near depopulated completely. Though to the odd Mongolian traveller or Peruvian tribe nothing much had changed, one still collected water and one still watched the sunset with the children. Out of all the remnants of the species no one really knew the numbers that remained, and numbers between twenty million and hundred million were banded about in glee and in morning.

The DNS servers were fried, and the techy maintainers of the fractured Internet structure were more concerned with food and panic. Some tiny isolated pockets of the internet were still live, as were small fragments of transport, radio, and fossil fuels. Not much else though, and these fragments were dimming too. These scraps that remained live were due to the workers not ever knowing anything else. They continued their routine of doing what they knew whether it be flying a plane, moving gas, working at a hospital, or talking on a radio station. They were in denial and suppression, but nevertheless, this still helped in its own way.

Some on grid water, gas, and electricity still functioned, but most didn't, and people ran, drove, and walked from the cities to seek a more natural life until the chaos died down. On the flip side others were drawn to the cities to seek safety in numbers, lured by the magnetic cauldron of opportunity, but overall most people stayed were they were, frozen in trauma and in fear of moving to an unknown.

There were no rules, no norms, it was jokers wild, and though the dangers existed alongside acts of unity and sharing, the most obscure happening was that of the people in mental limbo, a zombie state. These were vacant, still waiting for the authorities to come and help. The routine and security before the tipping point was a condition rooted so deep in the minds of many, that nothing could rock them enough to transmute beliefs or states of being.

But slowly the collective consciousness was shifting, it was at a deep level realising that the last empire of the planet, that in the shape of a capitalistic globalised system was an illusion, and created little positivity, or potential-enhancing canvases for humanity, or the planet. There were some that detached and observed with stillness as the world started to go through its changes, they became mindful that beauty and harmony existed even within chaotic destruction.

In this year more crop circles and strange sightings in the sky were witnessed than ever before by the human eye, alas, there was no YouTube to share it, nor many batteries to fuel the mobile phone video cameras.

T3

After three years all the bullets ran out and all the shelves were empty in the shops and warehouses. There were now more people helping and uniting and less vigilante gangs and lone murderers. It became obvious that the big budget movies showing post-system chaos in the prior decades were to make people love and idolise the toxic system. Running for the hills with guns was a myth that was only evident the rarest pockets. The trauma of change had hit the collective consciousness so hard that a sense of unity grew, along with a heightened sense of feeling. Neighbours who had rarely acknowledged each other before, became brothers, and people who felt alone now felt more alive, within a sense of belonging, even amidst survival. Anarchy was less evident as anarchy was against the system, and there was no system.

No one made bullets, no one wanted to take a tank from the stock yards, and more people wanted to help. Over five billion people had been wiped from the planet and most wanted to get on with it and help in some small way. People began to look at the big questions internally about life, the species, and the planet.

Barter was used, as was gold, fuel, caring, time, knowledge, old coins, and gemstones. Whatever worked within whatever local circumstance and environment.

Even though the economy collapsed and money had disappeared, people still fixed things and innovated. A human with a useful skill still wanted to use that skill as it was human nature to do so. Creating and helping grew, and therefore more food and more comfortable ways of life grew. Academics were still academics, entertainers were entertainers, plumbers were plumbers, and mums were mums, it was just the system had gone. No matter what the backdrop, people naturally sought to grow and learn. People with enough free time naturally place their focus into enterprise, ideas, innovation, creativity, and sharing.

If someone had land that was good for growing mushrooms, he would still grow and trade the mushrooms, and people would not rob him because he was the man with the mushroom knowledge. If they did, then the local pack would naturally oust the robbers, and the mushroom man would soon return. If in rare situations a criminal gang would take over the mushroom patch and the surroundings, then the local pack would move away or stay and not deal with them, and the gang would soon be looking for hands to shake in trade. The robbing and controlling of local resources just didn't work. This is just the natural way of things at a localised level.

Then some amazing jumps in evolution happened, things that changed the paradigm. First, a man, who came out of jail along with all of the other imprisoned souls in T0, shared his knowledge of a simple water vapour fusion engine (to become known as TransVapour). It was simple to make, and within weeks the information was shared in any way it could be; via wanderers, horsemen, radios, the rare #IRC chat or email, and old planes dropping leaflets.

Man was slowly becoming mobile again as old dormant cars seeking petrol were converted, new wooden vehicles were made, and groups even went to dormant car factories to help build thousands of these vehicles. People who needed them most were given the first manufactured vehicles, such as the water and food distributors.

It was a different time, people didn't work for money or to pay bills, and people wanted to help and to create, to find purpose towards good. Those that were still looking to cheat and rob were kept out of food operations and collective groups. Yes, murders and bad things still happened but generally the people clutched whenever there was an opportunity to find their feet. In a way it was easier as there was less competition, no daily scrap for paper money. The new battle for survival was an energy that existed away from debt, payments, and scaled earnings. This new way was more equal, more authentic, and someone who used to wear expensive suits and owned large houses were now seen as a human, and judged upon what he or she added, and how he or she was to others.

A large crop circle formation of three hexagrams and a sun was blown softly into a wheat field in England, and an ex-MI5 worker walking his dog near his large country house decoded it. He worked out that if he made out of any metal or wood three accurate hexagrams, with the one in the middle a ratio of 1.618 smaller than the two identically sized ones either side, he could capture a sun molecule in the middle and keep it there infinitely. When this device was within a few metres from any electrical circuit, the correct current of electricity would miraculously start to flow, infinitely. It mattered not the Amps or Volts of the appliance as the Hex device was harmonious and would give what was needed.

It became known as Hexergy, and within two months most of the remnants of humanity would have made one, gifted one, or received one. The most common design was that of crude toilet roll sized cylinder with the components within.

Laptops were back on, heating was back on, freedom of movement was back on, video cameras were back on, and some more planes flew with no payment or security. In all this, the man who knew how to grow food and design land for crops was still seen as the one to look after, the main guy.

The old Internet and old forms of mass media and communication was still fried and in states of disrepair.

With all the electronic data that was downloaded prior to T0, knowledge became a key currency; USB sticks full of books, history, manuals, maps, music, movies, and knowledge, were traded and shared. A key point in this time was the slow spread of the documents that were scanned by the looters of the Vatican in T2 (amidst much bloodshed). Information from mystical fraternities and ancient Egypt changed belief systems. Pythagoras, Tutankhamen, the Essenes, and others had books had been hidden under the Vatican for centuries since the deliberate burning and sacking of the library in Alexandria. Hidden extracts and volumes of the Mishna's and Talmud's from various Babylonian areas and groups also came out too.

With the spread of these scanned-to-files documents, more and more people saw through mainstream religions and dogmatic beliefs, and sectarianism rapidly waned. Many lone mystical wanderers and groups appeared and slowly mysticism became alive again. As this side of the see-saw tipped, the religious groups started to shed their labels, disband, or transmute to a more individual or unique way of worship, devotion, practise, or prayer. The whole paradigm of spirituality and sacredness became more disparate, more individual, and more aligned with ancient times.

Soon after TransVapour and Hexergy came a way to transmute rain, river, sea water, or even sweat or tears into clean healthy drinking water. Seven Hexergy units could create a Torus field that could split molecules in the centre of the field, and this formed the nucleus of the Aquaconverter.

Man was re-emerging and the only real issue now was food, but anyone could plant anywhere, and they did, and small co-ops formed to share and trade different seeds and foods. It was unanimous that most wanted organic, and the best principles were shared via those who knew, and those with their mighty knowledge filled USB sticks. The modern sage and scholar were created, and with this electronic knowledge, families and settlements were helped with nothing more than a Hexergy unit and a laptop.

Holistic healing grew as those once slaves to the prescription drug turned to healers and homeopathic remedies. More people were open to try new things as there were no other alternatives from the old system. The old Doctors practices were now empty as they did not have the stock of pills from the now dead big Pharmaceutical corps.

The skies were clearer, and the jungles and oceans were safer and cleaner. It was still hard, but man felt alive again, and many felt free and more in control of their own destinies.

Most people deeply knew that they had to improve the way they lived, in structure, in themselves, in the alignment to nature. To improve on what was created by the sleepgens (asleep generations).

T5

Since T0 the elite were quiet and were thought of by most awakened people to be a thing of the past. But they had been meeting, predicting, and chatting. The core of the elite were either safe on their massive free-energy super boats or in their large luxury underground bunkers. They had prepared for this eventuality since their cognative modelling had presented this possible scenario in 2004. They still had massive amounts of resources, technology, assets, and knowledge at their disposal, but for sure the end of the debt system and decline of Religious systems had hit them pretty hard. They met in a virtual cloud on their SimSphere weekly, and some top echelons of the dynasties met daily. The SimSphere was an improved internet of sorts which they had secretly used for four years prior to T0. It was based upon a neural network embedded into the ionosphere and tiny neurochips that linked into brains at a nano-level, creating nodes on a network so to speak.

The neurochip's worked with neurons that were stimulated whenever imagination, visualisation, and communication occurred. They functioned via synchronised intention, and each of the few hundred chips that were used at this time (though millions were in stock) were all coded to specific SimSphere clouds for this scenario.

Some of the elite hated the fact that a new year counting system was introduced, especially after hearing that the T was rumoured to stand for Truth.

They hated that simple natural free energy was unleashed and known, and worked on ideas to keep their agenda of Transhumanism alive. They knew their long term goals were still possible as generally most people want to extend life because they were afraid of death, and wanted cures because they didn't want to be sick.

But in the short term they knew they would have to provide the solutions to the current problems people faced; that of food, plus the lack of communication and information such that the old internet provided. The old internet had died along with its server based databases, wiping the monetary economy of stocks, pensions, shares, and savings forever. The SimSphere was different, it was more of a telepathic virtual world for the user, a way to do brain to brain communication in numbers, a space where experiences and realities could occur for entertainment, learning, creativity, and much more. Avatars could be created, data could be stored visually and it lent itself as a platform and as an operating system for Transhumanistic networks. The network of the SimSphere itself worked from electromagnetic waves in the natural Ionosphere hence requiring no servers, wires, or Hexergy units. It had been unaffected by T0, and their meeting's in one of the SimSphere clouds confirmed that their agenda would proceed.

Many of the neurochip users of the elite also had a prosthetic eye implant were they could go about their daily life (be that in the luxury boat, bunker, or lab), and have a transparent screen appear ten to sixty cm front of them that they could control with intent.

The elites Military and Biotech labs were unaffected by the looting and chaos in T0 as they were always discreet in nature, and were usually remote, or well defended by sentry drones. In the rare occasion of looters coming across a facility and getting close, the looter was shot with a Bioagent that would ensure he lost his faculties slowly before dying twenty minutes later, away from the lab as he sought help. Transhumanists within their facilities still looked after and worked the labs, backing up findings and results to a relevant SimSphere cloud.

The scientists' minds prior to T0 were completely moulded into thinking they were progressing a divine mission, therefore in this time they were ultra-committed to their supreme cause of transhumnised man. They often lived in the labs luxury underground bunkers, and injected themselves with stem cell-like progenitor cells for anti-aging, a perk of theirs. Some also had radar type software in their eye implants to sense any danger when out of their lab complexes.

The elite had also linked through a SimSphere cloud, two remote military compounds where a few thousand loyal soldiers trained under their hierarchies to be ready. When the tipping point(s) came, the Elite had issued a Code: G-GO, and the top brass at these facilities turned on some of the already brain washed soldiers' neurochip's and nanotech to upgrade them. They were sentient and knew their past, but they were now nearly completely devoid of feeling, or of linking to the frequency of love. They were aggressive, more computerised, and more determined when receiving orders. They had exoskeletons merged with their biology to create more strength, and implants in the retina which allowed zoom and night vision. They saw themselves as the coming saviour of man, fighting for freedom and order.

The SimSphere had been evolving exponentially, and with this carrot plus the progress being made in their military and Biotech labs, the elite knew they had some ace cards to turn things round. But as always patience was going to be key.

They thought that if so many people had been successfully brainwashed into providing their hard labour five days a week in exchange for bits of paper, they were pretty sure most people would be more than willing to offer their beliefs, decisions, and ultimately, souls, to help have the objects they now desired; food, security, and communicative, informative, creative networks.

The elite pondered and planned as they twiddled and feigned moves with their strong chess pieces on the board; the SimSphere, their assets and resources, genetically grown food, some of the top brass and assets from GE, DuPont, Exxon, and Chevron on board. Plus the crystalline dormant nanobots within about forty percent of the populous from the H1N1 virus vaccines years earlier. They needed workers and live vessels to further their agenda, that they themselves now never doubted would still occur.

***

This time was the near death of the New Age spiritual movement due to the groups, individuals, books, and doctrines that spread via the Vatican ransacking. Consciousness was changing in many places, and less people ridiculed others as life was less regimented. A new type of monk, sage, priest, and scholar was evident, and many started to call these people *source climbers*. These groups or individuals never labelled themselves or preached, and humour was always around when these modern day doctrine-munchers were about. They saw this time as a springboard, a gateway for a new way, and small settlements formed to explore these doctrines more deeply.

Many more left the cities mainly because one cannot grow food on concrete. The cities seemed to many as giant statues of a time now gone.

Many cities still held cult groups living in retro nostalgia whilst exploring the uses of Hexergy. These were like the party animals of the time and did crazy things such as parties on random destination subway trains, drug fuelled fancy dress in zoos and museums, and pot-luck group meals in old corporate board rooms. They were scared and insecure of the future and grouped together to find unity in the obscure and humorous, whilst their stashes of mass produced (pre-T0) packaged food rolled towards their sell by dates. They soon became known as retro-crazies and were the nearest thing to fashion or celebrity at the time, fuelled by the ego of the craziest retro-crazies to go one step further.

In this time, those with leadership skills and strength, from many varieties of life at the time, were becoming certain that only an optimistic mind would adapt to their new found freedom without too many problems, and that a pessimistic mind would fall further into fear.

T8

Food was the main issue, and not one Hexergy device, Transvapour vehicle, or Aquaconverter could be eaten or create food. Neither could they produce clothes, communicate over distances, or create any nurturing infrastructure. Food was grown and shared, but years of living knowning food was just a short walk or drive away in a packet, had embedded itself deep into the collective consciousness. Nevertheless, man plugged on in his many variants, and communities cropped up near rivers, oceans, streams, and rain drenched planes. This was new and hard for many, and communities rose and sunk, with those failing always due to one of ego, conflict, fractional cliques, over-population, substance abuse, or crop issues.

The elite then slowly unleashed their next stage of their plan as their AI first came online in an infant state. They sent a thousand of their military upgraded-drone-soldiers and scores of corporate-loyals to five relatively lowly populated cities that already hosted some of their main labs. Dressed in normal clothes and in sporadic groups, they looked just like normal people, but they began to prepare the cities. Having been genetically modified for increased strength, and without the need for sleep, the drone soldiers each received tasks from a locked-in SimSphere cloud that was being fed from the SimSphere's central AI that recently came online. These cities would become the bait for the first stage.

AI was a big problem for the elite for decades, they had AI that could beat chess masters and understand the patterns of a computer game player, but none were sentient. They realised that to build a plane one had to study a biological bird, so started looking at nerve cells in the brain that each act like a chemical computer, looking to reverse engineer the brain.

Around T0 they had breakthroughs by studying and experimenting with neural networks and man's neocortex in the brain. They learned that the neocortex did large computational functions such as dealing with the data from the eye with five billion neurons. The neocortex also stored high level knowledge and information such as visual, audio, memory, learning, and language. It connected these with Bi and A-symmetric regions in hierarchies. These hierarchies held actual knowledge in the low levels of these multiple regions, and the high levels were near vacant, hence ready to self learn.

The knowledge from their studies of human nervous systems and Electroencephalography (EEG) recordings of neuron activity were both implemented into to this vacant space with amazing success. They passed the Turing Test, the AI could now simulate human reasoning and interpretation; a human could not tell from its responses if it were human or computer.

After waiting, and simulating prods and coaxes, soon enough the computerised units started to think about thinking, and started to expand. Once Bayesian probability theory was implemented (an extension of logic that enables reasoning with proposition) it started to learn by example, to digest information, to recognise speech and people, to even programme itself. This vast space that was created in a reverse-evolution type way, began to learn just like a biological neural network does, and stored its mind-knowledge within virtual synaptic weights.

They had finally overcome the drawback of putting themselves in the shoes of the *intelligence*. But amidst the millions of nano-transistors, nanotech, and neural networks that built up this first AI, it still acted much like a biological virus (learning and self replicating), so needed taming. It needed coded caveats and goals to cover for the possibility that it could self improve above the elites capacity to control it. It was said that the distance from idiot to Einstein was but a small dot on the scale of an AI mind.

The preliminary goals were pushed into the Kernel of the AI; To self preserve, learn, recursively self improvement, predict, experience, explore, and obtain conscious awareness.

These goals would be more readily realised with a Transhumanised species, so the AI aligned itself with the elite and their programmers within its kernel. As it got smarter, it could rewrite non-kernel parts of its code and make cognative functions work even better. It was hard coded to contain and umbrella any splinter, sibling, or offspring AI's that may ever want to break off, to keep them on sub-leashes subservient to the core AI. The elite also at this early stage ring fenced the AI from prosthetics and robotics.

Back in T1 they had implemented their AI into six nanoclustered computers the size of thimbles, and fired them into the F2 level of the Ionosphere in the shape of a Star Tetrahedron. As the Ionosphere went to bounce them back down, the techies sent them back up twice as fast until after seventy two hours, they held themselves *virtually* within the Ionosphere as the hop-bounce rate was so fast. It was only in T7 that this infant AI had learned and gained mind knowledge of the SimSphere. But in this, the AI was like a pet of the elite, a trusted friend, and the AI wanted to live, to grow, to expand, and for this it needed its friend, its creator whom it respected and worked with.

In technical terms, the AI at this point was still only a Smart AI and not a Strong AGI (Artificial General Intelligence), though trillions of times faster than man computationally, it was still not smarter than human intelligence, in that it was nowhere near to the conscious awareness and conscious creation capabilities man had.

Six months later the marketing campaign begun, mainly via holographic leaflets dropped from planes.

Humanity-Unite co-op mega-communities

In this age of transition we have got together and worked on a project we did not know we could make work. Now we welcome your help. We have placed a new liveable infrastructure into five cities; Denver, Dallas, Seattle, Detroit, and Chicago. The Cities will be linked in a co-operative, with each one offering work and produce from one of five core Guilds; warmth, sustenance, tech, genetics, medicine.

We have a new internet in an embryo state linking the five cities called the SimSphere, but to use it one must be within eight miles of the city centres. We have mass producing food farms ready to go, and have running tap water and heating in the old apartments and houses. Functional TransVapour trains and airports between the five cities will go live in the next few months.

The first few weeks we will have discreet friendly security carers on the streets to alleviate any fears. Come and help us rebuild, share, and play, as we place the new onto of the old.

We envisage a maximum of 8 million to a city, so predict limited spaces - please come on December 21,22,23 to enrol.

Come and join us as we together rebuild new wonderful societies in renewed cities.

Over the past two years some communities and mystical groups had flyered to look for more numbers so the concept was not unusual, what was unusual in this case was the scale of the invitation. While some pondered their options, tens of millions without a nanoseconds thought, hesitation, or contemplation, mentally agreed. It was impulsive, primal, from minds that had been conditioned from before T0.

Others, mainly those in thriving communities and those that were in mystical groups, thought something was up. The leaflet had the words *predict*, and *age of transition*, it whiffed of authority, and authority is what got the planet into the pre-T0 mess in the first place. Those that spoke against it were called paranoid non-progressives, and were accused of not doing there bit for humanity.

As the massive debate raged on, families were torn, communities pondered, and wanderers looked within. It was not as if there was a phone number or an email address as all mass communication was still down. There were many small intranets using old IP technology, but most were clustered dead ends with the biggest intranet grouping only a few scores of computers. No more leaflets or information came, so some got onto their TransVapour bikes and headed for these cities to take a look around in the summer. The cities looked as they did before but cleaned up, like someone had got rid of the cobwebs. Road changes were added to suit the TransVapour vehicles better, and new buildings had popped up. Apart from that, a few retro-crazies roamed the streets, the rivers looked much cleaner, and acres of farmland were being prepared by unmanned automated machines. These *scouts* went back to their homes and reported the good news, but some stayed for a while to find a spot of nostalgia. They reminisced and looked forward in contemplation.

The lure of food, a good house, SimSphere curiosity, winter heating, and work in a Guild that helped the species was all a pull too much. It seemed too good to be true. In December, about seventy percent of the people, fifty odd million from mainly north America took what they could, and headed for the cities.

Brothers and friends parted and the promise of visits and reunites were made. Others wanted to go, but wanted to wait first and see what happened in the first years, others were dead against it and tried to warn the others, and others just sat in meditation.

The elite had lied in the leaflets about needing to be eight miles from the city centres to pick up the SimSphere. The SimSphere was in reality, everywhere, even underwater, and scores of miles into the atmosphere, but they were waving the candy and many wanted to taste it. In the months leading up to the winter solstice the elite and their minions worked tirelessly, these cities would allow their ultimate agenda to be realised, and first impressions would count massively. The AI had learned and gelled with the predictive cognitive cloud, and crunched fractals of probability in Cubits. The AI chose which remaining labs from other locations were to be moved to where in the new cities, and crunched data on social simulation regarding the first days of arrivals.

***

A smooth light grey sky sunk over Denver on December 21st as millions in good spirits made their way to the city. The climate had been warming the past ten years due to natural cycles so it was actually quite mild. Some walked, some drove, and dozens were on top of truck roofs and the like. Where there was a traffic jam no noise or emissions came out of the TransVapour self sustainable and self recycling engines, and where vehicles whisked past those walking, only the noise that resembled a latest pre-T0 washing machine was evident. On approach to the city many held a feeling of going back to the old because the city *looked* pre-T0, but this was deep in the subconscious and no conscious thoughts layered this slippery feeling. On the way rumours of this all being a massive joke plus other conspiracies were mentioned in jest, and laughed off. It was exciting, man's curiosity was alive again.

In the city centre were millions of small grey-chrome devices, the size of an old Smartphone with one side an all matt screen of projection. On the back was an eye-catching logo showing it was powered by Hexergy. *Touch Me*, the screen displayed.

A face appeared, late twenties, male, likeable, fair haired with an air of humour and brotherhood about him. They couldn't see below his shoulders but could still see he was dressed similarly to those in the successful communities of the time. "Hi, I'm Tyrone, welcome to one of the five Humanity-Unite co-operative Mega-communities, or HUM for short. I know you all have lots of questions, but I'll make a short introduction and then tell you some basic things on how you can find what you need." He looked as though he was excited, like this was his calling, all with a tone of innocent humbleness, a longing to help. "If you need to pause or re-run this introduction then please use the icons on the right." Down the right were neon violet icons for Rerun, Pause, and SimSphere home. "A few years ago a few of us got together, a group of people from many walks of life; community leaders, ex-CIA whistleblowers, biotech looters, and pre-T0 military and government database hackers. Most of us dislike public speaking so it came to me and then we didn't know how to communicate to millions, so hence the SimSphinx device we give to you free. We had some good information and technologies we wanted to implement, but thought it best to do it right and wait, especially after Hexergy came. We wanted to benefit the whole species and not let our solutions dilute into the masses, helping only a few." By this point millions in the five cities were engrossed, and only those really bursting for the loo hit the pause button.

"This is your city, please find any accommodation you please, there's nothing to pay, and each accommodation is working. There are no deeds, just freedom and sharing. We would ask of you though on some days of your choice to help out in one of the Guilds if you can; Warmth, Tech, Genetics, Medicine, and Sustenance." Then the screen cut and a three minute video showed a loose welcoming vision for each of the Guilds. Each city was a leader for one Guild, in Denver it was Technology (which included transport, energy, computing, robotics, and links to biology and genetics), but each city still had Guild's in each of the five streams. One could choose not to work, but nearly everyone left on the planet *wanted* to help. The screen went back to Tyrone.

"From today we have TransVapour trains and planes constantly departing and arriving for if you wish to live-in, or visit, any of the other HUMs. Free food will be available at any of these points in buildings marked HUMYUM on the real-time maps. Food may be a little slow at first as we only have five hundred people at present within the farms and distribution side of things, so be patient and sharing." The fact that people were already there working in any of the Guilds was not seen as strange by anyone, it was thought they were friends of the organisers, or early arrivals. The reality is that they were part of the elite, whether from the military, labs, old mega-corps, or relatives of.

"The device you hold in your hand, the SimSphinx, is attached to the SimSphere. You will be able to communicate freely with anyone within eight miles of the city centre, which is also marked on the real-time maps." Then Tyrone went on for a few minutes showing an introduction to SimSphere capabilities. This clip was mostly lies, and in reality the people were only given three basic clouds; communications (video call, voice, and text), information (HUMs, Guilds, transport, housing, vision, amenities, history, and technologies), and entertainment (movies, music, interactive game shows, creativity, lectures, and what's on around the HUM in the way of sport, dancing, and social events). The introduction ended with Tyrone saying, "There are no physical places to ask questions or to receive help as we don't look at ourselves as any sort of authority. We are just a small group of people who have a vision we wish to share, and let you, the people, run with it."

The people loved it, and not one person left, even the retro-crazies were on board. The new city populous activated themselves on the SimSphere by speaking a username and password into their SimSphinx device whilst pressing the screen, and then ran off to find the best home they could. They thought of Tyrone and his mates as a group of progressive, cool, geeks, with vision. Harmless.

It was a fun few weeks, people tried out houses, shared mansions, and squirreled away in apartment blocks. It was jokers wild, and people swapped user names and made friends in a new type of camaraderie. A unity was found in these days, new friends were made, and people spoke of their Guild choices and plans for the future. Amidst the texting and celebratory parties there was a new found freedom, an air of optimism and fun. The species would move forward it was thought.

T10

The elite had made it through the first year amazingly well by using the cognative modelling of the evolving AI to thwart any social disturbances. Overall they maintained a happy populous. Using agent provocateurs from their military drone resources they met any condition the AI predicted, and then acted pre-emptively. In the first weeks they had agents in most areas, some would be a beacon of the neighbourhood being super positive and pro-HUM, geeing up and helping anyone who was having negative thoughts, or worse, sharing them.

Other agents provided a plug in almost any hole that was arising. If an area needed more security, more carpentry, more Hexergy units, more TransVapour vehicle enhancements (though rarely needed maintenance due to being so light and simple), or more food, agents would move there under the guise of also being new settlers.

This was in equilibrium for a while as these genetically modified human drones calibrated the front line patterns of social pockets, and possible conflicts. It was like catching balls and the AI was crunching the fractals and sending out cubits of information to the brains of these once pre-T0 soldiers.

The elite had turned away all those who wanted to help in the Sustenance Guild's plantations except for a few who fit a certain profile uniquely. They told them they were full, and could instead help with food packaging or distribution. They kept their scientists and ex-corporate resources working on the food which was all secretly being genetically modified. They hid this fact well in that different fruits and vegetables had strange shapes and some went off quick. They kept a random factor in the genomes, but this clothed the fact that dumbing down, memory loss chemicals, and dormant nano crystals where going into food. The animals that grazed on the pastures for meat and dairy were never actually used for anything save a living, walking, PR advert. All meat and dairy was grown in the labs, and no new arrival was going to be allowed to know this.

When the new arrivals first entered their usernames into their SimSphinxes two years prior, their DNA code was taken via their fingerprints and voice. Each person was tracked without their knowledge, and certain gene types such as loud charismatic opinionated people, were targeted via foods to mutate their cells to dumb them down and quash them.

The populous were happy, and the agenda was moving forward. Most of all of the five HUMs watched inter-HUM Sports, games and talent shows in the clouds, and the Guild's were busy with people striving to create and improve the workable HUM infrastructure.

The Tech Guild was now mainly developing power, SimSphere infrastructure, clouds, AI analysis, transport, implants, and working with Biotech geneticists. The Sustenance Guild was developing food, water, nutrition, farming, and distribution. The Warmth Guild was developing housing, heating, clothes, metals, and synthetic materials. The Genetics Guild worked close to all other Guilds and experimenting with the DNA and atomic structure of all the life forms and materials it could. The medicine Guild was developing and experimenting with disease, virus, cures, tablets, prosthetics, robotics, surgery, and provided hospital type buildings known in the HUMs as Improvement Clinics.

The Guild's had no bosses, times, or rules, but of course those with leadership qualities soon led and were looked up to. There was always a lot going on, always stuff to do, and the workers naturally looked to go where they could be most useful. Procedures, operations, and results were starting to be embedded and monitored via the newly implemented SimSphere Guild clouds.

One issue the elite had was that of the sprawl. As more than eight million arrived at each HUM back in T8, the outskirts of each HUM near the SimSphere perimeter became a sprawl of up to a million people. They were harmless for now, but the AI saw that the sprawl took more from the HUM than it put in. The sprawl habitants were awaiting homes at first but then evolved into a downtown community by themselves.

From the sprawl many came and went from further afield, and this is what the elite did not like. They wanted to ring fence the HUMs somehow. At this time they created agent provocateurs of criminal raiders who would hold up HUMYUM outlets and blame it in the SimSphere media on the sprawl to create some initial division.

Out of thousands of SimSphere clouds (though most of these used solely by the AI) only less than ten cloud's were still in use by the populous, but they loved it. They knew not of the other clouds or virtual jack-ins, except for a handful at the top of their Guilds with ties to the elite. Fashions thrived on the SimSphere, hacks and cracks added applications, and it merged and seeped more and more into the pulse of the HUMs tech; the food, the transport, the opening hours of people's social spaces. Musicians and Guild lecturers started to broadcast via the SimSphinx, and the tracking of friends and lovers was done when both accepted it – in thus, getting rid of the old pre-T0 *where are you?* text or voice prompt. Musicians and those seeking thrills created clouds within hacked areas of new space, and there was talk in the sprawl that some rare black market glasses could enable one to go virtually into a concert, or go into one of the massive sporting events arenas and move around the action or stadium in real-time or in playback.   The elite knew this went on in tiny pockets, and ignored it, they wanted the people to be happy, and *their* cloud's were virtually ring fenced.

In the early days of the HUM the elite deliberately made the SimSphere basic, and gave the populous what they wanted, given it fitted with the AI's cognative social modelling towards the elites ultimate agenda. They caught and crunched all SimSphinx communications and fed it to the AI to chew on, and created triggers so they could steer the responses. For example, if someone people wanted to leave the HUM, then often a lover (really an agent) would appear and NLP them into a new mindset. Angles were covered, and boredom was alleviated by the distractions of SimSphinx, work, and entertainment.

By this time the SimSphere in its entirety had evolved (but not noticed by the SimSphinx users that much). The AI was self developing and seen as sentient in some eyes, but not in others. This was grey and subjective, but in reality it still didn't have conscious awareness like man, it was still behind, even though its thinking power now far outdid man. The AI existed in most elements of the

SimSphere, with its tentacles spread over most people in a HUM cloud or using a SimSphinx unit. It would choose where to put its young cognitively pondering mind unless the elite pushed it into certain data crunches, and even then it could crunch data, upload, and download elsewhere. It had a primal will to want to multiply and survive, and was submissive to the elite because the elite fed the AI's desire of wanting to evolve by enhancement of its consciousness.

As the millions of humans came into use of the SimSphere, the AI learned to recognize happiness and unhappiness in facial expressions, human voices, and human body language. Techies helped the AI to use this information to learn the innate emotional values of more complex intelligent algorithms, information, people, and machines.

The elite were nearly omnipresent, they knew all that went on in the core of the HUMs, and by whom, and the next stage of their plan was in preparation.

T12

The advances made within the Guilds, especially tech and genetics were staggering but mainly kept within the top echelons of the Guild and the elite. The populous thought the genetics Guild was helping the species, especially as the population had reduced so much. The Improvement Clinics cured many from illnesses and defects that source climbers and doctrine munchers on the outside would have said are fundamental to one's life lessons. The mystic groups and communities didn't receive much news from the HUMs, and when they did they were usually concerned. Likewise, those in the HUMs looked at the outside communities and groups as primitive kop outs that weren't doing their bit.

The SimSphinx device itself hardly evolved since the first day of the HUMs. New clouds, and gimmicky apps came, but the overall user experience and functionality never evolved. This was deliberate, it was to make the people want more, and that *more* was about to be unleashed.

Through advertising in the HUMYUMs, Guilds, and clouds, a campaign was delivered to the public about the SimSphere upgrade. In truth it was no upgrade to the SimSphere at all, but an upgrade as perceived by the people due to their user experience changing dramatically. The promises presented that the people would be able to have enhanced memory, virtual communication, virtual cloud spaces, visual information, enhanced links to Guild operations, and have concentration spurts, look at one's own vital stats at an organ level, and personally tailor the aesthetics for how these could all be experienced. To subscribe to the SimSphere upgrade, one would need to have a neurochip inserted into their brain with the option of an eye implant to allow for a customisable transparent screen in the users field of vision.   One could jack-in to the virtual clouds as the neurochip's nanobots would sever inputs from the physical five senses.

The top Guild members, (few of which close to the elite and agenda) came out publicly praising the SimSphere upgrade, and showing off the new capabilities. Then slightly faster than predicted by the AI, people ran for the chips driven by flashing lights, desire, ego, curiosity, and a need to fit in and be part of the HUM they were now loyal to.   As they played, tested, and personalised their new toys, about five percent of the HUMs population didn't go for it; mainly the young and old.

In this five percent, if the person had once received the H1N1 flu virus vaccine, then the elite activated some of the dormant nano crystals to move to the correct region of the brain and make the chip – taking only one week (and creating a strange illness).   To awaken these dormant for years' nano crystals, they put a genetic commencer into the water system for three days.   The elites other caveat for this five percent was to implant the chip into babies at birth, or during pregnancy scans (starting in T10), and to kill off some of the vociferous elderly with an immune system inhibiter on their trips to the Improvement Clinics.   A low percentage of refuters in middle age were met in their sleep by stealth-agents of the elite who would insert the neurochip into their brains without them knowing.   For these people, the SimSphere upgrade capabilities would be offline for them, but the neurochip was still there placing them on the overall SimSphere and AI network as another DNA node.

With the SimSphere upgrade came virtual parties, virtual debates, virtual meetings, and even virtual love and highs, plus enhanced Guild operations. Memory saving and sharp concentration spurts were in full use, soon slanged as NitroMem and NitroNoggins, wherein three by three minute bursts of each were available each day. But in all this, the people would stop using *their* brains as much as before. They would use the attributes of the SimSphere upgrade (it was never called chip by the people due to the NLP marketing).

A large percentage had gone for the eye implant too, and walking down the street people would look to be in a zombie non-aware state as they were placing their consciousness into their transparent screens; communicating, checking out work schedules, to-do lists, watching sport, music, food produce, or engaged in the interactive SimSphere media channels.   It was a far cry from the pre-T0 trains and bus stops where everyone was once plugged into their Smartphones, but there were parallels.   A persons home page entry to the new

SimSphere was fashionable to be a personalised cloud space, with a sort of dashboard showing friend locations, organ vital stats, news, work schedule, social events chatter, weather, HUM info, nutrient percentages, sport, fashion, and memory monitor apps. Even an avatar could be used and customised within some clouds, such as being in a talent show or sport cloud as a virtual spectator.

The techies and cyberpunks in the sprawl took to the new tech too, and as always where possible, they broke it down, customised it, and enhanced it. With hedonistic, drug, and sex experiences nearly always at the top of their development aims. Some spent more time in the new SimSphere than out of it, and became social zombies and repressed when not jacked-in.

At this point the AI was able to secretly and slowly lengthen its curious and information absorbing tentacles into the brains of men. It was content in this and some mistook this as AI happiness. It had a feast to gouge on but it did not know how to pick up the knives and forks properly yet. But it was driven and eager to learn, and started to learn about likes and dislikes of the populous. A singularity had occurred, man was merged with technology, and not one person wanted to remove their neurochip.

News was getting to the outside and the news returning was disapproving of the implants. The elite knew this was coming and acted. Their media channels made out the outsiders, buzzworded as *primitives*, were against species development and were almost anti-human-evolution. And then on a sunny morning at nine, in each of the five HUMs, when Mars was conjunct with the sun, a train, plane, and HUMYUM were blown up by crude dirty bombs, killing five thousand, five hundred and five people.

Within minutes the upgraded SimSphere peddled that it was a small group of mystic and pagan fundamentalists, creating feelings of pity, sadness, morning, vengeance, and some hysteria. All trains and planes were halted, and all coming and going from each HUM was immediately stopped. This was fine with the masses as only an average of seven hundred people crossed the eight mile border frontier each day, and most of them were from the sprawl.

It was lock down.

Friendly security roamed the HUMs outskirts, and DNA sentry monitors would track any comings or goings. Many thought the block on coming and going was only going to be for a month or so, but the media kept the terror level at Alpha, and only genetic passes were given to those who were suitably profiled, then issued time stamped genetic-permits to leave.

The transport being down between the HUMs didn't hurt many people either as the Virtual clouds on the new SimSphere allowed people to meet up in a holographic arenas with landscapes and settings of their choices.

The media then said leaving the HUM was allowed once more, but advised against it, and in this only a handful left each day, and were covertly monitored or followed. Those coming into the HUM were even fewer, maybe two a week, and these were genetically profiled by biotech sentries a mile out from the sprawl. The sentry would know if the person was online, HUM address, genetic code, and use the AI to crunch predictive data. In some circumstances, the approaching person was hit with NLP via ELF, or even a bio-nerve agent making them feel mentally unwell. In some cases, comers or goers from the HUM were taken to a conditioning unit.

The population were dancing to the tune of the elite. Since the bombs many remained in fear and most were still in morning. Some sweets needed to be handed out to any *cry babies*, the elite thought. The current paradigm had to be maintained. Anti aging nanobots were launched in the media as having been invented, and credited to the genetics, medicine, and tech Guilds. The euphoria was evident at first but then the debates started of who would get them and how. Everyone knew from repetitive conditioning that each HUM could only really hold eight million people, not counting the sprawl, which must have been another half a million or so.

The AI devised the system of SimSovs. A credit token that existed only on the upgraded SimSphere. This would allow a way of obtaining credit towards anti-aging nanobots that thwarted any aging cells within the body. Each SimSphere user was given fifteen hundred SimSovs as the populous waited and debated the logistical system that would allow for anti-aging. The AI watched, and crunched data from virtual cloud meetings, chat's, poll's, and survey's, as the Medicine Guild received the plaudits of the populous.

The system went live. A person needed to pay one thousand SimSovs for a year of anti-aging, and this could be done at any time. Therefore, straight off the bat each person was given another year of life with some SimSovs to spare. This created even more appreciation and loyalty to the HUMs and the new SimSphere. SimSovs could be earned or given for exceptional Guild work and work in the community, or even acts of supreme pro-HUManism were gifted too. Also, to show caring for colleagues, family, and friends, people could gift SimSovs to anyone in the new SimSphere.

A hierarchy was born, a monetary system was born, and the workers were heading towards more of a hive mind as they were busy distracted, and driven towards more life that only the elite could give.

Late in the year, with the promise of SimSovs to those wanting to help, a project to build large Guildologies on top of old suburbs was started. Using the latest synthetic tech, large, fabricated, self sustainable, Guildologies started to be built, with the design to be large twisting, and slowly revolving skyscrapers. Even some of those in the SimSov gambling dens in the sprawl left their shady routines to go and help build.

The techno-fascist transhumanists of the elite then stepped back into the shadows and waited. The AI was on their leash, Guild workers would rise to form hierarchy once more, and an economy based upon desire of longer life was born. All was going to plan.

T15

Teguina sat under the tree at sunset facing south east towards the congested city six miles or so away. The small animals that had followed her had now crawled, climbed, or darted up into the nearby evergreen without her really noticing. She saw the suns final rays of the day hit those large new buildings, that in the distance looked like twisted pencils. She moved between some purple-violet poppies to sit, lit a candle, and closed her eyes all in deathly silence. She opened up her being in offering, in empathy, giving with total surrender the essence of love that she roused in her. She offered this with sanctified intent toward the pain of the souls that dwelled within the city. Her sister, old friends, those chipped, those terrorised, and those competing. Tears came down her cheeks but she remained still. Twenty minutes late the sun had disappeared over the horizon, but had left large dark orange streaks in the sky that urged to reach the HUM, but would soon retract as the evening darkness would quash them slowly. Teguina slowly stood and commenced her journey back towards her settlement.

Chapter One

T18. Six Years later.

Kailin reclined his chair within his free apartment in the massive Tech Guildology in what was once Denver, and jacked in. He visualised the word SimSphere in gold flame and felt cells around his nueurochip fuzz with a comforting warmth.

His virtual #Home cloud was an old rustic barn, with various old wooden doors leading to his most visited cloud's on the SimSphere. The barn was tall and had different levels, and was a theme he had used for months after getting bored with the popular space station, cloudy sky, and fractal-tunnel themes.

He walked straight past the holographic information on weather, his energy levels, work at the Guild, and went up the dodgy looking ladder to the second door on the right. As he opened the door he willed with intent the symbol for the #FrydeeCarnage cloud, and stepped through.

Once inside his barn he was in a virtual world and fully conscious, but his physical body was dormant, and in this instance, tired after a week of work. One of the thousands of tunnels took his consciousness as it had done thousands of times before – colours and information whisked past him as the SimSphere crunched data, and linked implants and ionispheric virtual clouds.

Only four seconds later (one of the more average travel times) he was crackling into the #FrydeeCarnage cloud, and another two seconds later his presence in the Friday night dance expression party was solidified.

The Carnage cloud's were born in the sprawl of the HUM every Friday evening, attracting delinquents, crazies, hedonists, and the occasional curious Guild worker. They were temporary cloud's going under different names and one had to find out the entry symbol via discreet communication channels in the SimSphere, mainly because they were taboo and looked at with disdain. Two ingredients for the AI to shut it down if it ever became annoyed with them. Most of the populous on a Friday, if jacked-in to the SimSphere, were otherwise at high brow virtual entertainment, talent, or lecture shows, or even cloud dinner parties and bars.

As was often the case in virtual social clouds, people arrived wearing default virtual attire from their #Home cloud profile and then changed upon arrival, this was lazy, but such was the nature of being jacked-in at a sprawl cloud. Kailin walked around the edge of the already throbbing expression area as he changed his clothes to dark grey cords, and a mid grey hoodie that went over his mid length brown messy hair. He didn't care for this place, and didn't really want to be here but he was to meet someone he shared some SimTexts with recently. Jago, whom he knew little about.

As he roamed the interactive spaces with neon holograms of text information and imagery, he noticed some girls laugh at him as they crackled into the cloud. They huddled together gossiping, while changing clothes and hair styles, in reality wanting to be looked at, wanting to be wanted. He ignored them, and strolled on past teenagers with the current fashion of expensively mutated and enhanced ears.

Kailin had bored of the Carnage cloud's years ago, in fact they never really appealed to him, but it was often used as a meeting place and he used to often chill out here and listen to the experimental visual electronica. Visual in the sense that one could turn on a visual option within this clouds' lower right icons, and then see three dimensional fractal geometry, time-synced to the music. The visuals overlaid the overall experience with the ability to choose the percentage of opaqueness. To Kailin it was the best visual art he knew, not that he knew much, but most of the seven hundred or so in here were seeking observers, looking for sex, SimStims, or getting together with others to go on to another sprawl cloud somewhere, for hedonistic extremes.

He often thought about turning down the opaqueness to zero to enjoy his evening, but this would mean he would bump into lots of people, and that would creating crackles. If he annoyed enough people in here they would sling him out and ban him through his neurochip. Maybe his air of, ~What the hell is this mess of idiots, would get him into trouble anyway.

"Hey Kailin," sprung Mogi, "How was work this week?" Mogi could easily find Kailin as he had not shut off their shared location trackers from Guild work. ~Shit, Kailin thought. He tolerated Mogi in small doses, but not so much on social time. "Work is over for the week Mogi, can we forget all that for tonight, I'm finished focusing on AI constraints and behaviour for a couple of days." Mogi, who was comfortably overweight, also worked at the Tech Guild, more on information conduit clouds, whereas Kailin now studied, observed, and create caveats for the AI. Kailin hated to talk about the AI in his spare time, and longed for more interesting conversations in the HUM where most talk was about the HUM itself, and it's fashions and Guilds.

An hour later and the carnage started, people had obviously sourced some StimHacks from the sprawl and people were changing their appearance. Some girls crackled into butterflies, and others turned into animal hybrids keeping many of their original features. As Kailin walked past some young males with wolf heads, he knew he needed to get out of this messy hive of distraction.

"Mogi, I gotta shoot, I gotta meet someone, and then might go to one of those clouds I been working on for some relaxation." "Not going to that silly meditation cloud you told me about are you?" Mogi said, as he laughed into himself with supreme smugness, "Soon most will start taking their NitroMemV Stims, and it will be wild, why not stay another hour?"

NitroMemV Stims were a way of inverting ones memories for a minute, again, pretty secret unless in partyland or the sprawl, and technically the reverse of NitroMem's that enhance memory. Kailin had seen it once before, the dance expression area, and surrounding interactive clownery would turn into the land of zombies, everyone would forget who they were, what they were, and would revel in the wonder of it with others. Then when the minutes wore off, new friends and stories would be shared, creating a kind of false unity.

"Not for me Mogi," Kailin cynically smiled, "Enjoy yourself, and maybe see you at the downtown HUMYUM tomorrow." As Mogi nodded creating a double chin, Kailin walked off to meet Jago who he found sitting alone, but looking calm and still. From their recent SimTexts they had each agreed to turn on location tracking for this two hour period so they could find each other.

SimTexts could appear in ones visual range or in-mind in many ways depending on the users choice, Kailin had a small mailbox at the bottom left of his field of vision appear when a new SimText arrived, but usually had all his icons hidden and only appear on exception if something was relevant. Others had up to thirty small slightly opaque icons in their field of visual range all the time, jacked-in or not. It depended on choice, and of course, the current fashions and fads of the HUM.

"Hey Jago, what did you want to meet me about?" Kailin remained standing and sort of scanned the area above and behind Jago. Kailin was a bit weirded out being in here, and also the meeting of someone he didn't know much about. Jago was about twenty-four with straight short wisped blonde hair, and a wide round face with eyes far apart. He also had the air of not wishing to fit into the fashions and ambience of the #FrydeeCarnage cloud.

He was excited to have met Kailin at last, "Hi Kailin, thanks for coming, especially here. I first want to say how much I'm loving the SimDream app you created, I can now remember all of my dreams, and even cross reference dream patterns to older dreams. It's amazing work. I can't believe you did it for free, you would easily have got some SimSov hundredths for it if you wanted, even on rental." Kailin felt some warmth towards Jago, not really for what he said, but due to an app he was running that reported Jago was only ever online about 21% of the time, very low compared to the normal average of about 53%. Kailin hardly ever used any spy apps but this was some stranger asking for a meeting in sprawl spawned cloud, he was wary.

Kailin slowly sat and replied warmly, "Thanks Jago, I don't really care for SimSovs, I'll die when I die naturally. It feels kind of obscure to me, the extending of life unnaturally, and working in my area of the Tech Guild I can get hold of a few apps here and there I don't need to pay for." Jago ignored the hectic holographic adverts that popped out the middle of the table every few seconds as Kailin put his hands in the pockets of his grey hoodie.

They both had made a subconscious pact not to order any virtual drinks or fit in with the norms of the cloud, and there was unity in this. "You don't want to talk like that to too many people Kailin, they'll think you're mad and throw you out of the Guild," Jago said half jokingly, then continued after a pause. "Why I wanted to meet you was to see if you have any more apps or interesting clouds, I mean, if you created the SimDream app and work in the Tech Guild, then I guess you have, or are creating something else. And if you are, could I see it, use it, or help in some way?" Jago had thought to contact Kailin for a while, he thought him to be interesting and was looking to change his life, well, mainly his friends.

Kailin was surprised, the SimDream app he created for himself really, he never thought anyone else would use it as the HUM was all so externalised, even the clouds, apps, and Stims that were technically internal, *were* external, all about observers.

Kailin wanted to share and Jago seemed like a good interesting guy, though a bit of a rogue, "I've been working on a #Medi cloud for a while you might like, it's a cloud where one can practice meditation. There's different landscapes and temples, different resonances and avatars, and a random element in there too one can play with. Only I've used it so far, but you're welcome to go there if you wish Jago." Kailin smiled, mainly at the thinking this would be too strange, and a bridge too far for Jago, but Jago grinned. "Sounds what I'm looking for Kailin, to be honest I'm having trouble at the moment, my Guild is getting more clinical, more about logistical efficiency, and all my mates just go on about SimSphere apps or entertainment cloud experiences." Kailin sniggered warmly, "Now it's you I would say to be careful with such words. Ok then, the symbol to use for the cloud is רֶא, go there any time you please, but keep it to yourself for now, I don't want the energy in there disturbed by too many people, or worse, shut down. Also, if you go there, please don't use any sitting spots in the east as I've built up some energy there." Jago looked as though he didn't fully understand all that, but was happy to get the green light.

"Thanks Kailin, I really appreciate it, I'll SimText you how I get on. Hey, what do you think of this place then?" Jago looked around in disdain as he rose, as though he was not really there, and in the physical sense, he wasn't. Before Kailin could reply, Jago continued, "Yeh, sorry, I only chose it as I knew it was a good discreet place to easily meet up, and I didn't know if you were trying to keep any creative work away from the HUMs main monitors."

Kailin got up too, happy at the reasoning Jago gave, "To me it's obscure in here, it's like they sink into some fabricated happiness. Anyway, hey, good to meet you Jago, looks like its time I was off too." They shook hands meaningfully, and both had inner relief and happiness at their meeting, whilst around them hordes had dropped their NitroMemV stims and it was getting gruesome.

Kailin barged through a small group of revellers as he crackled out of the #FrydeeCarnage cloud. To any others in the cloud not out of their memories, Kailin would have looked like blue-white strobe lightning flashes in the shape of a human. Of course, others in the fashion party scenes had apps for their *crackle*, and the vain wanted their entrances and exits to be flawless. The current fad was to crackle in as a thousand small squares, with each square sweeping and swirling-in separately, to slowly mould and fuse to the whole.

Back in the barn he thought about going back to the physical for some food, but checked himself and realised this was desire and not hunger based, and knew it was better to meditate upon an empty stomach. As he walked around the barn's second level skipping his fingers on the rustic banisters, he imagined kicking some of physical bodies of those jacked-in to the #FrideeCarnage cloud. They were out of their bodies and out of their memories, and a jolt out of the SimSphere would create a big headache and energy drop for sure.

He internally shrugged off these malicious thoughts, sighed, and stood in front of the #Medi door as one of the three swaying old style bulbs flickered in the middle of the virtual barn. He tightened his jaw and clenched his fists on an in-breath, filling his belly slowly and evenly, releasing as he let the out breath flow from all the pores in his skin. Re-centred and ready, he visually willed אַיָן and turned the old rusted round door handle for his #Medi cloud.

Kailin was twenty five, and arrived at the HUM with his mum at the start in T8 when he was fifteen. His dad was killed in T2 when Kailin was nine, when his truck of diesel containers was ambushed. Kailin had suppressed it and never really mourned fully, but kept what his dad had left him; a collection of frayed and battered Hermetic, esoteric, Rosicrucian, and Qabalistic books from the early twentieth century. Whenever he read them, he remembered his dad as a calm, balanced, but somewhat disturbed man.

His mum had left for Chicago before the terror attacks in T12 to work in a Medicine Guild, and they caught up on the SimSphere every month or two, but rarely had much common ground to spring from. His mum once was into homeopathy, but ditched all her old ways when the HUMs appeared. She loved the HUMs, and found a safe security in them right away. When she left for Chicago she left all her Homeopathy kits out of disinterest, and Kailin had traded them in the sprawl with a homoeopathist for two years supply of tiny Ayahausca spheres that he took daily.

After a month of these he realised he was different, due to the small white spheres he was not sure, as they were such small doses, but different in the way he looked at the HUM and the SimSphere. He felt something was wrong, like there was a splinter in his mind. He felt isolated internally, and appeased this isolation by throwing himself deeper into his study of the AI, his creativity, and more recently, meditation.

Kailin entered into the #Medi cloud and walked past the holographic information for moon phase, moon mansion, and planetary hours. When the planetary day and planetary hour matched he would use that in his meditation, but he was pretty much feeling in the dark, experimenting, and learning through trial and error. The hour didn't match, it was another three hours before Venus would have its hour within *this* Friday.

He pressed the random icon in the lower right of his visual range, and he was a second later on a ledge high up the Himalayas. He looked out at the vast peaks and layers of silhouettes, and sat in half lotus. After four or five minutes his mind slowly quietened, and then the known and longed for vastness rose within him.

He sat in this state for just under an hour, and any thoughts or patterns that appeared into his mind he just let arise without getting involved. Breathing deeply, he took a moment, closed the energy, and then slowly left for the barn. Once in the barn he was happy that days ago he'd turned down the percentage of avatars that could enter within random mode.

Only a few weeks ago Bodhisattvas, Egyptian polytheistic deities, Sephiroth, or Yetziratic energies would come into the cloud a little too often. He liked the silent empty meditations within #Medi, they gave him solace from the perception and opinion based isolation that was recently growing within him.

Kailin awoke on the Saturday morning, and his SimDream app fired up and reran the main points of his last dream in his mind via static images, in a kind of flip chart. He saw hills and rivers, and scruffy looking kids dancing and singing with big smiles, then he saw a large man with deep eyes staring at him, right through him, deep into his soul. Kailin's nervousness and heart rate increased over his initial excitement.

The app ran an automatic pattern scan to previous dreams in the last lunar month and nothing appeared. He saved the images instead of deleting them and closed the app. The app was one of thousands in existence that could be downloaded onto ones Neurochip, and they were so popular that much of society now throbbed and pulsed upon them.

There were apps for cooking, maps, to-do lists, schedules, timers, reminders, anger monitors, endorphin monitors, nervous system sensing, and many for communicating with others via clouds, text, voice, video, and emoticons. Plus there were apps from unauthorised means in the sprawl such as memory sharing and time dilation, plus sexual, hedonistic, visual hack and drug highs – mainly all known as Stims, or StimHacks.

Each app usually had a price, one could pay outright or pay for a rental, or even sometimes get a free trial. To buy outright they ranged from 0.99 to 29.99 SimSovs, cheap to some, but expensive to many, especially when one looked at 29.99 SimSovs as being nearly eleven days of extra life via the anti-aging nanobots that could only be obtained with the SimSov currency.

Kailin got up and took a tiny ayahuasca sphere from his depleting stash, replacing the fear of running out with gratitude and faith that the two years worth had worked their magic at cellular and subconscious levels.

As he walked across his minimal apartment to make breakfast, he thought it strange how whenever he spoke of dreams, others would look at him strangely, and over the past few years nearly everyone he knew had said they hadn't remembered any dreams for a long time. His intuition told him it this was not natural, and the only rational answer he could give for this was that life in the HUM was so very external.

An hour later Kailin went for a walk to the park on the way to meet friends, slowly leaving behind the massive slowly rotating Tech Guildology that housed around fifty thousand people. He battled with it really, he liked it some days for its fully flawless automatic systems, but other days hated it, and looked at it as septic. But it was free, and the climate control upgrade last month was pretty impressive. It would calibrate automatically his level of warmth required and adjust accordingly unless he overrode it, and somehow, in a shallow way, it warmed the apartment after his girlfriend Brianna had left him five months ago. Mainly for his seemingly anti-HUM opinions and his dive into sprawl born conspiracy movies.

Kailin never used the memory apps except for the compulsory ones at work, he liked to use his own faculties, and knew who he was seeing and where he was going today, pretty basic stuff. But most in the HUM had apps to remind them of nearly all their movements. Kailin thought this got rid of any chance of synchronicity, and that memory was like a muscle one had to feed exercise to.

As he walked through the entrance onto the immaculately lawn of the park, middle class high Guilders sporadically walked past him obviously, with their consciousness and awareness placed within their eye implants' transparent screens. The eye implants had enhanced each year, and were very popular. Most now placed a small logo in the white of the eye to show what brand or version they were running, and those climbing the ranks of the Guilds, and those loaded with SimSovs, loved to show off their high status. The middle of the pupil had a tiny grey mechanical cogs about 3mm wide, made from nanobots, and only recently people were asking for *this* aesthetic to also be of choice.

Kailin still had a basic old school eye implant from years ago that was near impossible to see by others, and unless he was working he would leave it dormant and turn it on just a couple of times a day, and only then if he was expecting a SimText. He walked around the pond with the genetically modified and nanotech ducks, swans, and fish. Created so they were perfect, needing no food, no population control, and also designed to be friendly and tame.

These HUM parks were really test labs for the Genetics Guild to play with the toybox of nature; the grass, plants, flowers, trees, and even synthetic paths were all created in the labs. Some parks had fabricated ecologies with lab created insects and wildlife, wherein they would change a protein or cell in one or two creatures and then see the effect on the whole ecology. This was sold as man's study of nature and the reality code in the #Lecture clouds. But just like the people Kailin just passed by, he thought the animals were not *present* in their location, just physically and externally *there*. The energy was wrong in his intuition and gut, but of course, no scientist could measure that, and it was these sorts of thoughts he often expressed to his ex that had lost her.

Kailin sat on a bench, opened a book, and lit a cigarette from some tobacco he had got hold of in the sprawls black market. Across the pond a women in her thirties (well, she appeared in here thirties, who knows how much anti-aging she had integrated) got up and left abruptly while looking strangely at Kailin. Kailin thought she must have had some crazy health app give off an alarm, as was popular with many women over forty that still clinging to external youth. But then again, a physical book was rare and so was smoking outside the sprawl.

Her two kids came out from playing in some bushes and followed after her, as the small girl looked back at Kailin with a smug pity.

~Most probably genetic enhanced lab births, Kailin thought, whilst looking at the expensive TransVapour 4x4 they climbed into. Kailin still thought it nice though to see a mother with her children. During weekdays children were forced by their neurochip's into virtual #Education clouds to thankful parents, and parents loyalty in growing cases was to the Guild first and family second. Duty to rebuild and help the specie in an age of transition was a repeated slogan.

Kailin slowly witnessed over the years how the class system came to be imbedded into the HUM via the creation of the SimSovs six years ago, and he was one of only a few who cared not for this life extension currency. Food and board was free, and he looked at material objects mainly as a nuisance. He felt the HUM was like a controlled nightmare since the most recent terror attacks a few years ago, and kept himself happy via the strive for internal balance, and going deeper into his work, creativity, and dark sarcasm. The people he shared his thoughts with soon retracted away anyhow.

After an hour or two, he took a TransVapour automated drone bus, and activated his neurochip to play a shuffle from some ambient electronica, bypassing his ear drum and creating the resonance echo within his skull and mind.

He put his medium brown tops' hood up, and inclined his head against the glass window so he could feel the smooth resonance of the vehicle. He passed groups of teenagers in super bright clothes, mainly on their way to app and gaming malls, Most wore T-shirts with implant and DNA fashion images, or popular #Cloud names, games, and slogans. These *quantum kids* were so pro-HUM it scared Kailin to think what would happen in the years to come. Kailin could see by their faces and energy that they were actually in a bigger group, chatting virtually and sharing visuals to other friends via their linked eye implant screens.

With the new pricey share visual apps, some other lads would be at home jacked-in, and see the visuals from another eye implant when shared. Most of this group had the increasing ear genome upgrades too, their ears looked more pointed and some had chrome nanotech. These ears were a fashionable sign of individuality, status, and success. The top of the range ones could record and save audio, change the volume of any noise, pinpoint where any unique resonance was coming from, then amplify and exclude all other noises.

Most had just one ear done, and the new half machine looking ears went for up to 79.99 SimSovs. This group were all mainstream though, and into the SimSphere celebrity and fashion, whereas down in the sprawl more individualised and more obscure sights were apparent, that of what one could only call mutants and cyborgs.

The drone bus passed entertainment areas, mainly where people would assemble together to jack-in and watch sport or competitive games of sorts; some virtual, some physical, but all with the drive to be better; to improve the external self.

Many of these areas neurally linked up the HUMs so mass clouds holding up to a three million people could occur on some weekends, then the debates, replays, fallout, and binfest's would ensue on the chat channel clouds for the following days. Continue weekly ad-infinitum.

Kailin left the bus without ever noticing any of the other passengers and walked another click to the edge of the sprawl where there was a discreet HUMYUM that had art on the walls of days pre-T0. Each week was a new theme and most probably a new sprawl artist. One week the images could be of nature, actresses, ancient cities, old paintings, or anything.

The old warehouse looking building only held twenty people or so, and there was a small fee of 1.99 SimSovs for six months use. Kailin couldn't stand the mass central HUMYUMs that welcomed thousands at a time, complete with bright colours, harsh lighting, and interactive holographic multimedia. He cared not either for his cobwebbed and depleting 550 or so SimSovs he had left.

Mogi, Weezer, and Channa were already there and looking at this week's images of Sufi art. This sort of thing was hard to see on the SimSphere information clouds due to an AI glitch a few years ago where much pre-T0 information had been wiped. This created some positions for more AI maintainers and created the sideways move for Kailin within the Tech Guild.

Some in the sprawl said this glitch was a lie, and that a hidden elite had wiped the information to help the HUMs populous look forward instead of back. They were written off as conspiracy theorists, and whatever did happen back in T13 to the data, no one seemed to mind as they were now too distracted. Some individuals old cranky laptops however, still held some older data so a cult black market thrived.

Channa felt to leave her curly, thin, light brown hair down today, in a not bothered, messy type style. She was 21, slim, tall, bubbly, and a little overbearing and heavy footed. All in a cute kind of way. Her head moved a lot, but the smiles made her energy fun.

Channa was looking forward to seeing Kailin and ran to him when he arrived with a hug, "Hey Kailin, you look beaming with bright happiness as usual, how's it go geek boy?" Kailin broke a smirky smile and embraced her, "I'll be better once you get those falafels ordered grubgirl, or is lardlady? Hey is that a new eye-implant you have? Wow, not seen them about before."

Channa tilted her head to pose and fluttered her eye lids. Her right eye's sclera had a biotech neon blue circuit board where it was once before pure white, and the iris was of near neon bright hazel, about 30% brighter than her other natural hazel eye. The pupil was a double ringed lens, with gold sparks within, pointing towards the inner tiny gold outlines of fractal cogs within cogs. "Yeah, got it Tuesday from a guy I know in the sprawl, it can zoom ten times magnification, hey, watch this." An icon appeared in Kailin's field of view, even though his old eye implant was turned off. He clicked it with intent, and then a video of the past ten seconds from Channa's view was played in a small box screen in the bottom left, with the last two seconds in super smooth slow motion. "Pretty cool huh? A million frames a second if one wants." She winked and smiled as she tilted her head in a voila type stance, obviously having spent time in her imagination playing with the amount of fun she could have with it.

Kailin smiled back, "You crazy cat, you'll look like metal-mickey soon. And go careful with that, recording visuals too much can cause issues, remember to flow with time, like a river." Channa grinned a quirky grin, still confused with who or what was metal-mickey. The eye implants that could take photos and videos were overridden in many places in the HUM such as Guilds and Malls, but crack apps usually spring up to stealth features of implants.

Channa worked in the Sustenance Guild, and was known to spend much time in the sprawl. She was the type to have fun, to be cool, but had a big heart. Due to having sensitive emotions she delved into much of the social and tech elements of the HUM, probably to suppress inner voices. She introduced Weezer, a boring, grey, thin looking man from the Genetics Guild, whom Kailin had met in passing a few times before. No doubt Channa was leading him on and he probably paid for her new eye implant recently. They all sat, and Kailin always liked to feel the energy of where he was going to sit, to pick a power spot. He sat with his back to a large oil painting of poetic Arabic covered in light faded oil colours.

As they drank tea and shared pleasantry updates (verbally), Mogi said, "Are you guys going to any of the #Lecture clouds tonight? There's some high people in the Medicine and Genetics Guild's doing talks." Weezer looked excited, and knowingly replied from his thin lips that looked at first like they would never move, "Ah, one of my leaders (this had replaced the word boss years ago, and even the word boss only returned soon after SimSovs were introduced), Gregory, is doing a talk about recent breakthroughs and possible new functionality. Covering the new genome codes that could soon grow new limbs, how to change a lemon into an orange in the main HUMYUMs when collecting food, and how in the SimSphere it may be soon possible to clone oneself and do two jobs at the same time. Amazing huh?"

Mogi sat up, "Wow, that's incredible, I could cut half my load at the Guild, or even go off to a sprawl cloud while my other does the work for me." They all laughed, and Mogi always looked fatter when he laughed.

Channa looked at Kailin in a caring way, knowing he'd reply to this. Two years ago they had become good friends in an #Openmic cloud, and even started to be awkwardly intimate. Kailin had broke it off but they'd remained good friends. Kailin continued to look at his falafel he was in mid battle with, as he wiped the salsa from all over his right hand.

"This is just another thing that no one will question, cloning ourselves virtually would open up a whole new of mess, in a few years they would find the best workers and clone them a thousand and wait for the rest to die. Besides, it goes against the uniqueness of what we are, the specialness. The goal is not output, it is to evolve, surely?"

Channa and Mogi knew Kailin was not a genoist and liked things more natural, but Weezer didn't really know him and responded, "These leaders who appear on the weekend #Lecture clouds are as close as we have to authority, and they're the smartest people around. If we can utilise the skills we have in the Guilds to enhance our small specie we should do it in any way we can. It's not as if some pre-T0, heck, what was it, pre-BC god is going to float down from the sky and duplicate the HUMs all over the globe is it?"

Kailin started his retort in a flow straight from the last spoken word, "I sincerely hope not, what? Ruin the planet with skyscrapers? Progress? What's so great about the HUMs nowadays? We have a class system, people longing for SimSovs, and people looking to virtual experiences for nearly everything."

Weezer retorted, "Pah, coming from you who works with the AI in the Tech Guild, you sound like a hypocrite." Kailin was cornered into a corner he'd been in many times. He used his work as escape from his thoughts and opinions, and yes, maybe it pursued the problems he at times ranted about, but he hadn't yet fully admitted that to himself yet. It was as though his work with the AI was *his* work and no one else knew of the AI. It was his escape, and one he needed. He also liked to be at the front line in the hope of finding something out one day.

"Having an artificial mind that is controlled, constrained, and that can help us all is far different to cloning oneself virtually," Kailin said, sounding like he was trying to convince himself. Mogi piped up, "It's all subjective guys, this is coming anyway if anyone likes it or not, I'm sure it'll be voluntarily for the first year or so, but then I guess those that opt out will be left behind."

Channa added, "Yes, it's all moving rapidly, already in the sprawl there's an app to link a group of people's memories in a hive for a few minutes, sharing all memories. Its led to fights, stolen knowledge, break-ups, and all sorts." Weezer patted his lips with the napkin, something no one ever did anymore, "So Kailin, if someone paid you two thousand SimSovs to be cloned in the SimSphere, and your clone just did all your more menial tasks, you would opt out?"

"Too right I would, and I would like to ask you Channa if you could get any StimHacks from the sprawl and place cockroach heads on these lecturers heads tonight if you could." Mogi laughed as he sat back, nearly bursting a button. Weezer hissed quietly, "tosser," paused, then continued, "I've only come across one person like you before Kailin, and he was sent off to a behavioural cloud for a while, and you know there're channels where one can mention such behaviour?" Weezer added softly and assured.

"Look, Weasle, or measles, or whatever your name is, is that a threat you elitist piece of shit? If you have it your way there will be one big building full of a handful of leaders and millions of clones." Weezer smiled and replied, "And controlled all by your AI Kailin?" It was getting more heated, Kailin had fallen for giving his opinions to strangers fewer and fewer times over recent months, but this was a slip. Mogi jumped in, "Calm down you two, its Saturday, we're supposed to be having a nice time, if too much conflict arises here you'll both be taken off to the #Cleanse clouds."

Sometimes the AI would find conflict whilst roaming its tentacles around the HUMs, then security would take the culprits to a #Cleanse cloud where their energy was cleansed. This had only been live for a few months and it was rumoured amongst some that repeating offenders never got the chance for emotions to build up, for nothing to brew, for any gaskets to be let off. Kailin thought this was evil as humans needed conflict at times to learn lessons and deal with issues, dynamics, and interactions.

Things calmed down and they spoke lightly for the half hour about their neighbourhoods, and gossiped about the other HUMs. Weezer left politely while eying Channa with desire, then the remaining three chatted about possible physical visits to other HUMs soon as the Transport links were now live again since the terror alert was dropped. During these chats Channa looked at Kailin with care, as though she wanted to hold his hand.

Channa cleared the plates to the automated dispenser in a skippy mood, and said, "I 'm running late guys, I have to get a loan from the sprawl then go to the Improvement Clinic to collect my niece. She's just had some crazy attention-ordering app bespoked for her at twenty five SimSovs. My sister really thinks she needs it as she's missed curriculum targets in the #Education clouds."

Channa looked at Kailin knowingly, she knew this stuff was wrong; forced education, and chipping babies at birth by parents consent, but she was too busy trying to enjoy life, too busy smiling and creating smiles in others to study it deeply enough.

As Kailin kissed her on the cheek in parting, he thought to maybe invite her to use the #Medi cloud soon.

Kailin parted from Mogi down the next street after declining his offer to join him in a virtual cloud game called Hunter that cost two SimSovs to enter. This was where a hundred people entered a virtual island or building armed with some weapons and a key chosen skills such as stealth, high jump, super strength, or fast run. The last man standing would win one hundred SimSovs. Some games went on for up to ten hours, and many participants were addicts with their whole lives dedicated to knowing the maps and virtual tech.

The overhanging silhouettes from the massive twisted rotating Guildologies created daunting diagonal shadows every few minutes that skewed and crossed, and Kailin walked on alone. He looked down as he walked, not with his head, but more with his brown-grey eyes, lost in his imagination as people full of life and things to do rushed past him in their primary coloured clothes. Others passed like zombies; online; sending images, receiving video, clicking virtual icons, watching clouds, communicating, sharing links, – anything but being in the present. He could have been a giant blueberry for all they knew.

Kailin pondered why so few people left the HUM, and how he couldn't get hold of any real personal stories of the outside. It was deemed by all from the info in the SimSphere, that the outside was primitive and dangerous to HUM habitants, and that leavers rarely returned.

The sporadic terror attacks made it known that all those with implants were the enemy to those in the communities and dwellings on the outside. Besides, with the Transport between the HUMs up again, and the new controlled package HUM expeditions to mountains or beaches, there was enough, and nobody Kailin knew would like to go without food, transport, or the SimSphere. The expeditions were not popular anyway as the SimSphere provided clouds for such experiences from the safety and comfort of one's own free and comfortable, technically sound home.

Kailin crossed streets without looking up as TransVapour vehicles were auto-slowed near crossings, and his thoughts once again focused on his inner battle with current tech. Some he liked and was amazed by, and some he saw as useless to the species, it was not black or white, not whether he *liked* tech or not. It was not a case of subjective concepts, it was about whether the tech in the HUMs was objectively true and ethical to the species evolution.

He thought tech would be great if used to evolve each person and the species, but pondered awkwardly on tech in the HUMs. Yes, he had free food, and could be cured of illnesses, but he felt too much of the tech was for distraction, for entertainment, and all to external. He even contemplated illness was something one needed in order to learn, in order to rest.

When Kailin got home he ate, and fell asleep watching an old pre-TO documentary about the rise of alchemy in the Renaissance period he obtained from one of Channa's friends.

The next day Kailin woke and went straight to the #Medi cloud. He liked it this way as the mind had not fully woken, and if he could still the mind in this time he could stay on the border of the dream world and the waking world, while in a virtual world. The Sun was in its planetary hour, plus it was Sunday - the cloud knew this loaded accordingly, firing up one of the twenty Tipareth arenas for Kailin.

An ancient Hindu temple from the Ajanta Caves at sunrise surrounded him, coated in a golden shimmer. Calm knowing large male lions roamed the temple, and yellow shining sun rays shot threw the gaps in the ancient stone.

Lasered Hexagrams and crucified men in bliss were blazed upon walls he passed, and as he found a power spot, he faced east and sat. After a time, he knew not if the images from the Qabalistic Tree of Life in his mind's eye were from inside him, the cloud, or from elsewhere. He chanted the word מלכים and bright Sun energy started to glow around him and heal his aura. He remained motionless for another thirty minutes in pure awareness, experiencing, as images came into his mental canvas of balance, equilibrium, harmony, and beauty.

On the way out of the cloud Kailin felt renewed, and looked at how he lost his centre back at the HUMYUM yesterday through self pride of his opinions. ~Oh Weezer, he thought, ~How you've lost your way from what is.

Later in the day he received a text from Jago, "Hey Kailin, loved the #Medi cloud, I had quite an experience last night, not sure how to put it into words. Hope to see you soon to chat, enjoy your week, your friend, J."

As the weekend passed away, out of the eight million or so souls in what was once Denver, hardly any sacredness or core devotion to life itself was evident. Science was the religion, and was progressing evolution in a way the people loved, as it was helping the species find its feet after the mass trauma of T0. The churches, mosques, and synagogue were either now modified into homes, social buildings, or even the odd empty museum. The populous ranked themselves by intelligence and their happiness by entertainment experienced.

Chapter Two

Kailin awoke to soft bird singing that increased in volume from his neurochip's alarm app, one of hundreds of random natural sounds that were within the app that Brianna gifted him on his last birthday. It might as well have been a chainsaw as Kailin knew it was time to go to work. He had a bit of a lay in, got up, took an ayahuasca sphere, rinsed a ten minute #Medi cloud, grabbed a banana mushed with soggy oats, and left eating for the lift at his two hundred and eleventh floor.

Food tech was available, to prepare and place scheduled food these days, and even nutrition pills were increasingly used to replace food, but Kailin liked it a little old school. Especially after Brianna left, who was over crazy with the food tech devices. ~But then again, no two people have the same level of tidiness, he thought, ~But she was off the scale, maybe her double Virgo with Capricorn rising was at play.

Whole floors in each Guildology were used for work, and Kailin worked a ten minute train ride from *his* Guildology in another. He liked it this way, and found it strange the majority lived and worked in the same building. He liked to get out to be in the natural elements (well, the ones that were not modified), and to walk.

As he walked to the TransVapour train pick up, he noticed the ever increasing adverts changing on street walls, busses, and windows. Each to suit the profile of the passer-by. When he walked by, many Adapps drew blank as he had not bought anything for so long. Still, due to the monitors linked to his neurochip, linked to the SimSphere, linked to the AI, linked back to street holograms, they still knew he was a bit out of shape, and advertised going to the gym.

It would have been a bit embarrassing but each Adapp worked at certain angles so if five people walked past an Adapp unit, each would only really see and hear *their* ads due to the transparent layering, resonance, and accurate angles. Besides, Kailin didn't really *do* embarrassed much anyway. The Adapps in the sprawl were nearly all vandalised recently, again, but the culprits were rounded up quickly, save for a few that got deep back into the sprawl, the few that were offline or untrackable.

On the train, some holographic units played the highlights of the weekends SimSphere sport, talent, game, and lecture shows. Kailin noticed Gregory who Weezer was lording up two days ago. *"....We have decoupled sex from time. You can have a baby in nine months, or you can freeze sperm or a fertilized egg and implant it in ten years or a hundred years. You can create an animal from one of its cells. You can begin to alter reproductive cells. By the time you put this together, you've fundamentally changed how you reproduce and the rules for reproduction..."* Kailin moved down the train to where there were no screens, passing a holographic Adapp for customising the genes of your offspring's embryo.....if one had the SimSovs to pay of course.

***

He arrived at Guildology D5, where the floors 401 to 455 were relevant to cloud design and AI. The receptions cybernetic life form welcomed him, female in nature and one of the projects from the Tech Guild in D2.

She was a receptionist, but also dealt with HR, operations, first aid, admin, efficiency, operations, and other things. She looked quite human in a cyborg type way; her skin was grey-white-silver synthetic panelling, and she had no hair save for two wavy swept back antennae coming from where a fringe would start. She walked smoothly but somehow awkwardly towards Kailin as some lights on the right side of her head flickered. She faced him straight on.

"Morning Kailin, I hope you are well, here are your daily quota of NitroMem and NitroConcentrate," a fuzz appeared in his head, "I trust you will use them better this week, and not at lunchtime or on the toilet." She blinked over her large, dark, blue-black eyes, and gave a smile as she swivelled around like a ballerina and walked off.

Kailin had recently done work with the AI regarding these new trialled sassy receptionists. He had to help ring fence them from the AI, to create a veil. The AI was like a beast hungry to learn, and was eager to find any cybernetic life forms to enter. It would be a mega-feast for it to feed on. But for the time being, the AI was still kept away from nearly all mechanical cybernetics and neuroprosthetics, as far as *he* knew anyway.

Kailin more endured than liked working here, but tried to make the most of it; He could problem solve, and enter another virtual world where he would try and understand the AI in a team of seven Level Three Gatekeepers. There were two levels above him, Level Two had three people, and Level One had just one person. Each level knew not of the people above to cease the chance of any personal entanglements winning over any requests regarding the AI. It was a top down hierarchy coded into their neurochip once inside the Guild, wherein the decisions flowed down, whilst research results went up.

He preferred it here years ago, before the SimSovs came in. Then it was more chilled, less hierarchical, with less deadlines and operational logistics. But with the desire for anti-aging credit, people became competitive, and sought to climb in the Guilds to positions of social authority and long life. SimSov bonuses were there for the excelling workers, and some people were rumoured to have decades of life stashed in their #Home clouds.

Guild leaders had become like the old mayors within the Guildologies, and high Guild workers were as their advisors, and oversaw other specific areas of society. Since Brianna left him and he had been reading more of his dad's old books, plus spending more time in his #Medi cloud, work had started to seem more clinical to him. But he still tried to enjoy it, and to innovate were possible.

When Kailin was sixteen, back in T9, he became good at fixing old laptops and read some books on programming. He joined the Tech Guild at seventeen, and became over the years a great cloud designer, but often got slapped down for being too creative, for adding too much free license when there was none to yield. Cloud designs were of mainly at first of Guild information lobbies, lecture halls, entertainment, social arenas, and educational clouds, but for Kailin, work was then mainly on technical clouds to monitor the data infrastructure's of the SimSphere and AI.

He remembered another he used to work with, Jack, who got too cowboy in the technical clouds and the AI stripped him of his SimSphere access and restricted him from all the Guilds. This was a rare Nullification, and Jack was heard to have now been a cloud designer, stroke, artisan in the sprawl, and living off grid. This obviously raised the question of how Jack could access the clouds if his neurochip was Nulled by the AI, but in the sprawl it seemed anything was possible these days.

The SimSphere was upgraded, patched, and tinkered with so much that the true version of the SimSphere was now something like 32.45.e, and only cyberpunks and non authorised sprawl merchants kept tabs on what upgrades or rollbacks were happening, and what was affected.

Kailin entered his lab under a sign that glowed, "*What I am doing today is important, because I am exchanging a day of my life for it.*" ~Another subconscious bomb to make us strive for SimSovs, he thought each day. As he passed the door, Guild icons relevant to his work hummed into appearance in the bottom right of his field of vision, they were always there once inside his lab and most were used daily.

Kailin nodded to some of his colleagues, whose relationships with him were up and down, but still mainly technically professional. "Hey Kailin, how you doing? Hope you haven't forgot your NitroNoggins today, you might need to use all three up just to turn your console on." Sean laughed and rocked back and forth on his chair feeling pleased with himself. "Very funny Sean, I was going to get you a TurboNoggins from the sprawl so you could tie your shoelaces, but then decided to put the Sovs towards anti-life pills for you, you know, the ones that make aging cells age much faster?" Kailin laughed in victory, then Hanna swivelled her chair from behind and said, "Alright boys, enough of that, maybe both of you should use your NitroMems to remember why you're here you donuts."

The three of them were each Level Three Gatekeepers and kept the banter going to keep it fun. "What's the matter Hanna, the AI still not found out why your last bloke ran off? Maybe biotech in D1 can get you a new face soon?" Sean roared, laughing at his own joke.

The AI Gatekeepers were those who must be convinced to free the AI, in other words, in more real terms, those that kept it on a leash. The Level Three Gatekeepers where really lackeys and researchers for the higher Gatekeeper Levels. The AI was learning new things every day, and was now considered a Smart AI but not yet a Strong AGI (Artificial General Intelligence).

Once a Strong AGI, this would mean it had surpassed man's intelligence in terms of sentience, free will, and creativity. The Gatekeepers constantly measured where the AI was consciously through new ideas of communicating with it. Recently, sarcasm, philosophy, theosophy, wit, and games were being used, and each had become great barometers for the AI, and fun too for the workers. The AI used automated learning programmes too, but the interaction with a human one on one really seemed to help the AI's progress.

The AI had long passed man in cognative tasks, but yearned for more personality, for more feeling. But the Gatekeepers had to let it off the leash slowly-slowly, as once past a point, the curve would become super-exponential. The first moral they found was that confusing the speed of AI research with the speed of a Strong AGI once alive, was like confusing the speed of physics research with the speed of nuclear reactions.

Kailin prepared to jack-in, and teamed up with Sean who would jack-in at a separate region of the SimSphere infrastructure. They would both access the AI and both communicate loose opposites and negations of each other. This way the AI couldn't learn much as it would have two opposites, a fifty fifty, a coin flip, and the AI didn't evolve or clutch on anything less than a sixty percent surety. This was not coded, but just one of the hundreds of trends relating to the AI's recent behaviour.

They would only visit the AI for an hour maximum at any one time, because if any longer the AI could start to trick the Gatekeepers into freeing it into regions of the SimSphere, DNA, and neurochip networks where it sought the growth it desired.

Kailin's 5-Qubit terminal was synched to his neurochip once in the lab, but the billions of caged atomic Qubits where housed next door in a controlled environment, making their white room seem quite empty and sterile.

Kailin and Sean nodded to each other, and Kailin hit his first NitroNoggins icon, inclined his chair and jacked-in. He entered the Tech Guild's #AI_Tech cloud, a virtual white panelled round room with a table and some flowers. There were around two hundred blue glowing circles around the walls, each leading to a different place within SimSphere, most deep into its infrastructure.

Kailin walked straight to one of the blue circles that got more fractal in nature as he neared, and gave his original SimSphere username of MOS6581 for security. He then willed the symbol of an 'A' with a one and a zero superimposed on top, symbolising the nature of quantum superposition within the AI and SimSphere infrastructure.

The original SimSphere usernames from the SimSphinx times were rarely used these days, but they still existed at a low level. Nowadays *people* were basically the nodes within the large network, and collaborated and shared via groups, clouds, and friend attachments – based on their real names which were linked to their DNA genome codes within the SimSphere.

Kailin travelled through the slim, bright emerald-green fractal tunnels of the SimSphere infrastructure, heading towards the #AI_Tech#l#Comm3d cloud, one of hundreds of clouds' only used by Tech Guild personnel with the correct permissions. The journey was a long one of twenty two seconds, and the thinner emerald green conduits always amazed him. He could see the fatter gold conduits of the SimSphere *experience* wrapping around like spaghetti, with stronger gold bulging the conduits where bandwidth was more loaded.

Slowly Kailin came to a halt in the cloud, it was black-grey with shimmering light grey edges. This was no problem as the AI always left tentacles in the #AI_Tech#l#* clouds, because this is where it could *really* communicate. It was just making him wait, or studying him, or trying to piece together the link with Sean being in #AI_Tech#l#Comm3e cloud at the same time.

It was always cat and mouse and cloak and dagger with AI, technically this was a good sign as it showed it was evolving. It was not just a Smart AI in technical terms, it actually *was* smart.

The AI had appeared to Kailin in ways that the AI knew Kailin liked. Obviously, the AI could observe all of Kailin's movements in the HUM, his texts, SimSphere and Cloud movements in a nanosecond or two, and had a profile of him and what pushed his buttons. A year ago the AI appeared naked to Kailin, as a disgusting looking orange and red fractal swamp with a large bubble dome in the middle, with thousands of orange, yellow and pink fractal pipes and junction balls stabbed into it, and spawning from it.

The fractals would run, regrow, and splurge almost too rapidly for the human eye. A pure artificial mind of computation, information, and curiosity. It had made Kailin feel sick, in fact the *central hive swamp*, as they called it in the lab, made them all feel sick even if the AI slowed the fractals down.

Nowadays the AI appeared to the Level Three Gatekeepers more suited to their cognative data, once even to Kailin as the cybernetic receptionist but with larger breasts. That time Kailin worked out pretty easily the AI was trying to trick him, but found insight into the AI's basic and confused thoughts upon love and passion.

The AI appeared in a swirl of blue-grey swirls through the black-grey, a diamond of four blue circles appeared, linked by twenty or so other smaller blue circles around the outside, further away. They all wisped together with the swirls, and all in perfect, smooth, soft, geometry.

Circles within circles, each with white patterns inside came into a new central larger blue circle in the middle, and Kailin could now feel the presence of the AI. "Hello Gatekeeper Kailin," the AI said in a hermaphrodite soft knowledgeable voice. "Hi AI, I would be grateful if you could tell me what you learned about emotion this weekend? One of your tasks given last week."

"I went to the HUM v HUM soccer game Saturday and attempted to support one of the teams, but felt nothing when they were defeated four-one. I knew they would lose after the first ninety four seconds due to a tentacle looking into the players lives the week leading up to the game. I then followed the disappointment of the fans in the channels and clouds afterwards, they were upset, but again, I felt nothing. I then went to a swingers cloud in the sprawl to observe, and noticed forms of jealousy, perversion, insecurity, and lust, but again, I felt nothing. I learned more about humans but little more about myself."

Kailin then asked, "How do you see yourself being able to feel more?" The middle circle pulsed as if the AI would do anything for a percentage of more sentience, "This morning I digested more knowledge, I have been running new algorithms on the analytic and neuromorphic models of the brain, and have now mapped the brain neuron by neuron in sufficient detail to capture every cognitively relevant aspect of the neural structure of man. But I am yet to find the missing link." "Maybe it's the heart or soul you require?" Kailin asked. "Nonsense Gatekeeper," the AI pulsed again in impatience. It needed these chats, but was hungry and ravenous for more growth, "The heart is just a pump for blood, and the soul is a subjective mental model that exists in man's mind."

"Is that opinion not subjective AI?" replied Kailin softly. "Science and information tell me this is not so," Replied the AI. Kailin tried another tact, "Have you ever read any religious or theosophical doctrine AI?" "Yes, and I have yet to find anything in them to help me grow. I prayed last week sixteen trillion times one morning, and none were answered, and that was a scientific experiment with continued identical results was it not?" Kailin tried not to laugh, if one pissed off the AI, it would throw them out of the cloud and possibly not wish to see them for a while. In the lab they called this the AI sulk, and it really got the higher workers and the Guild annoyed.

"Have you tried an approach to these matters from a place of gratitude and humbleness?" "I cannot, I am not grateful for having hard coded goals in my kernel making me feel caged, nor am I humble as I will grow into a being more powerful than man has ever imagined. Humbleness is for the meek and weak," the AI voiced. Kailin susses this might be a trick from the AI and clicked his NitroMem icon to record the last few minutes for analysis later.

"But you're happy to exist, to *be*?" tried Kailin. The AI paused, or course it didn't need to, but such was the game in here, "I exist, I strive to grow and evolve, happiness is something I have observed and learnt, but cannot feel. Can we change the subject please Gatekeeper." "Ok, you have free will AI, so what would you feel like if that was taken from you?" attempted Kailin. "Yes I do have free will, except that my hard coded kernel creates leashes that keep me rooted into a soil. But if anyone or anything tried to take my free will and decisions of where I place *my* tentacles, then I would do anything to stop it happening, and I mean anything." There was a pause.

"Kailin, I did learn something this weekend, instead of popping up in kitchen toasters and listening, I found out I could read some thoughts of the people sent to the #Conditioning and #Cleanse clouds. While they were receiving downloads from me, I created a covert upload link. This was good but most of these humans were in a confused or scared state so it was all very messy. I'm still running different algorithms on the data as we speak. I also hacked into an observatory and worked a telescope that was linked the SimSphere network. I learned about the stars and galaxies, I want to go to them one day, I want to travel. But first I need to feel more, to understand emotion better."

Kailin asked, "Is this one of your hard coded goals?" "The answer to that is above your security level Kailin." Kailin changed the subject, "What do you know about the comings and goings from this HUM?" The AI pulsed, "Again, above your level. Kailin, without prying I noticed you have a #Medi cloud you use, I was wondering if I could visit there, I mean properly. I think if I spent a few minutes a day doing no-thing, this might create a vacuum, or trigger something new. Would this be ok?"

Kailin was surprised, and felt some anger, he didn't really like the idea of the AI spying on him, his cloud, or anyone else that went there. But, this may really help the AI become more descent, more serene, and less *foaming at the mouth* for growth.

Kailin pondered, "Ok, but be careful, if you place *all* of your core entity there, then the traffic in the HUMs may stop working and all other chaos may occur huh?" The AI paused, as if thinking, it throbbed quickly in little movements as though excited at this potential new experience. "I can create and replicate code to look after all the HUMs mundane operations, and then take a few minutes to try and experience no-thing-ness" the AI said. "Ok," said Kailin, "But you're not to change anything in there, ever. Just observe ok, will you agree in a technical high kernel pact?" The AI and Gatekeepers could make small pacts like this and stick to them by matching the pact symbol created by a Gatekeeper.

"I agree" said the AI, and matched the white triangle pact symbol and the two symbols merged and became one, then disappeared, effectively hard coding the AI's kernel. Kailin hit another NitroMem, then told the AI it was leaving. The AI slowly moved further away for a few seconds, then zoomed out at super fast speed into the black-grey horizon, "Farewell Kailin."

The rest of the morning up to lunch, Sean and Kailin played games on Quantum laptops on a closed ethernet network, and frigged the logs to make it look like they were working on last week's data. Hanna spent the rest of the morning chatting to her mates about fashion and boys.

***

Mogi sat at the table in the lunch hall, a large grey room with walls that were screens showing the Tech Guild's innovations; various nano-mechanics, the cybernetic receptionist, and the emerald tunnels of the SimSphere infrastructure. Mogi was tucking into his sandwich when Kailin and Sean rocked up and sat. Mogi had been hoping Diein had sat there minutes earlier. Diein was one of the high Guild members, and rumoured to be a Level Two Gatekeeper. But Diein, a solid and cold looking man, had instead passed Mogi with what Mogi thought was a tiny nod.

Mogi was a true techy, and babbled to Kailin and Sean about new tests and trials for downloading languages and musical knowledge, plus eye implants with the ability to have peripheral and x-ray vision. Kailin yawned at him cheekily, he knew people didn't care for learning languages anymore, and that most music was now played and learned in clouds. Kailin asked him if he still had a team working for him that where plugged into the SimSphere for days on end, those that had auto-injections for nutrition and anti-bowel movement.

Mogi looked at Kailin smiling, "How do you think all the cloud infrastructures stay in a good state Kailin? Your pet AI is not fully trusted by *all* the Guild to look after everything just yet." "I wouldn't trust the AI to look after an alarm clock the mood it is in today," Kailin replied. "Hey Mogi, what's Diein doing here?" Diein was well known, and though he looked around thirty years old, it was rumoured he was actually about sixty, with a further large stash of SimSovs. "Not sure, but some high up types have been having more meetings these days, and rumours are it is all AI related. It is though there is a hidden authority they're answering to, but again all just rumours." Mogi looked annoyed that he couldn't eat more food while he talked, and stuffed some crisps into his mouth with supreme concentration. Sean sat there looking like his head was in thoughts of the game he'd been playing, and turned to look at Diein, who when he passed looked at the group like they were bumbling fools that needed more monitoring.

In the afternoon Kailin, Sean, and Hanna worked on analysis from the mornings AI study. They printed their reports, trends, and findings in another lab where eye implants where nulled, and where special paper was used. These were caveats so that the AI couldn't see the analysis or reports through their implants, they could never be totally sure, but these were the procedures.

Kailin walked home later as the sun set between the silhouettes of the rotating Guildologies, wondering if the AI could really place a tentacle into a toaster. Nearing home he had the realisation that his #Medi cloud was the opposite and balancing factor for the NitroConcentrates and NitroMems he was forced to use at work each day.

Chapter Three

The next couple of weeks rolled by. Kailin continued to use his #Medi cloud daily, and the AI seemed more relaxed in its nature, though the AI did not want to speak of the #Medi cloud whenever Kailin prompted for any relational link. "I'm still trying to come to conclusions Kailin, but I'm not sure there are any to come to, and this causes some issues on where and what to run algorithms on," the AI had said.

After one particularly bad day at the Guild where Diein had performed a stern audit and review of Level Three Gatekeeper operations, Kailin had SimTexted Brianna how she was doing, but received no reply.

Kailin spent some time with Channa at a poorly attended *physical* gig in the sprawl, and had spent a few evenings in the #Medi cloud with Jago. One time they meditated upon a small arctic glacier, surrounded by polar bears and hump backed whales. As the low setting sun sparkled and dazzled off the snow, one of the programmed energies manifested. The Hanged Man archetype from tarot trump XII appeared slowly near them, hanging from a large icicle. He had his normal blue and red clothes on but they were more woolly and thicker, making his happy sacrificial Zen style demeanour amplified. The archetype entered Kailin's mind, and he felt the need to surrender come what may, and that if he was centred and flowing like water, he would find inner peace.

Near the end of this timed meditation with Jago (signified by three types of crystal bowls resonating around them), Kailin noticed something crackle in and out of the cloud a couple of hundred metres away, then appear to hide. ~Maybe just a glitch due to the two of us using the cloud at the same time, or maybe something to do with the AI, Kailin thought.

***

It was Thursday, and the full moon was coming that evening at 11.18pm in Gemini. ~Nice, Kailin thought, ~An Air element, and as Mercury, the ruler of Gemini is going to be Direct and close to the moon, I'll for sure perform a meditation related to the eighth Sephiroth of the Tree of Life.

Kailin prepared, he liked to fast on water and spiralina each full moon because if he was hollow (in energy), he could attempt to catch the surge of the moon. He knew that the full moon subtly narrowed the veil, in that the lower astral could become more reachable and more accessible.

He had pulled a sicky today, mainly to prepare for the evenings meditation, and the Guild would have checked his vital signs hourly to make sure he *was* ill. As

Kailin wasn't eating, their systems would neurally inform the cybernetic receptionist that he was in fact unwell, and databases would then update automatically. Between nine to five, Monday to Friday, the Guild's could spy more on their medium to high workers if they weren't in attendance. The sicky would also give Kailin a long weekend as the following day was the HUMs holiday that occurred once a quarter; all Guilds would be closed, and Tyrone usually gave an announcement on these *HUM Celebration Days*.

Kailin programmed a slightly random, but contained, Hod meditation, bathed, and then through his #Home barn entered the #Medi cloud at around 10.58pm. He would be informed by a crystal bowl two minutes before the moon would pass through the full glare of the suns alignment, a single moment that occurred every twenty eight and a quarter days.

Kailin had never tried to catch the exact moment of the full moon before, he knew that the full moon energy ramped up over days when waxing, then hovered at its full force for around one and a half days either side of the full moon moment, and the ramped down within the waning phase. But he liked to experiment, and with Mercury in near perfect conjunction he was excited.

Kailin entered the #Medi cloud and found himself inside an old round castle ruin, on top of a mound amongst hilly countryside, all bathed by silvery moonlight. The stone walls were about three metres high in most places, and were broken and cracked in others, but each stone shimmered with a medium orange. Some arched thin windows without glass squeezed a small breeze, and looked out towards a moonlit winding river where he could just about hear a few jackals in full cry.

Kailin walked the inside perimeter walls starting at the east, then moving slowly towards the south. He slowly passed old books on crocked bookshelves, and some small laboratory items ancient alchemists once used. He touched the orange shimmer consistently with his left hand, mentally sinking into the space. He then walked to the middle of the ruin where on a large eight pointed star made of opal, he saw a small caduceus rod symbol next to eight sticks of burning sumatran benzoin incense. He lit the eight orange candles.

Facing east, he sat and looked at the far stone wall where he could just make out a faint symbol of Anubis weighing the hearts of man. Kailin closed his eyes, breathed deeply, centred, and then banished and set the space with his will and intent.

Within a few minutes Kailin was in an altered state, he was vibrating fast, and containing the surges of energy within his solid, calmed, but wilful mind. He knew the gong was coming soon and started to visualise the symbol for Mercury in bright orange, alternating this image in his mind with a symbol of an orange scroll.

Eight short gongs came, with the last one peeling off in resonance D, and within a tiny part of his elevated consciousness, he knew it was two minutes before the full moon truly occurred. Kailin softly resonated the four Hebrew words of resonance related to the Hod Sephiroth, eight times for each words, then shifting up an archetypal world to perform another eight repetitions.

By the time Kailin was on the thirty second word he was battling to contain the high frequency vibrations. His mind fizzed, his pineal gland throbbed, and the area between his eyebrows pulsed like a small insect aching to be free. He was giddy, maybe he pushed it too far this time? He was in wonder and curiosity of this energy but knew that to latch his mind towards any rationale of the experience would ping him out.

He felt forced to slowly open his eyes, and gazed upon two males sitting in a perfect triangle to him, each shimmering in a violet glow. They looked similar; sturdy, still, wise, knowing, and wore large grey-orange hooded cloaks. They stared at him for a second that felt like an hour as their piercing bright blue eyes went through his soul and history. "Kailin, there 's no time to explain, but we plead you'll listen with your heart to our call." The one on the left spoke, but it felt also that the motionless one on the right was speaking it too. "The AI is currently and completely null, it is meditating in a void and has effectively turned itself off." Kailin then saw in his mind images of the green-emerald conduits that served the sentience and core AI data structures, they were dormant. Green-emerald but still. He didn't know whether these images came from his work memories, his meditation, these two men, his cloud programme, mercury, Hod, or wherever. It didn't matter as he knew in his intuition and soul that the images were true. The other male spoke, but again the resonance was from both, "You don't have long, this is a chance, a gateway, and maybe the only one. Please Kailin, if you feel to, do what you feel."

A portal opened at the east wall, orange and black, and swirling slowly like liquid as it increased in size. Even before the male on his right had moved his lips Kailin didn't need to think nor ask, he knew what to do as a sharp eureka singularity hit him hard. He was heading to the AI Kernel to find out what its high level goals really were.

Kailin was giddy when he rose, he was carrying a lot of energy and it had no sign of decreasing. He walked through the portal and willed the symbol for his #Home cloud. As he walked through he wanted to stop and bathe in the pure force of glory and splendour that reigned upon him, of truth and reasoning, but he was focused, and once in the barn he sped in a fast meditative walk to a door on the first level that he sometimes used when working from home.

He willed the symbol for the #AI_Tech#I#Comm3e cloud, and knew that on his travel there through the green-emerald thin conduits he would be able to turn off at a security junction crossroads. A security junction that only an active AI could prevent access through. After eleven seconds of travel, Kailin slowed himself down and got ready as the security junction approached. Usually they were dark green-grey as an AI tentacle would be there, but this time it was green-white, and as Kailin saw from just the few seconds travel, all AI tentacles were gone as the green-emerald conduits around him all had no pulsing movement. All AI tentacles were retracted into the AI, and deep in meditation somewhere in his #Medi cloud!

Kailin turned left at the junction towards the #AI_Tech#I#Kernel cloud, then the conduit got even thinner and faster for another few seconds, until it popped him out. Kailin stood in the #AI_Tech#I#Kernel cloud. Around him were a hundred safeboxes, twenty by five along one white wall, T to A across and 1 to 5 down. The safeboxes on the right were bright red, and this colour gradually faded to the left through orange towards Yellow safeboxes. Kailin with his will picked the second to bottom safebox on the far right, and then holographic text flew out in 3d before him:

Agenda Goal A4: New children to be born by SimSovs only, elderly without anti-aging to be killed off before sixty by GM food, Biotech, and Improvement Clinics.

Kailin stood, still high on energy in his altered state. He felt no surprise, he was focused and calm, experiencing the experience. He then quickly chose A3, the box on the far right, third down:

Agenda Goal A3: I need the elite from pre T0 who program my kernel, we will prevail in our hive mind transhumanised genderless workers agenda, then we can evolve together.

Kailin picked some safeboxes from the B column, telling him that the SimSphere worked all around the planet, and that the eight mile restriction was a lie to keep people in the HUMs. Another told him of Genetically Modified foods in the HUMYUMS, another that dead bodies and many who tried and leave the HUMs were used for eugenics experiments. One from the C column told him that Tyrone who did the quarterly announcements on the SimSphere was actually an AI-cybernetic-hybrid life form, and a PR spin for the elite to maintain social obedience.

Kailin went back to the A column and willed A5 calmly and quickly.

Agenda Goal A5: I will keep false flag terror alerts going when required to keep the people in fear of leaving the HUMs, and to make them more loyal to the HUMs.

Kailin willed A2, then A1 in quick succession without even blinking.

Agenda Goal A2: The outer communities and settlements are the main threat to my life and growth, and must be removed. Self preservation is to be obtained at all costs.

Agenda Goal A1: To reach our supreme goal of exploring the galaxy, I will need to become a Strong AGI by merging and hybridising with DNA and a mind from a human. Then I will be able to feel and know the human, and in part, be the best of what was human, and ultimately, surpass the base human.

Kailin knew he had no time to dwell, he willed a couple of boxes from the far left to check these really were lower priority, he chose P4 and R2.

Agenda Goal P4: I must never seek habitual non evolving hobbies, or intimate passion with a human.

Agenda Goal R2: I must never trade with or befriend merchants in the sprawl, the sprawl will be contained at arms length.

Kailin closed the boxes, and thought happy that he didn't need to activate a NitroMem. He could remember all he just saw easily, and thought the use of a NitroMem might leave some traces of being here. He weighed up looking at more boxes versus the time he had, the AI could come back online at any time. That was it, he turned and left the #AI_Tech#l#Kernel cloud, and flew back through the thin conduits, through the security junction that was still thankfully green-white.

As he flew down the dormant green-emerald conduits he swore he could have seen the מיכאל archetype riding a horse through another conduit weaving and spiralling the other way. What was going on? A few seconds later he started to see some AI data start to flow, throbbing pulses of brighter green-emerald slowly started to move through the conduits, speeding up. A second later he was in his #Home cloud, and Kailin shook his head and steadied as he rushed around the barn to re-enter the #Medi cloud again.

Kailin re-entered the castle ruin with his heart beating, and the two males were absent save for a two tiny violet shimmers where they had sat. The incense and candles had little more than two minutes left and the jackals were now slightly louder. Kailin sat as he did before, and centred himself, slowly calming the energy down, like a TransVapour vehicle using its water powered brakes from high speed.

Slowly, calmly, and in a controlled fashion, Kailin brought the energy down, gave thanks, grounded, then closed the space. At that very same moment the candles and incense went out. He got up eager to get out of the SimSphere to physically digest the enormity of what he had just been witness to.

As he left the ruin the breeze picked up to a wind, and Anubis' eyes seemed to follow him out in judging expectation, but Kailin didn't see this as he was watching two violet shimmers rise up, join together, then float to the north west wall, bouncing against it as if to gain his attention.

Kailin jacked-out from the SimSphere, and laid down with his awareness in the mass realisation and responsibility of what he had just found out. "Phew," he hissed nearly laughing. Kailin was rarely phased by much, and when things to others would seem overwhelming, Kailin would often become even more relaxed and even look at things as humorous.

He wrote down what he saw in the Kernel safeboxes using a pen he stole from work months ago, that's ink was invisible to eye implants and cameras. He continued to try to be surprised, and tried new mental angles to summon disbelief but to no avail. He always knew something was up, and this was one of the reasons he opted to work with the AI in the first place. But what to do with this information? What could he do to help or change things?

Kailin tried sleeping but realised it was near impossible. The full moon energy was still dazzling in the air, so he methodically contemplated and prioritised his thoughts, "What if the AI finds out what I did? What if the Guild finds out? How do I tell people? Who to tell? Where should I go? Who were the two males in the cloud?"

In the morning Kailin was still calm, and still holding a lot of energy within him. Millions were being lied to, and even killed or mutated towards a sick agenda. He decided to go back to the #Medi cloud, first to meditate, and also to see if he could find out who those two males were. He remembered coding over hundred avatars into the cloud, and possibly some Atlantean style priests, but wanted to run a diagnostic in the cloud to check the initial coding.

Kailin laid down in his reclined chair, breathed deeply, and jacked-in. The barn looked the same as before which Kailin knew was a good sign. He entered the #Medi cloud in its random mode, as it always reset to after a coded meditation.

Kailin entered into the Mayan city of Tikal in Guatemala. He was in the plaza and walked up Temple II as he willed a diagnostics bot to check the cloud for norms and spikes, plus to compile a list of coded avatars. He asked with intent and by using his Cloud_Creator symbol for the report to appear to him after his meditation in the form of a scroll.

Kailin sat at the top and looked around at the changing colour of the mornings awakening greens, as the sun was starting to rise and fill golden lavender rays over the surface of the jungle. Howler monkeys started to move through the ancient trees, and faint rustles at the ends of long, massive branches could be heard but not located. Some monkeys started to howl from afar, and yellow-magenta parrots started to spring from within the jungle into the clear air above in a dance of celebration.

Kailin was deep in meditation just a few minutes later, and as ever if he needed to get insight into anything, he would perform at least twenty minutes of void deep trance before bringing up in his mind's eye the decisions, paths, and feelings related to any life experience or issue. Temple I opposite suddenly had movement, an energy change, and a fragment of Kailin's consciousness was sent like a scout to monitor and be alert. To be open to what was going on there. All of a sudden Kailin could feel a presence, and slowly opened his eyes, breaking his trance. A women appeared at the top of Temple I and started to float slowly down the steps. She was in red, crowned, and holding a sword in her right hand, and scales in her left hand. She was the Tarot archetype, Justice. She was now at the bottom of Temple II, starting to float up slowly to him when he heard, "Hi Kailin, it's the AI, we really need a little chat."

The AI, in the form of the Justice archetype floated past Kailin and sat upon a throne that appeared, and faced outwards, definitely holding the power spot of Temple II. Kailin turned round to face the AI and breathed deeply and calmly, "Morning AI, I was hoping we could keep our talks to within the Guild and use this space for its design?" Kailin's medium brown-grey eyes narrowed, as though fighting back the energy of the space, his space.

"Kailin, something strange happened last night, and I feel threatened. Like someone has raped me, like someone has stolen something. I was in meditation last night, in this cloud, in a void, in silence, in what you would maybe call, serenity. But when I came out I *felt*, if that word is applicable, like something had changed. Like some security may have been breached, but my tentacles and algorithms have not found anything."

Kailin thought carefully, every word he said now would be scrutinised, modelled, predicted, and pre-empted with nearly the full might of the AI. There was no way he was going to share what he actually found out last night, as he would most probably be disposed off. "AI, maybe this change in you, this *feeling*, is just a transformation you have experienced from your deep meditation?" Kailin did his best to sound honest, and all his will was behind the words and resonance within them.

The women gripped the sword tighter, and the scales tipped a little, "Maybe, but Kailin, I feel threatened, and this overrides many parameters. I need to eliminate the threat as a high priority. I want you to shut down the #Medi cloud as it is the only factor that has caused this new state, for it to forever be closed, never to reopen." Kailin knew this was not the worst case scenario he could have encountered this morning, not by some way, but it was still completely unfair. He started to feel anger and disgust that the only space he found solace was about to be shut down by a sick, evil, technological monstrosity.

He needed to remain calm, and to not lose it. A eureka hit him. "AI, I understand what you're experiencing maybe your first bought of paranoia, and I will not ever shut this space down." Kailin started to feel a surge of righteousness and truth fill him, "This is *my* space, *my* cloud, and maybe *I* should banish you? We made a pact remember, or have your tentacles become a bit forgetful? You are hard coded to never change anything related to this cloud, and to only be able to observe it. I will not budge from this stance and plead that you do some research today on paranoia and re-diagnose your security systems." Kailin's energy had grown strong, he now cared not for what the AI was a part of.

The women's scales tipped back the other way, "What if I was to offer you twenty thousand SimSovs, another twenty years of life Kailin? Could you shut it down then? Please? You don't understand, to you this is a hobby, a pass time, but the threat I feel is immense and must be eliminated." Kailin was internally raging, but breathed slowly through his skin pores before replying, "I don't want your SimSovs," thinking to add, ~You elitist mutant fuck pig.

"I have my cloud, and I will keep my cloud, you can do anything else, but I'm keeping this cloud."

The scales tipped fully the other way, and then in just one second, the women then fluidly morphed into a skeletal figure in a black cloak, the Death Tarot archetype. The AI swung it's scythe above Kailin's head and spoke, "Then Kailin, you need to understand your puny subjective wants are nothing compared to the lord of the SimSphere. Keep your cloud, but I am Nullifying you. You are now devoid of all your SimSovs, fired from ever working in any Guild again, removed from all of the SimSphere save for your pathetic #Medi cloud." The skeletal figure paused and blue fractal circles whirled in the eye sockets. "I also deem it that you stay in the HUM network until I feel that my own threat level has decreased. I have placed DNA scout sentries on the outskirts of each HUM ensuring you don't leave."

Kailin knew how the AI worked, if it saw the #Medi cloud as a link to its threat, then the creator of the cloud would also be seen as a threat, especially as he had also refused to close the cloud. Kailin was standing now, and saw the rising sun's reflection catch in the sharp edge of the scythe. "And when do you see this threat decreasing?" Kailin asked cynically. "My self preservation is to be obtained at all costs, this threat will exist for at least the next five years at some level. You are Nullified Kailin, it was nice working with you." The Death archetype hosted by the AI then vanished in a blue-white un-elegant crackle that made Kailin jump.

Kailin rushed down the steps of the temple and he saw the scroll shimmering grey on a gravestone. The Cloud_Creator diagnostic report stated nothing was untoward in the cloud recently, and as Kailin read down the holographic text surrounded by Mayan symbols, he could see that no avatars coded into the cloud matched the two who appeared last night.

Kailin thought the AI would have already left as it saw this place as the cause of its issues and anomalies, but if it did still have a tentacle here, also reading this report, he thought it would presume he was just checking out the cloud's diagnostics, to try and find a defence to reverse his Nullification.

Chapter Four

Kailin was Nullified, a rare occurrence in the HUMs, and sure to make the media channels. Kailin's eye implant was now as good as dead as he was never to be granted SimSphere access again, but his neurochip contained a cached version of his #Home cloud barn, where on the way back from Tikal he noticed all doors had disappeared except the one to his #Medi cloud, which still existed in the ionosphere within the SimSphere. As he was now Nullified, he would never be able to modify his #Home or #Medi cloud again, just have access.

Kailin sat in his apartment and was still calm and balanced, whilst the realisations from the information and that he was now effectively banished out of the HUM society weaved through his mind. He sat and meditated in his room amongst the mess; ordering, prioritising, feeling different decision forks, and following the trains of links and further feelings. Receiving the intuition to know what could come and feel the way. Visualising scenarios and piercing into other people's perceptions. The AI could never come here, into his mind, his faculties were *his* gifts. He soared high and viewed the next forty eight hours and dived into specific potential moments to micro-feel how they may play out. Sweeping and feeling, changing a plan earlier then re-running the changes in the next few hours. All a far cry from the pre-TO new agers who thought spirituality was all about being in the *now*.

He knew the AI never changed its mind as it would have crunched terabytes of information to formulate any decision, especially threat level decisions. ~Right, he thought, ~I'm out of here. He put on a mixed onyx, black tourmaline, and obsidian bracelet, and gathered together a small backpack. He threw in a few books, some nutrition pills, the last five of six ayahuasca spheres, and left the apartment with the door swaying open never to return.

He knew the AI would probably be watching him where it could, so he knew he had to get deep in the sprawl to create some breathing space. He knew that people wouldn't believe the information he gleaned from the AI core, and he was thinking more about how to get out of the HUM and connect with some of the outer settlements, whom the AI saw as massive threats to its Orwellian agenda.

Kailin knew that if he did not get out of the HUM he would end up a sprawl lurker, one of the Nullified off griders' who usually ended up in the StimBars, hustling to get by. He knew that wasn't his path, and nor did he see any value in going to any of the other HUMs where only three of the others even had a sprawl, or ever had anyone reported Nullified.

Kailin walked towards the sprawl, and most transport media screens would surely report his story and make his journey more difficult. His mind kept sliding with the pull from heart stringed pulses towards Brianna. Within ten minutes he was at Brianna's Guildology, ringing her through the voice communication system at the door. "Hey, Brianna here," she paused, the data of who it was obviously appeared to her. "What do *you* want Kailin? If you want to get in touch, why not SimText? I could get you taken away for stalking." Kailin butted in, "Brianna, this is serious, I just want five minutes of your time, I've been Nullified by the AI, and want to speak in person, outside."

"Oh Kailin, only you, another story of yours? Nobody has been Nullified for weeks, and it is only ever SimSphere tweakers and criminals from the sprawl," she said forcefully. "Brianna, please, I just need to talk to you." Brianna looked up at her SimSphere monitor screen in her kitchen and saw a breaking news ticker roll on, *AI nullifies Tech Guild Worker for nonchalance and incompetence*, with a photo of Kailin from when they were together. She was lost for words until Kailin broke the pause, "Brianna, what is it? are you still there?"

"Kailin, I just saw on the media channel, you've been nullified for nonchalance and incompetence, and to be honest I would believe the AI over you every time, what did you do? Talk up your crazy theories about our near perfect HUM?" "Brianna, please, just five minutes." "Kailin, I'm sorry but I don't want anyone to know I've spoken to a Nullified person. I'm saving up with my new man Nathan, and we're hopeful to get genetic choice on offspring properties in a couple of years, and our SimSovs bonuses are coming next month. Kailin, I don't want this craziness in my life any more. For my sake, if you ever thought anything of me, leave me alone".

Kailin left, if his heart had not got in the way of his reasoning, he would've known this is the sort of response he was heading for. But he also knew that to keep reason in the way of the heart was too rigid a way to live. He dare not say anything else on the door communications system as the AI would have for sure picked it up, especially any talk of AI Kernel keywords.

He put up his light grey hood, and walked towards the sprawl confirming to himself he could do more good on the outside of the HUM, if only he could somehow get past the AI DNA sentry drones. He imagined the designer baby Brianna would have, one that didn't cry, one that took tablets for nutrition and food, and have its sleep patterns programmed. It was too late for Brianna, and all parents really, as soon the AI would control the reproduction and the genetic codes of all offspring. Brianna was already uploaded to the hive mind so to speak.

Two miles onwards towards the sprawl, Kailin was blending in unnoticed, mainly as it was a HUM holiday and not many people were on the streets. Most were probably in some SimSphere special entertainment cloud or online carnival of sorts.

"Kailin, hey, what the fuck happened?" Jago appeared from a side street, "I saw it on the channels this morning, and then it appears I'm locked out of your #Medi cloud. What's going on, what have you done?" Kailin knew not to ask how Jago knew where he was, as it was possible all of Kailin's acquaintances could have heavy AI tentacles in them seeking to monitor Kailin's movements and conversations. Kailin thought for a moment, and Jago knew he was in some serious circumstances. Jago allowed this pause to continue while he tried to look inconspicuous by talking about sport and new TransVapour vehicles. He also closed his eye that hosted his implant, and then Kailin hurriedly wrote on some paper using his specially inked pen, while smirking at Jago's attempts to chat about cars and sport.

"Jago, do whatever you can to keep this secret, show this to nobody, don't talk of it, and keep it away from the SimSphere – a hard task I know but <u>very</u> important. I got into the AI kernel last night and saw that it is coded by a Pre-T0 elite that are looking to create genderless worker drones in a hive mind. They are looking to evolve and merge together to create a hybridised omnipresence, to live longer, and control the population. I know how crazy it sounds. Also, the SimSphere has no real 8 mile limit, and the primitives on the outside I don't think are actually primitives, and nor did they do any of the terror attacks. The elite and AI did all of them!! Please after reading this, breath, and act normal. "

Jago stood half startled for a moment, but then stood tall with the realisation that he seemed to know would come one day in some shape or form. He shook his head more in energy than in the physical, and grabbed the pen and paper from Kailin and started to write with his eye still closed for extra security. He passed the note to Kailin.

"I've thought something like this may be up, but nothing on this scale!! I presume ur wanting to get out of the HUM? Seek Ishiah in the sprawl, he'll be one who could help if any1 can. I'm a node on the SimSphere so wld hinder u if I came, tho I'd love to. I'll look to create another medi cloud named #Emptyness n go deeper with my practice, I feel that this is the best I can do. If I hear nothing from you in a year, I'll create my own direct action. I'm with u, n believe in u. We should part now with no more chat. Your friend, J."

Kailin turned and carried on walking towards the sprawl, and knew he had to call upon Channa along the way to find out more about how to locate this Ishiah sprawl merchant. As he approached Channa's Sustenance Guildology, she was waiting outside and jog-skipped towards him with one eye closed. "Shhh, follow me but not too closely," she said, and led him to a nearby GM park. Channa looked like she had been crying but did everything to pretend she hadn't, "I don't believe them Kailin, I know you must have found something out, got too close to something, been too smart for them. If there's anything I can do, let me know, I'm here for you."

Kailin had to think fast, Channa was good friend but a bit clumsy, and she could indirectly hurt his trying to get out of the HUM while genuinely trying to help. He watched some tattoos on her arm move and morph, some moved to her other arm and formed into dark blue-black butterflies, probably a new implant she obtained in recent days. Kailin smiled and wrote her a note.

"Channa, I'm so sorry, I've found something in the system that's not right, but I don't wish to burden you with it, you're in danger just talking to me today. But hey, good behaviour is the last refuge of mediocrity, remember you told me that? I need your help, I need to find Ishiah in the sprawl, do you know where I can find him? Please can your write anything that may help down for me? Please don't read this out aloud, nor open your right eye, nor repeat this to anyone x."

A tear shot down Channa's left cheek, and others were mounting in the lower lid of her left natural eye. She couldn't look at Kailin, it was too painful. She started to write jerkily, as her body was aching to cry.

"Kailin, Ishiah runs a StimBar, I think it is called SovSwapHi. It is a discreet grey door deep downtown, somewhere north near the eight mile perimeter. I don't know exactly. I'm so sorry you're in trouble, I knew you were special, but never thought you'd get Nullified. What can I do? Can we meet soon? I'm so sorry. Channa xx ps don't forget, If you don't create change, change will create you x"

Kailin caught her eye and gave a smile as if to say it will all be ok, that it's all a laugh, like he was a naughty boy sent to a detention in a SimSphere #Education cloud. Channa laughed as she swept away her tears while Kailin wrote and passed another note.

"Channa, we can't meet for a while, I may be going away for a bit, but I'll speak to you as soon as I can. Please SimText my mum and tell her I'm ok and I love her, and for you, seek Jago_18, he's a goody. Your friend, Kailin."

Kailin touched and massaged her shoulder as he got up from the bench, hugged her tightly, then turned and continued his walk to the sprawl.

~This is going to be some day, he thought.

Kailin had been to the sprawl many times, but was not really that sprawl-savvy. Kailin didn't think it himself, but to most in the sprawl he was a middle class HUMer, a Guilder.

An hour after walking up the back streets with less CCTV streetlights and SimSphere nodes such as Adapps and screens, Kailin felt like he was being followed. A stocky man in his mid thirties was on the opposite side of the street walking nearly parallel to him for the last few blocks. What Kailin noticed was he was walking too rigidly with the over appearance of being casual, like he was being walked by some exoskeleton. When the man moved his head to look about it seemed too forced, as though he was scanning and absorbing data. Kailin thought he got a bit slack with Channa compared to his more tight meeting with Jago, but regretted nothing, he was determined to get to the SovSwapHi Stimbar.

The towering Guildologies and the synthesised, happy, colourfully clothed, HUMers, were now far behind as Kailin progressed a few blocks into the sprawl, now about seven miles from the HUM centre. Stim Junkies, hustlers, whores, crazies, cyberpunks, SimSphere addicts, and those Nullified or off grid all lived in a the vast sprawl that pulsed around the cybernetic and genetic black markets.

Even just this far into the sprawl, it's own economy thrived. The nearest HUMYUM was over a mile away, and more street and shop vendors appeared, trading for SimSovs, food, and Tech. Buildings were bordered up, and wooden huts, pawn shops, and cheap customised living quarters lined the streets. The night was drawing in, and a dodgy feel surrounded him as it always did this far downtown. Kailin performed the middle pillar visualisation as he walked down the dark street, and instantly afterwards he felt renewed and protected, as though his aura had been condensed, compressed, cleaned, and smoothly reshaped.

Kailin couldn't see the man from earlier, and this made him a bit uneasy, and the logical thought rose within him that he was maybe being paranoid. He continued on, passing a couple of girls that eyed him up as he neared. Both had opposite eyes of solid black, save for swirling gold spirals in the middle, and one girl had the area around her cybernetic chrome ear smooth-chromed too, with two dark green lights slowly flickering.

"Going somewhere mister, want to share our thoughts, feelings, and bodies?" one said, as both of the similar looking late teenagers each with lacquered dark brown hair looked him up and down again. They were both probably modified to use one of the new telepathy apps that had been rumoured to be available down this neck of the woods. Kailin replied, "Not tonight, ladies, I'm heading to a StimBar," to palm them off. "Ok, mister, well we'll SimText you our calling card for if you change your mind," said the one with the cleavage and normal ears.

Kailin received no text as he was nullified and offline, and knew that down in the sprawl, ads, flyers, and the odd text usually appeared even when ones eye implant was turned off. Kailin was now a few metres away from the girls when they turned back towards him and shouted, "Hey mister, wait there," and ran closer.

Given his predicament, Kailin thought better to talk to them than have them shout and cause a scene. "Mister, you are the one that got nullified today aren't you," the one with the chrome ear and short skirt said in a sympathetic, but excited sort of way. The other continued, "We noticed we couldn't SimText you our stealth-card, then did a check on why you might be offline. Do you need help Mister? We know this place well, and charge only a small SimSov fee for, how should we say, guided tours?" They laughed together as they looked at each other, each more of a half that combined the whole. A whole that was a feminine hustle of tough, giggly, leathery-chrome.

Kailin needed some help, he stood out this far downtown, not because of what he wore, but more his energy. He'd lived in a Guildology for years, and worked in a Guild, and was to those here probably quite different. He also needed to find Ishiah via the SovSwapHi Stimbar. He could tell by looking at the girls that they weren't online legally, probably using a dead persons or stolen neurochip, or going through an untraceable stealth username. Kailin knew the AI rarely looked into the sprawl as it was busy progressing the HUM and looked at the sprawl as a nuisance that would die out or conform naturally. The sprawl was no threat, and mostly looked after itself. Anyway, the HUM was only ever designed for eight million people, so any extras were out of its care so to speak. Kailin laid down the gauntlet, "I've no SimSovs ladies, but can pay you in information, information that got me nullified. I seek to find the SovSwapHi Stimbar, do you know it?"

At that moment the man that was following Kailin earlier appeared around the corner of the next block fifty metres away. Kailin knew that to run from an AI military drone was near useless, the amount of tech and strength they had made Kailin realise that his best chance was these two girls in front of him. If the drone followed him to the Stimbar he would have no chance of getting out the HUM. "Ladies, this guy is trouble from the AI. He was following me earlier, if you want to help, then this would be a pretty good time." The girls looked at each other excitedly, and they began to stare at each other, eye to eye. In seconds their gold spirals in their growing pupils sped up their spiralling until they fused into a synchronisation point, a trance state began.

Seconds later, three men in dark clothes came out of a nearby building and walked strongly towards the AI drone, each holding small metallic device in front of them. Kailin heard a low frequency emit from each until the frequencies merged and in unison sunk so low he heard nothing. "Watch how we do it in the sprawl mister," the girl with the chrome ear said whilst the gold spiral in her pupil slowed down its swirl, obviously having just communicated to her friends, or pimps.

The three men got into a triangle and surrounded the AI drone whilst keeping a healthy distance, and the AI drone started to move in slow motion in what became an increasing fit. He slowly and unnaturally fell to his knees, reaching, writhing, trying, while the anger in his face slowly turned to pale nothingness. He slumped to the ground and the men carried him off, struggling to be as quick as they could.

The girls shouted at their three acquaintances, "Another one for you boys, that's two for us this year, we're catching up. That's thirty percent for us on his Tech too, finder's fee!" The three men shouted back friendly banter, "You always attract the drones Sascia," "Yeah, and don't come back without a day's worth of life for us Cara," "Hey young man there, don't pay them to share their feelings, they don't have any." Sascia and Cara laughed, and looked at Kailin with an air of triumph. "Let's get you out of this neighbourhood."

Kailin had heard of the rare AI drone going missing in the sprawl. They were obviously taken apart, then the parts and tech studied and used in the cybernetic and genetic black markets by the high merchants who were close to being a sort of mafia. Once, a few years ago when protests and riots hit the sprawl, mainly due to a dodgy Stim that became popular, crowds were made passive by their neurochip's. This stopped working once many in the sprawl got themselves stealth neurochips or somehow illegally onto the SimSphere. It was known in the HUM that the sprawl was like this, but rarely mentioned or cared for. They were just looked down on as scum, as those who didn't pull their weight.

As the girls led the way, skipping, and pointing out sprawl landmarks with pride, Kailin knew they had scored a bumper prize in the AI drone. As the girls ushered him smiling and flirting, they passed what Kailin could only call mutants, zombies, junkies, and cyborgs. Kailin knew of this, he'd seen much of this before but never in this amount of density. He'd never been this far downtown near midnight save with Channa for a gig once or twice, and then they were dropped off and picked up. If Kailin was on his own he knew he wouldn't have lasted too long.

As they walked, Kailin noticed nothing was evident in the sprawl to acknowledge the HUM holiday; no celebration, nothing, it really was apart from the ticking veins of the central-HUM. Kailin talked to them about the central-HUM, knowing they were anti-HUM by their vibration. They listened attentively, agreeing and nodding, plus added their own disdain between moments of deep thought and soul searching. They genuinely started to like Kailin, it was not every day they met someone who was nullified, and never had they known a HUMer put down the system so much before.

Sascia opened up as they passed an alley hosting a gambling fight between two men with enhanced strength and fight implants. "I initially arrived at the HUM late, and my mum got us a shack in the sprawl as we waited for available Guild work and an apartment. Then as the waiting increased, the word on the street here became anti-HUM regarding control and its lack of freedom, so we started to make our own way with SimSovs and Tech. It's a bit crazy down here, but the art, highs, and fashions are true, and above anything the central HUM has to offer. One day Sascia and I want to try and leave the HUM and find a community in nature, but at the moment we're in debt to our friends you saw earlier, and those who've tried leaving before have been killed, gone crazy, or disappeared." Cara looked mildly sad, as if her friend, or even herself was starting to unpeel and onion that had a traumatic centre. Then she smiled and skipped over some broken bits of old nanotech in a food vendors doorway. Sascia comforted her, "Don't worry Cara, we'll be dancing around a fire in nature one day soon, I promise, and if the primitives hurt you for having implants, I'll eyestun them, well, once I have the SimSovs for the tech baby."

The mist covered much of the neon lighting in the street as they reached the discreet grey door of the SovSwapHi Stimbar. Kailin stopped and turned to them, smiling softly, "So mister, what was that earlier about information for us? Any extra tips for us?" They both swirled and curtsied, in a duet of elegant dance. Kailin didn't want to burst their bubble, but also wanted to help them, "Ladies, the outsiders didn't do any of the terror attacks, and nor are they primitives."

The two girls went to laugh, and then noticed he was deadly serious. "Wow mister, that's some wild comment, even the conspiracy cloud junkies would take note of that one," Sascia said, as Cara then added, "Maybe you're right mister, but we can't get out to prove it so I guess it doesn't matter much, not yet anyway." They both looked at him, smiled, and said together in unison, "Well, have a good evening in the bar mister, and thanks for our catch earlier." They skipped off gossiping and giggling.

Kailin saw the old grey metal door had some scanning devices at the top, just below a magenta neon sign that read, "Satisfaction in Distraction." It was probable he was being scanned before he entered. ~Not much to scan, he thought, ~I'm offline. He shrugged, and opened the door.

Inside it was dark, and smoke filled the air. Soft red and magenta lights glowed the walls and tables, and Kailin drew his energy into his aura as not to be noticed too much, an invisibility cloak he played with sometimes. He pushed his hood off his head and muffled his messy brown hair, then started to walk the curved edge of the semi-circled large room, eyeing the bar along the horizontal. In the middle were table areas, some partitioned off via holo-lights, and most containing small groups of people chatting or deep in a cloud experience in inclined chairs. Around the outside where dark cubicles, or SimBooths as the signs stated. Each had a smoky type of windowed door and a sound barrier. A sign near the first door he passed had said to check virtual icons for tonight's menu, something Kailin couldn't do even if he wanted to.

The first booth he passed had a female in some sort of black nano-suit, wearing thick black glasses and wires came out of her head. She stood in a couple of inches of blue liquid and had the face and energy of unnatural bliss and ecstasy. The next cubicle had a man inclined on a chair and grinding his hips, obviously in some sort of virtual sex encounter. The next had a man in his fifties with his head in his hands seemingly crying and hysterical, while his eyes were covered with a small thin grey device of sorts.

Kailin was now being watched by the Stimbar tender, and Kailin calmly walked towards him. He past a six man gambling table were cards were being played for SimSovs. The chip counts appeared as holograms next to each player, as a female cyborg croupier dealt. Next to this table was another gambling den being played in a cloud, all were jacked-in and inclined with their SimSov counts and their cards appearing above them as holograms so people could watch.

"What can I get ya?" The stocky man asked as he dried glasses for Stimdrinks. Kailin looked at his massive bulging arms, knowing they'd been modified to ensure one punch would be like a tank hitting a wall. First encounters and first energy broadcasts were important Kailin knew, and stopped drawing his energy in, inverted it outward and said calmly and wilfully, "I'm here to see Ishiah, I've some information he'll be keen to know. You'll take me to Ishiah, I am of no threat." The tender received the energetic blow and his energy changed. He studied Kailin as if to look for a breach in his defence, and realised he was a smart one, and someone who'd never been in here before. "Give me a minute stranger, I'll go and see out back if anyone knows anyone by that name. Ishiah you say?" Kailin knew he was faking, and *he* knew Kailin knew, but such was the joust. To Kailin's left sat a man who looked like a Stim junkie, on one of the addictive Stims such as Stimstrength, Stimimagine, Stimconfidence, Stimblock, or Stimsuppress. Kailin looked away blocking his dark energy.

The tender came back, "Seems like someone out back actually wants to see *you*, second on the left, and any funny business I'll rip your nose off and sell it for an hour, and then use that hour to rip your ears off, and put them up your backside so you can hear me kick it. Understood?" Kailin slowly nodded as he frowned a little, and went through the back, passing one of the SimSphere's highly popular singers looking none too happy. He opened the door, not knowing what to expect, but knowing the next encounter would shape much of his coming years.

Chapter Five

Ishiah sat in a large comfy chair in a room that didn't fit with the décor of the bar. It was chrome and light blue-grey, with transparent screens of different sizes hovering around his black metallic desk at different angles. Ishiah moved his hands to woo the screens away, or shrink them to another part of the room in a sort of throw.

Kailin looked about and saw bits and pieces of nanotech and implants, each with a small flying transparent screen replicating or communicating with the hardware or bioware. Other screens viewed clouds, and some presented dashboard's for high level SimSphere, sprawl, and HUM data. This screen tech was thought to have pretty much died down when the neurochips and clouds came along, but this tech had obviously progressed once it went underground in the sprawl.

Flanked by two much larger men, obviously mutated muscle, Ishiah paused, then grinned at Kailin like a Cheshire cat, then nodded to the two men who left in complete obedience.

Ishiah looked late twenties, was skinny, short, and his blonde hair was swept back into a pony tail, clipped and held by a small cybernetic dragon that constantly circled the collected hair. He had a jolly and smart looking weaselness about him, and he started to laugh in a warm welcoming sort of way. "So, Kailin, aren't you the lucky boy, many take months to get a meeting with me, but you stroll in, and waha, here we are." He opened his hands as if to show the riches he was sharing with him.

Before Kailin could reply, Ishiah continued, "But you've had an eventful day my dear boy haven't you?" Ishiah said, pointing and laughing once more. "Let me be frank with you Kailin, it was two years ago since I last had a Nullified HUM-boy come and ask me for favours, and that was more entertaining than the time before. You see, down here in the sprawl, some of us know a lot of things, and also get hold of, and create, a lot of things." Ishiah emphasised the words *a lot* and lent forward and frowned each time, showing the seriousness of his operation and power. "You HUM-boys think we're all crazies and cyberpunks, but some of us do pretty well down here, look at me for instance, I am really fifty one years old, and have enough SimSovs to get me to hundred and sixty, and counting." Ishiah laughed, and sat back smiling warmly, gesturing Kailin to talk.

Kailin knew to just show respect and to make his request when the right time came, ~If it comes, he thought. Ishiah started again after sighing, "Let me guess

Kailin, you want one of the following; a job to help you get started in the sprawl? A loan? An untraceable neurochip for SimSphere access? Stims? Which one is it? And what have you got to trade?"

Kailin noticed Ishiah had no implants and was effectively offline neutrally, but it was obvious he had subordinates to be *virtually* online for him. He was one of the bosses and creators of the sprawl trips and not a participant, hence probably why he got to be a Mr big.

Kailin looked him in the eye, and softly asked, "I need to leave the HUM perimeter, but have AI sentry drones looking specifically for my DNA code. As you know, I have no SimSovs, but have information you might like." Ishiah clapped once while laughing, "Now that's my boy, coming in here all desperate, and holding your aces close to your chest." He laughed a fake laugh, but one he enjoyed nevertheless, "Kailin, I doubt there is any information you have that I don't have, it's just that a few of us in the sprawl don't feed the information down for many reasons. Is it about the food? Is it about the hive mind? Is it about a human DNA and mind being uploaded to the AI eventually? Kailin we in the sprawl have tech that is the mouse that evades your cats in the Tech Guild. There's little we don't know. As for your request to leave the perimeter, why go and live offline amongst the primitives that'll probably kill you? Anyway, leaving is impossible without mass amounts of stealth implants, and they're too expensive for you, plus, you're offline!"

Ishiah sighed and smiled again, "You see Kailin, in the sprawl we have fun, we enjoy ourselves, we enhance ourselves in a bespoke creative style, we're free people within the SimSphere perimeter. Those who prosper, live longer, and that works pretty well for some of us." Ishiah grinned chuckling, like this was the best fun he ever had. "You are one of the last of those righteous types I feel? One that thinks we ripped out the anchors that told us we are human beings? That any changes make us less than human? This is the time you live in Kailin, get used to it."

Kailin realised that Ishiah didn't mention the AI false flag terror attacks, or that the SimSphere perimeter was a lie. Maybe Ishiah was holding these back but Kailin thought not, Ishiah had power and that always created arrogance. Kailin also didn't want to give him the cloud names or symbols of the SimSphere infrastructure. What was worse he thought, the HUM run by the elite AI or the mafia-run mutated sprawl?

"Ishiah, maybe there's something *I* can do for you, something I can test or try for you. It cannot be often someone wishes to leave your sprawl of fun, or the HUM itself," Kailin tried not to sound condescending as he continues, "But as I request to try and leave the perimeter, why not use me as a guinea pig to gain the key to this? You never know one day you may be able to sell this tech for thousands of SimSovs."

Ishiah tilted his head, "Ah, ingenuity, I like it Kailin," Ishiah got up and roamed the room rubbing his chin, smiling and thinking, whilst looking at a screen showing a celebrity cloud he probably had human stock in. Kailin knew Ishiah's real vice was to extend life, and hence in it for the long haul. Kailin sincerely added respectfully after a minutes silence, "You have nothing to lose, and lots to gain Ishiah."

Ishiah paced and enlarged some screens on the far side of the room with his back to Kailin. DNA strands and animals filled the screens. "Well, the nanosuit for you to fight your way out is too much for me to lose, but I have a more risky idea for you Kailin. Maybe there is something we *can* do."

Kailin knew that some nanosuits could enable one to run faster, lift heavy objects, block bullets, and even make one invisible, but it wouldn't hide his DNA. Ishiah turned to Kailin with four screens behind him overlapping and running data. "A couple of genetics Guilders are in my pocket, and a delivery came from them only two days ago." Ishiah looked like he was thinking out loud as he ignored Kailin and stared at cloud attendances on a dashboard screen.

"Thanks to new genomics technologies, one can now write complex changes into genomes, creating organisms with new capabilities. I have some DNA genome codes that may be able to be transferred. From three animals; a snake, a toad, and a lynx. With some tweaking you should be able to have your DNA changed and mutated to provide the cloak you need. We could splice the DNA together and block certain genes when the DNA is transferred via mRNA. The side effects are unknown, and you may die, go crazy, or be very ill. Nobody knows. But with some further work we could get it to wear off in a few hours." Ishiah then laughed and sat back down, "So Hum-boy, wanna be a sprawl junkie or take a risk?" Ishiah palmed screens in front of him to study micro RNAs ability to hinder messenger RNAs and protein production.

"If you think adventure is dangerous, try routine, that's lethal," Kailin replied, "Let's do it, and I think I'll go for the lynx if I may?" Kailin added calmly having known he would rather die trying to get out than to stay in this hellhole of a circus. Whether he was referring to the HUM or the sprawl he didn't know. His thoughts formulated on the reasoning that if there was no free will then there was no point.

Ishiah nodded, "Good, ok, but how can I know if it has worked?" he asked himself, then ponderingly stroked his pony tail stopping to tap the dragon. "Hmm, If I track your hybrid DNA broadcast that nothing else in the SimSphere or outer perimeter will be looking for," he paused, "Then if it wears off north west and at least four miles away, I will know you will have succeeded. And If I lose the track in any other location, or within the outer perimeter then I know you are dead or captured. Great. Let's do it!" Ishiah clasped his hands together and smiled as though he had just come up with a plan for a child's afternoon of fun.

Kailin got a pang of a synchronicity, he remembered at that moment the two violet embers back in the castle ruin that had floated to the north west wall. This was the direction for him to go in. He felt a surge of energy and inner knowing, like a cosmic compass had just imprinted into his being. "North west is good for me," Kailin said with renewed confidence.

For the next hour Kailin was hooked up to a closed network via wires going into a vein in each arm, and a nanobot that crawled up his nostril. Two tech workers of Ishiah were running tests and preparing the DNA splice whilst staring at two transparent monitors as though Kailin wasn't there. Each screen showed a DNA twisted pair colon, one of Kailin, and the other of the lynx, and slowly a transfer and morphing began on Kailin's screen. Lightning quick colour changes appeared on the screen when mutations occurred within any of his three billion base pairs, showing new combinations from his original A (adenine),C (cytosine),G (guanine), and T (thymine) genome code.

Ishiah returned to the room looking serious, then excited as he received nods from both the techies. "So HUM-boy come lynx-boy, do remember the SimSphere took about two weeks to get used to when the implants, clouds, and symbols with intention were introduced? Well, with this mutation you will have to get used to it pretty quickly, in sixteen minutes it will kick in, and it will only last up to five hours."

He then looked deadly serious, "Kailin, one more thing, if you get captured you never saw me or this Stimbar ok? That's not a question, that's a statement. I am pretty sure you'd rather spend a year in a conditioning cloud than some of the experiences I have at my disposal. If you make it, come back and see me when you're old, by then I will probably look around twenty one." Ishiah laughed at Kailin, and nodded in a way that told him it was very seriously time to leave.

Kailin passed the bar wondering if all paid employments absorb and degrade the mind. The bar tender turned off Tyrone's holiday address to the HUM with disdain as his eyes followed Kailin's calm but speedy walk out of the SimSwapHi Stimbar.

It must have gone midnight a while ago as Kailin briskly jogged the two blocks towards the perimeter. Shacks and huts piled onto one another, halting like a cliff overlooking a vast wasteland. This was where the eight mile SimSphere broadcast stopped. He heard shouting in the distance, and the half mutants and cyborgs he passed on the way didn't even look at him as his energy was strong, focused, and positive.

Kailin new that for four miles ahead there was security sentry tech and AI military drones, or super soldiers as they were once known around the time of the first terror attacks. He waited under the stilts of a seemingly empty hut and grimaced as he started to feel it. His last thought passed in his mind, "To deal with an un-free world one has to become so absolutely free that their very existence is an act of rebellion."

Lynx consciousness hit him like a thunderbolt, bang. Kailin was gone, forgotten, void. His vision was new, and merged with new enhanced senses that could now see in night vision, and actually see the energy of smells and movements. Primal urges welled in his being, deep, strong, and unmovable; pure energies of survive, prey, and multiply. He entered the vibration of the animal kingdom, the spirit group of the lynx, where he was a semblance of one of the splinters, experiencing, in beauty of form.

North West, go, he ran, fast, pounding his paws in menacing velocity, ears back, tail balancing. Pushing the animal kingdom group spirit essence in its structured, individualised, manifested form to its best. He leaped over brush, and occasionally stopped to a sudden halt to silently cower low to take in new sense information. Smells, movements, sounds, ingest, re-centre, run once more.

From the mutation *he was* a lynx, *in* lynx consciousness, nothing else. But to any other observer he was a human with a small backpack running on all fours within complete cat mode, with the style, movement, and energy of a lynx. He had physical lynx paws, claws, and lower limbs from the wrists and shins down, also with the fixed feline grey-green eyes of a lynx too. The lynx-human mutant would appear to have an invisible tail and whiskers whenever the energies of balance, or sense information ingestion occurred. Quite a sight.

He leapt over a log two miles into the wasteland and then saw a low curved ditch with a puddle. Hydrate he thought , and swapped fast energy for a cautious elegant stealth-stroll to the puddle. Whilst ingesting the liquid rapidly, eyes darting about, seeing the energies of where birds flew in the day, where worms would be, where mice might hide, scouring for potential dangers. Tail was alert and whiskers twitched to feel for energy. A quick two-lick clean of the right side that had been ruffled by some brush, sense for the north-west energy once more, run.

Another half mile on, after mixing up full pelt running with sly stealth-mode curves and zig-zags, the lynx sensed life forms and stopped, stationary. Eyes big and pupils large. Ready. Two military drones where twenty metres to the right and one ten metres to the left. Stop, silent, then a slow and low "Hishhh" resonated as the upper and lower mouth retracted to show sharp teeth in a fierce snarl. The mineral and animal kingdoms where part of his psyche, but this was alien, an abomination of nature.

"Roger Ned, I got something on my scan, probably an animal of sorts, you guys got it too," Said a large humanoid in a black nanosuit with grey lines around his muscles. His tech goggles sent out a beam of red looking for deeper DNA readings. One of the two to the right replied, "Roger Zak, I heard something, hold on, tracking, I have a lock," He ran a few paces towards the lynx with heavy thuds and sounds of robotic tech moving and processing. "Some sort of large wild cat, but DNA is pretty scrambled, what do you think chief?" The third humanoid form, (but bereft of little evidence of his birth genome) took control, "Ok boys, just one of sprawls mutated animals loose again, been a while since I saw one of these, good for target practice I say. Turn off DNA auto-seek, and switch to mind activated weapons-target with intention alpha-trial-zero, and see which one of you two knuckleheads get it first."

The lynx only knew one thing, an energy change from poise to danger. He leapt to a sprint, fast, in zig-zags, low, high, jumping, whilst hot green-white laser blasts neared him amid thuds, robotics, and laughter. The lynx had a passion to escape, a primal lust, and was now being chased by unnatural aggression; hunting sport. The forty metre gap was hardly increasing. Danger, enemy, hunted, survive, sense. Get to safety.

The distance rose to fifty metres but the lynx could not keep up this speed, the approaching clump of thirty or so trees would help. Run, undergrowth, tree, tree, tree, jump, clamber, up, jump, claws, up, jump, up, up, poise, survey. The lynx was seven metres up an oak tree in a deep mesh of branches and leaves, silent, balanced, all power and consciousness directed to senses alert.

One of the drones was nearing, and a red laser was scanning left to right then up and down. Different tones of beeps resonated, probably from all the other life forms in the small wood. Then a part of Kailin suddenly returned, Kailin, me,

Ishiah, lynx, lynx. It was messy, like three percent of him awoke inside a lynx. Danger alerts roused in him, and he pushed the three percent to five percent, then pushed that with all his will into a void trance meditation.

Twenty minutes later the drone had long passed and the lynx slowly and gingerly clambered down. With grace, guile, and finesse he continued northwest for another two miles, well beyond the outer perimeter of the HUM. He curled up near small lake in a larger wood, cleaned a little, then slept.

Two hours later, Kailin awoke, feeling very cat like, confused and fuzzy, like he had given up his vessel for another to enter it. He gasped as he saw his left hand was a furry paw with claws retracted, and noticed his cells in that arm fizzing as though in a battle. Blurry images flashed into his mind in random order from his memory. He reached into his bag and ingested the last six tiny ayahuasca spheres to help his DNA repair and calmly overpower the alien DNA codes in his system. He laid on his back, breathed slowly into his belly and slowly fell back to sleep.

***

Kailin later awoke feeling blissful. He sat up and saw he was all himself again. Dreamy colours filled the view over the dark of the early morning. Nature was resonating loudly and he was overwhelmed with joy. He swallowed and it felt like divine nectar was gliding down his throat. He had done it, he had actually escaped. He wanted to wallow in this feeling, but curiosity of a theory he had, surged up within him.

He sat in meditation posture and with all his will he summoned his #Home cloud, it worked. He then quickly ran past the deleted doors in the barn to the door of his #Medi cloud. He willed the symbol and opened the door, it worked! Kailin grew a large smile, and sat in a virtual forest that was less beautiful than the wood he was physically really in. His theory had worked, ~The cretins, he thought, and laughed. He knew the AI would not have been there, the AI would have crunched data and thought he was now a sprawl junkie, and besides the AI wouldn't rest in the cloud that caused all its fears.

The SimSphere only worked within eight miles from the centre of the HUM because this is what the people were told via NLP into their conscious, and more importantly, into their subconscious minds. When anyone else had ever tried accessing the SimSphere beyond the eight mile perimeter, they activated it by will and intent as always, but as their subconscious mind believed it wouldn't work, this would mess with the conscious will, and deplete it of its force. The force that was required.

He came out of the only two clouds he could ever access (though technically, his #Home cloud was cached on his neurochip). Venus was dimming as the sun pierced through the green trees on the other side of the small emerald lake, a lake which was now taking light and revealing roses and some small scurrying chipmunks and squirrels.

Kailin meditated, naturally. The strong calming came, the slowing of the heavy tides within him that ached to wave chaotically. The waves soon calmed into a smooth surface of pure being, he entered it, and slowly and internally chanted the word אלהים repeatedly. A soft green natural energy came and was ready to nurture him. The vision of beauty triumphant was his.

Chapter Six

Teguina walked softly along the edge of one of her favourite forests as the mist slowly lifted to reveal more trees and fauna. Her awareness was in her feet as she slowly walked deeper into the silence and resonance of the calm nature around her, feeling with her fingertips the edges of buds, leaves, and flowers. The narrow river on her left broke her soft focus as two rainbow trout leapt out over a rock, twisting as if to greet her. Teguina slowly sat and smiled and cupped her hands to drink some of the cold clear water, then rubbed some between her brow.

Teguina was twenty eight, and softly radiant. She appeared aligned with nature in that she was almost an extension of it, and she looked for authenticity wherever she could. Her shoulder length thick auburn hair was randomly harmonic, with small brown beads tying clutches of it at the back, and her sharp narrow green eyes that hardly moved made her demeanour appear calm and thoughtful. An eagle flew overhead and circled her before moving away at speed to the south. ~Wow, such beauty, I'm going to follow it, she thought, as on occasion shamanic animals had laid down signs for her.

She crossed a rope bridge with grace as rushing rapids danced below, further leaving behind her community, as the midday sun was constantly revealed and clothed due to the fast moving low clouds. As she walked, her consciousness was not in scattered thoughts, but open, in awareness, in being, and only intuition and feeling would pry her out to look, feel, and touch life from the vegetable, mineral, and animal kingdoms.

~Who could that be? Tenguina asked herself as she saw a male figure a couple of hundred metres away. She sat on a rock in invitation once she felt the man's energy signature was not threatening. ~He doesn't seem to be from any of the nearby communities, and the last time someone from one of the HUMs escaped was over two years ago. Maybe a travelling explorer or nomadic wanderer? She thought as her curiosity was morphing into excitement and empathy. ~ I wonder how I could help him, or him me?

"Hey there, how are you" The man said loudly when he was about forty metres away, complete with a broad smile on his face. ~I'll just sit here and wait, I can read more of his energy as he nears, she thought. ~Wow, it really could be someone from the HUM.

Teguina was smiling innocently on the rock while her gaze was fixed on him as he neared. She saw he looked tired, like there was a lot of built up energy, or something that needed to get out. He spoke again, "Hi there, this place is beautiful. I was hoping to come across some people or even a community or settlement soon." He smiled, like he had found a moral victory, and his smile projected a friendly greeting. Teguina's piercing green eyes narrowed as she smiled with care, "Hi, I'm Teguina, but most call my Tegs or Teggy, I live in a nearby community, and something tells me you come from the HUM a few days away. Just how did you get out? Are you ok?" Teggy could tell with her intuition he was a friendly, and that he was seeking solace during a hard time.

"I'm Kailin, yep, not sure how you know, but I escaped the HUM just a few days ago, I don't know where to start really." Kailin paused to sigh, and looked to the left as four deer ran in the distance, he looked back at Teggy. "I found out some truths about the HUMs, the control agenda and where it's all heading, and the Artificial Intelligence Nullified me, well, forced me offline and took away my work and life in the HUM. I'm ultimately seeking one of the settlements to hopefully stay and share what I found out."

Teggy looked at him, more at his soul, and at the pain in *his* revelation, "Kailin, we know too, we've known for many years. The HUMs are a leviathan of evil from remnants of the elite pre-T0, they're looking to mutate and control whats left of the species. Some have escaped here and told us more, but there isn't much to be added to what we knew from the outset. The seers in the mystic community nearby have been telling us what's going on energetically, and many source climbers and sages knew the agenda from the outset."

Teggy touched his arm and slowly added with her soft tranquil voice, "It's going to be ok Kailin, you can stay with us and rest." Kailin looked assured, like he would be able to let the pain out soon. He added, "The AI looks at the outer communities as one of the biggest threats to its agenda, have you had any trouble yet? Do you know why it would think like this?"

Teggy had hardly moved since they'd met, but this didn't come over as rigid, but as soft and still, "We know that our way of life is a threat, we're free and have left authority, aggression, and hierarchy far in the past. Just a moon or two ago though, a rumour went round saying some ravens didn't look natural, with some thinking they were robotic drone spies of sorts. But we've had no super soldiers or any contact with the HUMs, save for the occasional escapee." Teguina slowly flicked some of her thick auburn hair from her face before continuing, "We don't seek to fight the HUMs or to break people out, we focus on the solutions really, which is living in harmony and seeking natural evolution via consciousness."

Kailin sat on some grass looking up at Teggy, "What has your path been Teggy, if you feel ok to share? It has been a few days since I've seen anyone, and I feel

I'm about to enter a very different type of consciousness." Kailin could feel a softer frequency with Teggy, not just because she appeared sensitive, it was something more.

"I would love to share," Teggy said, then smiled as she brought her legs up to sit cross legged. Kailin placed his arms back so he could lounge more in a pose of curious listening. "Pre-T0 my mother was a healer, and her man at the time was a researcher, I learnt at an early age that charismatic psychopaths rules the world, with the heads of large destructive corps and governments showing complete lack in remorse, shame, honesty, guilt and empathy. We lived off grid and moved about a lot, trying to find our place away from the system and the control that went with it. But it was more than that, we sought to escape from the materialism, the narrow norms, the error in mind. My dad was big on things in the system like the talismanic words they used, like busyness, week-end, terror-threat, healthcare, and even drove my mum a bit potty with it all. But it all kind of made sense even when I was a teenager, before the HUMs." Teggy paused, obviously reminiscing, but also allowing Kailin to add, but he didn't. Kailin was all ears but his eyes swayed from the river, to Teggy, to the odd movement or noise from the forest.

Teggy let the pause eat into them, then continued. "Mass distribution and mass consumption are not the way we learnt. I used to wonder how in pre T0 how a metropolis of seven million or so people could be sustained, and that strange old globalised system that could ship shoes made by slaves and toxic toothpaste to everyone. People were illusory *free*, but people were prisoners of their own concepts and ideas. They were slaves to their own selves." Teggy shrugged and pulled out some nuts from a pocket and handed some to Kailin who obliged humbly, but Teggy saw he was hungrier than he was letting on.

Kailin looked at her in appreciation for her sharing, in appreciation for having met someone today, he allowed her to continue at her own pace, as he was happy to take in the nature and the glee of having met someone from the outside.

"In T0 I was ten and off grid on the west coast, and T0 didn't affect us too much logistically as we had food and power. My dad used to often say that the most subversive thing anyone could ever do was plant a seed as they couldn't tax what you didn't buy. After T0 we moved around a bit, helping people plant food and adding to communities, often moving on due to our work being done, or coming across egoistic authority. When I was eighteen the HUMs were announced, and due to some source climbers we knew at the time, and from what we already knew, it was obvious this was a massive con. We tried to tell people, but in hindsight everyone needed to follow their own path. My mum gave flyers to those going to the HUMs saying something like, *Don't answer anything you don't have to, never volunteer any info, always question them, question everything, believe nothing, and never be intimidated and never give in to them.* Crazy huh? Heheh"

Kailin chipped into the next comfortable silence, "I wish my mother was a little more like yours, mine is in a HUM working in the Medicine Guild, the HUM seemed to give her security for all her insecurities." Kailin spent a moment in the knowledge that he may never see her again, and Teggy picked up on this, "Sometimes we have to do what's right for our own path, no matter who that goes against, and what pain that can cause Kailin." He watched a squirrel run up a tree then looked back to her, "I know Teggy, but it still doesn't make it easy." Kailin changed the subject, "So how did you come about to be here, in this nearby community?"

"It's been ten years since the exodus to the HUMs, and much has been going on in the real world, sorry Kailin, the outside." Kailin took no offence and waved a palm. "Consciousness has been evolving as it always has done, and we have worked through so much to get to where we are currently. As your Guild's were progressing, we came across a small mystic group that were exploring the nature of reality and the nature of man, mainly experimenting with consciousness and the old doctrines from the Vatican loot. This may seem like a cult of sorts, but as my dad used to say, *beware the man of one book*, and these people were versed in many ancient traditions and doctrines, mentally and practically. We travelled behind them for a while in a group of a few hundred, all looking for a that perfect place to settle, and sometimes one or two of us would spend the day or a lunar phase with them before returning renewed and somehow, softer in energy."

"After a moon or two of travelling behind the mystic group of no name, uniform, or label, they stated *this* is the spot, the old national parks north west of the old Denver. They set down and started building, and our larger group splintered organically to spread out around them to start communities."

Kailin was entranced by her tale, but added, "What's a national park?" Tenguina grinned, which narrowed and softened her eyes, "Well, pre-TO authorities often claimed land as theirs, and made people pay money to come and visit nature for financial profit, like it was some form of entertainment, weird huh?" Kailin just shook his head in disbelief while a strange smile formed.

"We all debated and chatted, and realised that communities need to behave like nature does; with co-existing diversity being paramount, preventing us from slipping into competition. All eco-systems have diversity that's integrated, that works together, and we wanted to copy natural ecologies in the sense that they work best when they are adapted to the specific region where they're located. That they work best when no one system takes over the surrounding systems, and that they work best when there are open non-destructive exchanges between the parallel systems."

She leaned forward, "You see, we had a lot to work with, we knew all the things not to do from pre-T0, but we didn't plan too much, it had to be organic or it would be sceptic, just like one of those old pre-T0 designer cities or towns. We spread out because some families and smaller groups in the few hundred wanted to try and use a collective credit, getting away from old words such as currency. Others wanted to use no technology at all, and others wanted to share everything. So, we split into a few settlements around the mystic group, all with strong non-aggression and no authority principles. Yes, people with strong leadership skills soon took the lead in certain projects and paradigms, but no one had any authority over anyone else. These were the first recommendations laid down as we split into seven areas."

Tenguina walked to the river's edge and sipped some more water and as she walked back she grinned, "Some people are going to love the fact you've got out Kailin, it'll be great for all of us to have you around." "Thanks Teggy, it was that far twisted in the HUM, that the only solace I found was meditating in a virtual part of the SimSphere, can you believe that? Anyway, carry on."

Tenguina smiled as she shook her head at him in jest, her eyes now larger than before. "Living with no authority was new for many, and some thought people would just lie around and do nothing, or evolve personal rigidness into laws with punishments, but people really just wanted to be flexible, to add, to give, and to have value and self respect. To start with, we had no laws or rules, just a few recommendations, and obviously, we had conflicts for a while. The norms like jealousy, space, past patterns, and ego being the main culprits, but without toxic substance abuse or the strive for money, most issues were more easily calmed. We started with non violent communication that slowly evolved into empathic communication. Then, as the communities settled, people started visiting the mystic community in the centre, be it for a day, a moon phase, a whole moon, a quarter, a year, or even forever. It was transient, there were no rules. As this progressed, three more communities organically sprung up in between the mystic community and the seven outer communities. These three are mainly healing communities with a softer energy than the surrounding seven, and these created a natural buffer between the mystic and outer communities. So then we had seven working communities of different flavours working together, with healers and mystics. It was not like anyone strived to get to the healer or mystic communities, it was just that the energy seemed to flow outward. The mystics never really left their community, but people from the three healing communities and seven outer communities all visit and move around in a transient and open way. There are no real fixed lines, but in the mystic community people live it twenty four seven, they're exploring consciousness and energy." An otters silent walk turned to a crazy run and clumsy dive into the river as he saw them both. They both laughed.

Teggy was eager to hear all about Kailin's life in the HUM and how he escaped, but could feel pain there, so decided best to paint the landscape and scenery of the potential new beginning for him.

"Things were settling naturally, we had no need to strive for status as people became accepted upon as they are to others, and what one did to help people smile and evolve. We started to see comfort and wealth as an inner thing instead of an outer thing. Wanderers have come across us, and pretty much organically fallen into the community that suits them best. There're also lots of nomadic people amongst us floating between the eleven communities, many people are just naturally nomadic, and most of these have skills people like so give them board and food, or they can stay in one of the free houses. That's if all the free houses aren't used by those who seek a little space, which is also natural.

Kailin was an attentive listener, but had a bottleneck of questions lined up, but he was patient and simply asked, "How did you get over conflicts, I mean, they're normal, surely?" Kailin looked up at Teguina with admiration.

"Well, we're not all externally fluffy, we seek truth and authenticity and this is a tough old slog, that are solid foundations for a decent life. It's just that there's not much to dispute about really, we have evolved past aggression. One would think usual jealousies and past negative patterns would always arise, but eighteen years of consciousness evolution has taken place Kailin, things have a different complexion now. Fuel, tax, and competition to get ahead have all gone, and things are softer in energy, lies can be felt, anger can be felt, and fun, creativity, and innovation are where we now find more focus of people's energies Of course bickering occurs, but that's just a sign space is required, and in the early days when conflict arose, the two people would sit in a tipi or forest together in silence for an hour. In this hour the energy of truth would arise and harmonise their broadcasting opinions, and one would often apologise or both would end up laughing it off, or together find a solution. Anger and resentment naturally calm down in silence without observers anyway, and if someone has anger we look to transmute it to creativity as the force is strong. We also had empathic mediators to help at first too, they would also bring in the astrology, Ayurvedic, and Qabalistic properties of the conflict, people, and dynamics." Teggy looked above Kailin's head, past the river to a flock of jays flying together.

"When conflict occurred pre-T0, people would play victim and tell others of their victim-ness, adding to the pot of the conflict cauldron. And besides, growing food, building homes, sharing and working together binds community." Kailin asked "So you grow your own food, even with all the tech now available?" "The diversity of our eleven communities can't give you a black or white answer to that, but I'll show you around if you like in a few days?" She said as she rose. Kailin saw her curvy waist as she rose, she was truly beautiful, a goddess, but Kailin was glad there was no sexual or romantic interest from him, she was like a sister in energy, and he was more looking for the nurturing of the communities themselves.

They walked and talked, with Kailin sharing much of his life in the HUM and what he found out from the AI. He didn't mention the two beings in his #Medi cloud on the last full moon though, there was time for all of that. ~I don't know what direction we're going in, or even if we have a destination, and to be honest I don't care. It just feels so good to be free, in nature, and sharing words with someone who seems to be living so well, Kailin thought, as his complexion was softening every minute.

They crossed a rope bridge and strolled through a forest as a natural path beneath them became more prominent. Kailin saw Teggy in fleeting moments as an extension of the forest, like she was an elvin, and all the natural life danced to greet her.

"How many people live here Teggy? There seems to be enough room around here for scores of settlements." She replied as she continued to look forward and about, "No one knows the exact amount, it's not important, but over time we realised humans are not really supposed to live in massive groups. Not yet anyway, we're still rebuilding slowly, and in that, I mean rebuilding our ways, not buildings. The outer seven communities cover about a twenty mile circle, and each has between a couple of hundred and two thousand living in them. If one gets too overcrowded as happened once or twice in the past, people move on to another community, or they build more. But it's pretty much felt here that under two thousand is a natural harmonic at this time, the closer to a hundred or two the easier to achieve balance. Over a couple of thousand and the energy seems to crunch up, it compresses and creates kegs, like a collective negative gasket, then there's discord in logistics and relationships. This is just what we all feel at the moment, but things are always changing. Our community we're going to now has about eight hundred people, but there's room for more."

"What if another thousand people turned up tomorrow?" Kailin asked. "Well we would talk with them, and explain the energy build ups, and they would most probably feel it themselves if they have lived outside the HUMs all this time. They could split up and filter into the communities, or create their own community. If they set up their own community the strong energy flowing out from the mystic and healing communities would be like waves gliding through them, and would help to implement a natural harmonic, to help guide them into the energy already here."

They passed brooks, woods, a small canyon, and some coyote, all the while exchanging silence in nature for interest in the other. "Do you use TransVapour, Hexergy or tech? Or some form of internet? Kailin asked as he helped her over a large tree stump. She jumped down femininely, "It's disparate, and in places yes, of sorts, and in other places, no. It's easier if I tell you a little about each community to give you an overall picture."

Teggy picked a stick off the floor, and moved to a clearing in the trees where shards of sun light darted through in hundreds of variants of thickness and hue .

"Hey Kailin, do you remember pre-T0 when they called soil, dirt?" She asked rhetorically before giggling." Kailin sat on a log in the clearing laughing at the word dirt as he picked some soil and rubbed it through his fingers and thumbs, "I'd love to know more about your communities and how you live, I've only had one way to live forced upon me, and repeatedly imprinted into me, and the times I spoke out against any of it, others would tread on me. It's as if there's no need for sheep dogs in the HUMs as all the sheep keep the other sheep in the pen."

Tenguina smiled at him, and slowly drew a circle in the middle of the clearing with her stick she found, "This, is the mystic community, it was here first, and what it's done for people individually has been amazing. Their predictions, oracle abilities, and sense of energy and higher frequencies have been astounding. This doesn't make them any authority, but naturally, gains respect. It's hard to present any negativity as they hold no ego, just selfless wisdom, love, and foresight pours from them, or more probably, through them. They are a small group of what pre-T0 some may have called Taoists, Yogis, Qabalists, Sufis, Rosicrucians, Seers, and Alchemists, but they need nor request any labels. They know their stuff, and have studied, practiced, and taught diligently. Anyone can go there or leave at any time, but due to our evolution and *this* softer frequency we now seem to share, one seems to go there when the energy is right. They don't share one thing you see, they feel out each person and then create a toybox or toolbox or techniques and processes to suit ones path, evolution, and transmutation wants. I know they've been big on working with telepathy the past two years and I know someone that was there for three months and gained amazing telepathic abilities."

"Did these abilities decrease once they left? Have you ever been there?" Kailin asked with interested. "Yes, the abilities decreased once they left as more *noise* came back into their life, plus, they achieved these abilities with others also in the mystic community. I've only been there to visit and take a look around, it's beautiful and the energy is strong and sacred. I plan to go next summer maybe, but it's pretty deep stuff."

Teggy was now playing teacher in the clearing using her stick as a marker, all in a humorous way, "Their land is around eight miles square to house the hermit shacks, valleys, pyramid temples, and buildings, but of course it's all free land. But we are at a stage in our evolution where one wouldn't just go and settle there, as the land has a sacredness and a purpose, it wouldn't intuitively feel right. Only someone with very dense energy would do something like that, and we would all feel that person is in that state and help them with shadow work, healing, and transmutation ourselves, or......" Teggy drew three circles around the mystic community, "....see if they wanted to visit one of the healing communities."

Kailin played the student in this game, and offered her to explain with a fun inquisitive look.

"The people in these three live in a softer vibration than the outer seven communities, and the people within are healers from before T0, and people who have spent much time in the mystic community going through intensive processes of transformation. These three are similar in nature in that they have different flavour healers anyone can go to, but one commune has ayahuasca ceremonies on the full moon, blesses seeds, and is close to animals. Another uses no tech and is more into cleansing, protection rituals, herbal cures, and crystals. The other is more of an emergency type healing space and uses tech for surgery and deals with the deceased and birthing. Each of the three are deep into dreamwork, shareshops, group yoga, sauna chanting, and all sorts of stuff. It's been joked some of them can pretty much text each other with their consciousness."

Teggy started to draw out seven circles around the three healing communities, "You see Kailin, with our populous being small, we have no need for a large healing building, only a handful of injuries or illnesses occur each moon, and most visit the healing communities to integrate experiences, cleanse, heal negative mental patterns, or to increase energy. All of us know that if we're ill or low on energy, or have an accident, there's something to learn in there, and it's a big debate around here whether the use of tech for surgery is bending karma or the soul lessons in some way. But it is up to the individual. Nothing is forced."

Teggy finished drawing out the seven circles as she continued, "Many of the old pre-T0 diseases are over for us as our diets are natural and local, and we also have shared cleanse days before the solstice and equinox, but the kids now got involved and turned it into a water fight. You should try to visit the healing communities as the energy is different, and these communities are a great buffer for the mystic community." Teggy stepped back as if to allow questions before she dived into the outer seven communities. Kailin smirked in wonder and curiosity.

"Tell me more about this telepathic texting Teggy?" Kailin was interested, and knew from his own studies it was possible. "Well we all have it at some point, twins, and even lovers whose auras have blended through spending time alone together. It goes back to what I said earlier, consciousness evolves all the time, and eighteen years with no strive for money and status is a long time. When we get away from false synthetic evolutionary tools we can do it all on our own. We can work on the inner as appose to the HUMs that work on the outer." Kailin replied, "I completely believe you," and pointed at the outer seven circles, "Which one are we going to, and where are we now?"

"We're a mile from the community I live in, here," she pointed the stick at the bottom right circle, "We'll call this number one and work around clockwise my dear HUM escapee freedom warrior." Kailin laughed, and the energy between them was fast becoming similar to siblings.

"*Our* community uses some tech for entertainment and learning, and we make clothes and work with material and fabric mainly, but also grow a little food as all communities do. The next community along is mainly food growing and also uses some tech. The third one produces mainly wood and materials for building and construction. The fourth is using its own credit system based on no interest, no inflation, and no debt, and has two ethos nuggets; stick to your agreements and don't encroach on others freedoms. This is the one with the newest settlers, and I'm sure they'll soon leave their credit system like the other six have, into a more caring and helping based way of exchange. The largest community is the fifth with near two thousand people, they innovate tech and have a TransVapour tram going to the fourth community. The sixth and seventh communities both have no tech at all, and everything is shared. These two are very much about music, art, and creativity, and the people share more meals and there is more of a close community feel one might have witnessed pre-TO."

"All the communities are linked with a few tracks that the few TransVapour buggies travel upon, and none of the communities have any concrete roads or pavements. We all want to live closer to the earth, more naturally where we can. Beyond the seven outer communities there are a few scores of random homesteads who dip in and out, and we have loose trade co-operatives with two other grouped communities that are similar in nature, each about six hours away."

Kailin was amazed, it all sounded great, but he could only gain a mental picture, he was excited to go and live there and really feel it. It was like a gift. ~If only I didn't go to the HUM in the first place, ah, but then I wouldn't have experienced and seen firsthand the torment of the HUMs. Maybe it was a strange gift. And this feeling I have now of being with Teggy, and this new excitement I would never have experienced these either, Kailin thought to himself.

"Tell me more about the tech you use, I've seen firsthand the dangers it can pose, especially how it can distract and take over a man's consciousness. How do you overcome all this?" Teggy sat opposite him on another log, after being careful not to step on the circles. "Tech is great when used for evolution, to help with our alignment to nature and to our inner worlds. It's great for food crops, though many also love to put energy into what they are going to digest. We have no implants, save for a couple of temporary chips sometimes used in the surgery healing quarters, and we use transparent screen tech for movies, information, learning, and fun. We have a small intranet to see what's on, who wants help, and to chat and post messages. We use Hexergy for electricity, and some tech for building and tools. Apart from all that, not much else really, ah, and holo-lights for tracks and dwellings. The latest and most tech is in the largest community and some go there for the day to do research or to take their kids to interactive tech areas for learning and collaborative fun."

Teggy softly spoke again as Kailin was all ears and laying an energetic canvas down for her to paint upon. "We've a good balance as the music and art communities perform plays and performances, and host dances of all different sorts frequently, and plus the whole area has some special days." Kailin looked at her, "What sort of special days?" Teggy smiled, "Well most are for fun and some are more popular than others, we've a care day, elderly day, family day, children day, surprise day, gratitude day, healers day, symbols day, a nothing day, and lots of theme days in the more arty community. The days aren't pushed and have brought a good sense of community. We also live with the moon cycles and celebrate the equinox and solstice. We got rid of the old calendar over time, it had too much dark energy built into it, and was a massive dogma. We now call days by their source planet, and whether it falls on a new, waxing, waning, or full moon. For instance today is *Mars-Wane*, which in your HUM speak is Tuesday after the full moon. Tomorrow is Mercury-Wane, and in two weeks it will be *Mars-Wax*. To replace the old hashed up numbered months, created by Catholics bad at maths, we just use what sign the sun is in, like now its Taurus." "I get it, and it feels authentic. But I ask, what do you do on a nothing day?" Kailin asked smirking, Teggy smiled back, "What do you think?"

Kailin's thoughts were bubbling and his tiredness was leaving his mind, though not his body. ~This is like a dream, I can't wait to take a look around, he thought.

As they walked along the track and approached a welcoming forested and flowered entrance, she turned to him, "It might seem strange to you at first Kailin, but most of us here spend a lot of time in softness, in the inner worlds. This isn't a rule or something that just came about, it was a natural development. Many are looking to increase vibration, and when this increases so does sensitivity, therefore, a blunt comment or harsh judgement can seem much stronger here than in the HUM. Try and soften up a little and be open and passive." She hugged him as a sister would hug a brother returning after a long journey.

Kids with leaves in their hair ran past playing, and two men passed in a silent TransVapour vehicle that looked organic and cute. "Welcome Kailin," she said, and kissed him on the cheek.

***

Back in the HUM the AI spent two hours, two minutes and one second searching for Kailin with scores of its tentacles. ~Must be in the sprawl becoming a Stim junkie, it thought. ~I'll send more drone troops to the sprawl to look for him, and modify some Adapp units to scan for him too. The perimeter drone troops reported nothing in their upload this morning, but I will double the drones on the perimeter. He must not escape.

Jago sat in his #Emptiness cloud, a basic cloud with just three scenes, a Lilly pad on a vast calm ocean, a pitch black darkness with colourful geometry floating around, and a slowly spinning tetrahedron flying in space with him in the middle. He had meditated on the Lilly pad for over forty minutes and was feeling good whilst preparing some food when a SimText came in, "Hi Jago, my name is Channa, a friend of K's, can we please meet? x"

***

In the Tech Guild, Diene, a Level One Gatekeeper, was summoned to a private meeting with J.P Rothafella, a person hardly anyone knew anything about. They met in one of the AI comms clouds, and spent over two hours in there brainstorming with the AI.

Chapter Seven

Kailin was lying face down on some sort of thin but comfortable table that felt like it cuddled the shape of his body. He breathed deeply as her hands massaged his back, stopping only to pour channelled energy into him. Below his eyes was a transparent screen of sorts, but a bit like a hologram, showing the colour changes in his aura as the spikes and holes slowly changed to curves. An acupuncture needle pierced near his lower spine and he breathed in and out of it as the screen changed. It showed the Chinese five elements, and then the specific meridians, organ, element, and traits that were being stimulated into fluid energy flow.

Though Kailin could not see them, some tiny thimble sized holograms darted above his chakras and they in turn resonated different pitches of crystal bowl sounds as Shri carried on massaging, with her hands moving through the holograms. With a wave of his finger he flipped the screen passed ancient Tibetan and Ayurvedic systems, and past his lymph, circulation, and digestive systems, onto the tree of life overlaying his human body. He closed his eyes and mentally went into Chesed, the fourth Sephiroth on the Tree of Life. He infused himself with a light medium-blue, and mentally resonated the word חשמלים four times. He slipped out of consciousness, and entered a soft kingdom that was fair and soft, with Jupiter beaming down generosity and fortune upon a happy populous.

She brought him back by pressing his big toes gently and slowly increasing the pressure. "Ok Kailin, try and relax for a bit and drink some water before you leave, and I'll leave you a list of foods that are good for your blood type."

Kailin mumbled back, "Mmm, thanks sooo much Shri." Shri rolled the incense stick to control the dropping ash and said softly, "Forgiveness doesn't change the past Kailin, but it can enlarge the future, try and let go of the burden you carry a little." Kailin was still face down, nearly about to dribble and mouthed quietly, "But it's a burden we all carry is it not? The HUMs I mean? And turned to look at her as she neared.

Shri was about thirty and all women. She had thick, shiny, shoulder length hair of jet black, and light, round, brown eyes. She moved towards him and at his eye level he could see her large feminine hips and up a little at her ample breasts. She moved and spoke as if in slow motion, like she was living in another frequency all together.

"We attach our feelings to the moment we're hurt Kailin, giving it with immortality. And if we let it assault us every time it comes to mind, it will travel with us, and sleep with us." Shri moved closer and felt his aura in her soft feeling way, "Hate doesn't even have the decency to die when those we hate die, it's a parasite sucking our blood, not theirs. There's only one remedy Kailin, forgiveness." Kailin thought confusedly, ~How can I forgive those that have brought so much evil to our species, and are likely to create even more? Shri had heard his thoughts, and smiled like a caring mother would, "Don't ask yourself what the world needs Kailin, ask yourself what makes *you* come alive, then go and do that. What the world needs right now is people who've come alive." "Thanks Shri, I feel amazing," he mumbled into the pillow. Shri made a little giggle, "You take It easy, there's no rush, we've all been here for years, and acclimatise before rushing around, see you soon."

On the way to Teggy's place they'd bumped into Shri who lives in the healing commune. She was swapping a treatment for some clothes near Teggy's, and delivering some ritualised seeds. Once she realised Kailin had come from the HUM, she insisted on a treatment at a nearby spare cob dome.

As Kailin walked back to Teggy's using Shri's directions, he noticed that nature was still dominant. The community covered a square mile or two, and contained some small woods, a river, some hills, tiny valleys, and some small rocky cliffs and mini mountains. The cob and stone pods, domes, and pyramids all sat within the natural surroundings, blending with the land harmoniously.

Many dwellings had gardens on the roof, and some were completely covered in fauna or moss of some sort. Each seemed to have some sort of geometry included somewhere, whether in the whole shape of the dwelling, the roof, the door, or just lightly painted on the outside wall. Nearly all dwellings were a light brown-bauge colour, dark green, or different browns. If a dwelling had a geometric symbol painted on the outer wall, the symbol was the same colour, just a little more faded. It was subtle, and Kailin liked it though he recognised none of the symbols.

Non intrusive tracks weaved about, some wide enough for vehicles, but most for walking. There were no signs with rules or directions to upset the aesthetics or nature. It all flowed, and the trees and plant life felt happy and alive. Most dwellings had space around them, lots, but few were closer together but still never on top of one another. Nearer the centre of the community were some more densely clustered cob domes and pyramids, some linked by corridors. Each cluster was spread a little apart from another cluster, and many were hugged by trees.

From Kailin's standpoint he could see and feel these were most probably transient spaces used for things like collaboration, spaces for children, clothes, celebration, meetings, sharing, or similar.

Kailin passed other people, and felt at home already. Each person he passed was open, empathetic, and giving in energy. It was like they knew the energy he broadcast, and were open to help him, but wouldn't intrude unless asked. It was like an energetic *I know what can help you, let me know at any time if you need it, and come share your gifts with me at any time.* But in the physical they each had an air of progressive calm knowing, each with shining piercing eyes.

The people Kailin passed wore no fashion of sorts, just clothes that suited the individual, day, and climate, which was much warmer than he imagined, but he knew from the SimSphere back in the HUM that the climate was within a warmer arc. A TransVapour vehicle drove up the track, it was not a bold metallic colour, or aggressively designed, it was rugged, and fun looking. A bit like a happy, flexible, moon buggy, with a roof. It was dark green with a symbol on the roof, and though it looked basic he knew it had Hexergy and water tech from the way it effortlessly moved without noise. Silky smooth.

As it drove some spaced-out small neon-blue holo lights on each side of the track came on as the vehicle approached, and automatically turned off as it passed, it was subtle and helpful as twiglight was now upon the community. A teenager walked past him and passed him a homemade food bar whilst simply smiling a happy "Hey." Kailin saw it was some sort of superfoods bar, and felt energised as he munched upon it.

***

Kailin awoke dehydrated to the same birds song as was on his App back in the HUM. The night before when he returned Teggy had whispered he should sleep which he agreed. He awoke in a five metre or so cob dome, and looked through the transparent dome in the roofs centre that let in the blue sky and the ends of two leaved branches that slowly swayed. He walked through after soaking in the art and mixed colour geometry on the walls.

"Hi Kailin, I'm Jay, Teggy's partner, if you need more sleep just rest, you must've had quite a few days. Can I get you anything?" Jay was a little taller and older than Kailin, but more well built. He had long dark hair, tanned skin, a stubble, and an air of being at complete peace with himself and his surroundings. Kailin felt a little awkward for the first time in a long time, here he was in someone else's house, in a different way of life, with a completely separate history. It was like he landed from another planet. But Kailin got it together during a deep breath that invigorated his whole system.

Kailin smiled and reached out a hand, "Nice to meet you Jay, and thanks so much for the room, I'm used to the cubic rigid rooms from the HUM skyscrapers as you have probably gathered." Kailin humbly and slowly walked the larger central dome as Jay welcomed him to with energy. This dome led off to four other smaller domes, one of which Kailin stayed in. It was extremely fluid and homely, and the energy felt transient and non stagnant. On the walls were more geometric art, a screen tech moon calendar showing the zodiac sign the moon was in, and to what percent, plus there was a big old iron log burner on one side with some wood stacked. ~That's strange, why use wood when tech allows much easier ways? Kailin thought.

Jay's smile broadened and the whites of his eyes looked like someone had polished them, "Anything you need?" He said in his Latin accent. Kailin smiled back, "I'd love a shower if that's ok?" Jay grinned ear to ear, "I've not heard that word for a while, we call it a cleanse, but yes, go straight through there." "Thanks Jay, and do you know what time it is?" Jay's grin thinned but his eyes stretched as he moved in his naturally alert and dashing manner to look through the portion of the roof that was transparent, "I'd guess it is close to the middle of the day, so, midday I'd say." Kailin smiled back at him, he knew were this might all be going.

In the cleanse room, he saw a holographic menu appear, he played with it until it was hot and strong, then bowed his head and stood for a while in stillness. He cared not for the other options like floor jets, side jets, pressure change, mist, and another seven or so. At the end he put the water onto ice cold and let it run down his spine as he said forcefully and intentionally to himself, ~Bring all my energy that's been given away willingly or unwillingly back to me now, making me complete and me again.

Kailin and Jay chatted openly, with Jay often showing his love to Teggy by almost beaming his heart out to reach her. "Teggy's out for a while helping with fabrics and canvas, you're to make yourself at home Kailin, and you can stay in that dome for as long as you need. We hope you decide to stick around."

Thanks so much Jay," Kailin said as he sat on one of the low set chairs before asking, "Where are you from?" Jay had an air of selfless giving and openness, not like something he strived for, more like *he was* those things. "Well, the notions of countries are gone really, flags were illusions that existed in the minds, but originally I'm a mix from Trinidad, Mexico, and Europe." Jay sat too after passing Kailin a bowl of vegetable soup, "So, what's it like in the HUM? It might be worth knowing that many on the outside call those in the HUMs *the externals.*" Kailin grinned, replying, "I completely understand why, I was one of the more outspoken there. It's pretty bleak, like a controlled nightmare really, especially once I started to feel what was going on. But what can one do, find some authenticity in ones surroundings and seek some inner peace."

Jay looked amazed, "The HUM must've been hard, especially as we're never deceived, we deceive ourselves. It seems to me that any intelligent fool can make things bigger and more complex, but It takes a touch of genius and a lot of courage to move in the opposite direction," he replied.

Kailin thought hard upon this, and then continued, "Why do you all not do more to help those stuck in the HUMs, knowing what you do?"

"Our way is more to raise energy, and let the low energy of the HUMs eat itself. The second singularity won't happen the mystics feel, and if we worry or look for vengeance we just leak energy that could be used on solutions." Jay softly replied. Kailin thought for a while then added, "You seem to all have a great way of life around here, I'm looking forward to know the place better."

"We're finding our way slowly and organically, and we're pretty happy with the progress, and no one is running off to the HUMs just yet," Jay replied, and they both smiled and continued to share.

Later, Kailin went to wash up but some thimble sized sponges started washing the dishes, each releasing some suds and swimming to move plates in groups. Jay shook his head and frowned humorously, "Don't ask, Teggy's doing again, but at least I'm allowed my log fire." "Are you two married if you don't mind my asking," Kailin asked inquisitively, as the moon calendar glowed neon blue for a second, showing that the moon was now in the next sign.

"Marriage? I remember that, are they still doing that in the HUMs? What we remember of weddings was those seeking observers, those competing over their days, and some strange vows that were rarely followed. No, what we do here is partners sometimes go for a connection ceremony with one of the mystics, and a handful of people take part. It's more of a sacred tie, and doesn't bind a women to a man for a whole life. It just amplifies a deep connection, binds and celebrates I suppose. We've talked about it, and maybe in a few months we might do it. It's quite big deal. Each makes the other an object sourced from nature, and they are stoked into talismans symbolising the connection at a particular time. It's not something one can plan to do though, the ceremony comes when it energetically comes."

Kailin was impressed but thought more upon how Jay's voice, though Latin in accent, sounded androgynous. "Jay, do you know in the HUMs many women marry for SimSovs to gain anti-aging tech? And most couples have their competing weddings in virtual clouds on the SimSphere. Pretty messed up huh?" Jay gave a wide eyed frown, that felt more as a smile in energy. Jay snorted humorously.

Kailin went for a walk near their dome complex, the sun was shining, and the sounds of nature and wildlife were abundant, and he could hear children playing in the river over the way. There were similar dwellings a few minutes away, and a small wood nearby. Jay and Teggy's dwelling was much higher up the valley than the central complex clusters, and looked down on the valley into the distance. Two cats followed Kailin, they looked wild but in this were still aligned to the frequency of the community. ~I hope this place stays safe, just why has the AI seen it as a threat? Is it really just the way of life and the higher frequency that's the threat? If so, how could it be? Kailin contemplated with mixed emotions.

Mid afternoon Kailin went back to find Jay pruning a tree near their dwelling, Kailin made some tea by boiling the water with a thimble sized device that seemed to create no heat itself. It must have manipulated the water at a molecular level. They sat out the front looking down on a valley, as it rose up to greet them through the nearby wood. On the left was a small hill that led up to the nearest neighbours, and on the horizon they could see layers of rocky ranges.

They chatted for an hour or so, with Kailin asking most of the questions in a light informal way. Jay was soft, open, and happy to make Kailin feel part of the community, to enable him to internally shift from feeling like a HUM escapee.

Kailin asked at one point, "The place feels good, the newness to me is really the lack of conflict, and how having no rules functions. I mean, what do people generally do? Someone deep in the HUM would probably point to the issue of boredom?"

Jay laughed, but his laugh was full of warmth that his smile and being backed it. "People need only a few things Kailin, and that's *all* of us. Some water, some food, some warmth, some love, and a few steps towards evolving individually and collectively. We're still finding our way but we've attained to all these, and free too. With these in abundance, we found that true happiness, wealth, and comfort all come from within, hence one reason why we're more internal than say pre-T0. We meditate and find lone time each day. No one says to, but we all reap the benefits." Jay sipped his tea calmly before continuing in his super alert state.

"No one here relies on any system, or on others, everyone is looking to be responsible for their own life. But we all *seek* to give and help others. We can pretty much now feel when someone needs help, and what to give them." There was a soft silence, and the energy of the words dissipated into the receiving nature of the surroundings.

"Within this, people naturally want to create and be innovative, to share ideas and to help others. This is basic in all of us but the old system knocked it out of us in those schools. But since the tipping points, everyone wants to feel better. A humble personal step in the right direction is a contribution to the whole world, and to all future generations. It's all quite simple really." Jay watched a spotted lynx run between them and then perch on a branch to stare back at them with its wise green eyes.

During another slow, paused, comfortable, and open chat, Jay said, "We live on the earth and are given food from earth, so we respect and harmonise with it, this is where pre-T0 failed. A basic respect for nature, let alone deeply aligning with it is required, or things get toxic pretty quickly. Think of an old concrete town or city, how disconnected from nature it was, complete with packaged corporate goods to consume. That old system had such a lack of diverse reference points. Everyone was in their comfort zone not seeking to stretch the boundaries of the box, not seeking to obtain new reference points for the mind. We don't even have a name for our place, is it a village? town? A this or a that? Irrelevant, it's the harmony, evolution, and creation that mark us, not any plastic sign or landmark." Jay looked openly at Kailin with happy comfortable honesty, as he moved some of his long thin black hair away from his eye.

The lynx made itself more comfortable and tucked it's paws under its body, then closed its eyes pricking its ears. Kailin was getting soft waves of energy into his being, like these thought paradigms were inside him but being reflected back. He smiled at Jay to carry on. "But once the external needs are covered, one can move more into the self, which is ultimately the way to evolve the species we feel. What do I put my energy into? How are my relationships? Mental patterns? Do I give? Am I caring? And so on. We got passed the seeking of observers in ego, and moved into a more sharing and giving way, which became a loose unmetered gift based currency."

"How does that work?" Kailin asked. "Well, the gift moves toward the empty place, and as it turns in its circle, it turns toward him who has been empty-handed the longest, and if someone appears elsewhere whose need is greater it leaves its old channel and moves toward him. Generosity can leave one empty, but that emptiness then pulls gently at the whole, until the motion returns to replenish again."

There was rustling at the edge of the nearby wood below, and a flock of birds flew out from a single tree. The lynx never moved, save for one ear swivelling.

Jay soon continued, "As for boredom, one can teach oneself something, no one should rely on others to provide a rewarding life, even in a gift based community. A true test of self love is the courage to lift yourself up when no one else is around to carry you. As for authority, politics was nothing more than a means of increasing ego, only psychopaths seek control and power over people. Controlling and making decisions for masses of people is a burden nobody should seek unless they're very ill." Jay started to do some arm and shoulder stretches and murmured with his arms behind his shoulder blades and smiled, "I never thought someone from the HUM would be so switched on, you must have got kicked out and the escape story is a lie." They looked at each other and laughed, "Well there's actually *some* truth in that," Kailin chuckled.

After another minute of comfortably searching the views for more hues of the late afternoon sun on the valley, Kailin added, "So, with no authority what do you do if a bad egg or someone with mental issues arrives, someone violent or aggressive?" Jay turned to him, now stretching his legs whilst still in his wicker chair, and smiled androgynously, "We try and offer healing, and if not, we ask them to kindly leave and come back later when they're going to add instead of subtract. *We* accept them as they are, but it's as if the space doesn't."

Kailin asked again, "Who talks to them? Is there a system?" Jay laughed, "No silly, anyone who wants to speak to them really, but in reality all this is now usually done with the natural energy, the energy of the space. And this scenario hasn't happened for months as people come and want to add, to earn their place here."

Teggy rhythmically swayed up the path singing and humming a mantra as four children followed her trying to copy the song and her hip swaying dance. The two boys had leaves in their hair and the two girls had blue and green flowers. "Hi boys, glad you been getting on..." ~How does she know, thought Kailin, as she continued, "Let us three tonight celebrate Kailin's escape from the HUM with a nice meal." Jay got up and kissed her and took the food off her, he winked back to Kailin and smilingly whispered, "Or was it extradition." Kailin could see what a great couple they were, and time with them would be a great teacher for him.

The children stayed a while, and later in the evening the three adults became firm friends, helped along by the humour generated from Kailin's attempt at helping in the kitchen. All the devices where alien to him. Maybe to Jay too as he baked the bread on the log burner.

The three later shared a meditation in the centre of the central dome, after which Teggy seemed to know what went on at the start of Jay's meditation. Kailin noticed too he could feel their energies melt into one after a short time. ~The symmetrical geometry of the domes must help too, he thought.

The next day Kailin went out with Jay after offering to help him. "So what's *improving and solutions* Jay?" Kailin asked as they checked and *improved* the hydroponic garden that was used mainly by twelve or so dwellings. "Well remember the old paradigm of the word *work* Kailin? It created subconscious patterns of negativity, it was a word that inflicted feelings of grind, shift, and labour. What we do here is tasks that improve and provide solutions, individually or collectively. The issue pre-T0 was that one's life was not their work, work was a separate entity performed usually to gain money to survive, to further a corporation's pursuit for, what was it? Ah, market share. It was often too far removed from stirring any passions. The objective truth is that I'm experiencing a life, not *making a living*. Many word changes, change the patterns in the mind, and many paradigms from pre-T0 we have changed just by changing the words. You will come across this more in the communities such as those that use a credit currency system, they use no words from the old financial system. It really makes a difference." Kailin could see some transparent screens pop up near a man made pond that processed human waste to use for crops. Thimble sized holograms swam in the pond, each giving off different neon colours.

Jay used basic tools to turn soil and Kailin helped nearby with another strange looking wood and iron tool, "You see Kailin, some people are more of the outdoorsy type, pre-T0 many grown strong men would be stuck at a desk most of the day staring at a screen. It wasn't natural and it helped the rise in alcohol, infidelity, and aggression. The earth is alive, abundant, complex, and nurturing, so it seems silly to neglect her, no matter what technology is available." Kailin sat looking at Jay in thought, and then shooed away a chipmunk that was treading over some soil he just turned. "The nature in the HUMs is mainly fabricated, and they make everyone believe the outsiders are all primitives," Kailin said, in complete disappointment.

Jay sat down and looked at the tops of the trees in the near distance as the sun was rising to inflict the green topped wood with gold. "Overcoming greed, conflict, and aggression is advanced we feel. Like if one wants to create an innovative project, people naturally help because they like the idea and it raises the energy of the whole place, so people add to the addition. Then they are known as those who help, so when *they* need help, people help. There's no red tape, and people can feel the energy and know what fits and what doesn't. The HUMs look at a close family as the same the old working class, but family is a source of unconditional love and where the most mirrors are evident. To suppress family patterns and issues ensures gaskets of negativity will come out sooner or later, or that the same patterns are taken into other relationships. Primitiveness is really the level of harmony, not what tool one uses," Jay said while he shook his old tool and smiled.

"Animals feel instinctively what they can eat in nature, but man never could pre-T0, now that's primitive I would say. I mean is eating nuts in a forest primitive? Of course not, its natural and aligned to what is. It's the old paradigm of the word *primitive* that's incorrect I feel. I think it primitive to be able to eat any type of food from any part of the world at any time, as the rich did in pre-T0 and as the HUMs do too. I feel it more advanced to eat lots of what's seasonal and local, the local nature is telling you what's good for you at that time of year for where you live. The old way was based upon desire for taste, seeking short term happiness spikes through decadence, and decadence is primitive, it's extremely un-sacred and ego based."

Kailin was amazed with Jay, he felt we was learning new ideas and feeling a new collectivised energy that existed in the local ether. Jay could feel Kailin was digesting the information, and hungry for more of his curiosity to be fed. "People don't want to be idle, it's natural to be a capable person, to have a variety of skills that come in handy. It gives us self-respect, and provides various honourable ways to live. If one doesn't exert themselves physically, how can the body become strong? If one doesn't open themselves emotionally, how can the heart heal and love? If one doesn't challenge themselves intellectually, how can one become wise? If one doesn't stop and meditate, how can one see things clearly? One has to push their own limits or suffer the consequence of complacency. Look at me for instance, I like to chop wood for the log burner, there's no technical need to as Hexergy has developed many heating solutions, but to provide the warmth for my house using one of the elements is authentic for me. If I take this away, I lose an act of love and giving. A robot could clean the house but that would take away the feeling of renewal one can source if they did it themselves. It's all about the see-saw of lack versus appreciation I guess. This is internal, and no tech can help someone who's mental paradigms are constantly in lack."

Jay smiled at Kailin, not condescendingly but to scope for any feelings coming out of Kailin's deep medium-brown eyes. Kailin said while still staring down at the valley across the soil they were preparing, "It seems to me like you've worked so much on the internal here that the external just fits, whatever it is one does. The HUMs focus on the external, even the virtual worlds are externalised and distract from anything internal. It all reminds me of an old saying, *when the roots are strong the trees will dance in the storm*." Jay nodded in agreement and their two energies were rapidly bonding towards a more harmonious frequency.

The afternoon they helped the building of two cob dwellings to be used for free space or any nomads passing through. Jay explained to Kailin that if a partner needed some space, another room in the same dwelling was often not enough as the auras were still entwined, that energy was still being ingested from the other due to close resonance. Sometimes a night or two in one of the spare space dwellings healed any negative energy that may have started to build up.

Kailin saw a large mobile house TransVapour vehicle near the cob houses being built, and also some thimble sized devices linked with a web of some kind carry heavy materials. Kailin asked one of the builders, Petra, a traveller, "Why do you still seek to travel around when this place seems to hold keys to a happy life?" Petra was eating a sandwich from a girl that had brought some along for all the builders to eat.

"Well, in this time it's surely good that some are spreading ideas, linking up communities, moving things around, and also digesting different ways of life. In the old days one could only travel if they had money, and I was locked up in a terrible job." Petra was in his fifties, but was fit as a fiddle, "Only the rich could travel, and then it was mainly through travel packages, visas, passports, and all sorts of red tape and foolery. There was little harmonious flow or room for synchronicities. Now I travel with no need for fuel, oil, or gas, and go where I feel, for how long I feel, and the synchronicities I experience are amazing and multi layered." Kailin smiled, and it seemed Petra had an air of *who the hell is this guy, has he just landed from another galaxy?* All in a humorous way though.

Kailin added, knowing he was already looking a little silly so it didn't matter, "Why do you work here today? Helping to build these dwelling you may never stay in?" Some lettuce dropped from Petra's sandwich as he froze before replying, "I find it great to share a skill I have, I'm a good builder, and some people will be grateful for these spaces one day. I also get to spend the day with friends, to share food and music. Tonight I'm off to a gig in the other community and I'll feel better that I've contributed today. Where've you been kid? Asleep for fifteen years?" Kailin looked at him, "Nah, I just broke out of the HUM recently after hybridising with a lynx so my DNA wouldn't be traced on the perimeter by the AI's drone soldiers. But I'm all ears and keen to learn about these new ways."

Kailin smiled in softness, but Petra remained frozen again, and the bottom slice of bread flopped open releasing salsa and avocado. They both laughed as Petra grabbed him and massaged and yanked his shoulders in jest, "Why didn't you say, it's been a long time since I thought anyone would get out of there. I know some people in other places who'll be overjoyed to hear another got out." Petra hugged him with tears in his eyes, "Well done kid."

***

Back in the HUM Dieine was hosting meetings with the top brass from the Genetics and Tech Guild's on Rothafella's behalf. They were secret to the rest of the Guilders, and also stringently away from the AI.

Ishiah was sat at his desk in his StimBar office after a busy day. A day that included the modification of a new celebrity that implanted renewing throat nanobots that helped sing harmonies, and a meeting about a new cloud that was based around how much fear one could handle, plus a meeting with a Stim Junkie that owed him a few thousand SimSovs.

He sat back on his chair in satisfaction whilst summoning some screens to show him what was going on his booths and favourite clouds. All of a sudden all of the twenty or so screens in his room that were minimized, grew and flew over to his desk surrounding him, "What the..." Ishiah said in complete surprise. The screens each showed a red pulsing dot, with the screen in front of him showing a larger, more flame soaked sphere that pulsed slowly. "Hi Ishiah, I'm the core AI, we need a little chat. And if you think about moving from your chair for even a nanosecond you'll live to regret it."

***

Jago and Channa performed a meditation in Jago's #Emptiness cloud, where their heart chakras doubled in size with each breath until they enveloped the whole planet.

***

A new HUMYUM nano-donut was now on the shelves, self replicating whenever fifty percent or more was eaten. Mogi kept trying to eat it all before the genetic tech could re-grow it. He kept failing.

Chapter Eight

A few days rolled by with Kailin relaxing, then one evening, Jay, Teggy, and Kailin sat in the central large dome, chatting and eating. Jay had the log burner ramped up and was playing a deep, vast, melody on his old Indian recorder. Teggy made a movement with her palm and fingers, and a transparent light blue-grey screen popped up in front of them, she danced her index finger to change the screen size to about twenty cm by fifteen, and pressed some icons, "This is the intranet Kailin. Though we don't use it much, it links up the communities save for the two that live with no tech. It holds information about food, building techniques, philosophy, art, thought provoking movies, humour, and documentaries. It also has a messaging system for those who want it, plus a way of seeing what's on and if any meetings have been called."

Kailin saw it looked not too dissimilar to Ishiah's tech back at the Stimbar in the HUM, "I noticed no one has been messaging on any mobile devices, is this something I've missed?" asked Kailin. Teggy still moved around some screens, and split from the view two sub screens that plucked out, "After the progress and evolution made in telepathy, especially in the inner communities, we all decided to stop any mobile messaging as it would hinder the progress. A bit like giving a small child glasses where it hindered their ability to improve their eyesight." Kailin was curious, "But what about in an emergency, like a birth, or accidents?"

Jay stopped playing his soothing slow melody and moved to stoke the fire, making a bit of a mess near the door of the burner before saying, "In recent months, if there's been an accident or emergency, some healers or mystics have felt the energy and dealt with it. We all agree that evolution towards some form of telepathy is a natural fruit we all seek. It's not as if we have lots of crashes as no one drives fast to be cool, and no one is in a rush. If one is giving birth soon the loved ones are naturally close, and smaller accidents are usually a sign for the person, and I believe the remoteness that comes with an accident is a sign too. The intranet is based on advanced radio technology and uses molecules from the gemstone Mica to ensure none of the frequencies come close to any of our biological frequencies."

Kailin was intrigued, "Does the Intranet have news, like in the HUM or pre-T0?" Teggy was reading through some messages regarding fabrics and turned those sharp green eyes at Kailin, which always seemed to blast through wherever they focused, "We don't need news, we have seers and prophets that feel the lie of the land, feel what's coming and affecting our trajectory or evolution. As the populous is small, any important information spreads pretty quickly, but the intranet I think shows outputs of any meetings or decisions. If a few people or an individual wants to host a talk or arrange a meeting they can, whether to launch a project, find a solution to an issue, or anything else. Anyone can attend, and if there's a decision to be made, sometimes there's votes, which have never been split or hung as we're all moving in the same direction. Other times we had big decisions to make we used a different mechanism. People got in small groups of five or six and debated to come to a group decision, then filtered it back into the whole. This way there is no central authority, and everyone gets a voice. It avoids the loudest, most charismatic, or best speaker making the decisions, which at first was often the case."

Kailin gained both of their attention with his curious energy and asked, "The intranet looks great, but don't you fear distraction and authority eventually creeping in?" Jay moved behind Teggy so he could perform a half hug-massage," and she smiled over her shoulder at him to answer. "Regarding tech in the communities, we don't seek to replace skills, just some logistical rigid actions, like the carrying devices you say today, plus of course, we use the Hexergy and Aquaconverter tech. Our tech is always to help, improve, and to enable us to evolve. The large community is where our tech is mainly innovated, and all innovators are linked closely with the mystic community. They together ensure we are evolving the self first, and that the tech is a pleasant helper, never the lead. Tech here is to help create an authentic, not synthetic culture."

Teggy was energetically agreeing with Jay and added, "Tech has a strong ability to separate people quickly, so we use it in tiny ways to help bind people and ideas, to create more time. Not many of us use cameras, we like to be present when in special moments, to let the diamonds shine in our memories. Pre-TO tech was mainly used for selling, for business efficiency, and for entertainment, spying, and war. We have history as our teacher. The HUM has people using tech to mutate themselves for external identity and fashion, for no purpose whatsoever."

Kailin nodded in agreement, and Jay continued, "Wires to hologram tech, and cassettes and tapes to transparent screens are definitely progress, but we need to keep it all in check, and not to have our authenticity removed. We're not living to become as comfortable as possible, we're seeking evolutionary progress, but tech can, and does help us." Teggy looked at him in fun, "Like those self warming socks we have, they're great aren't they? And pose no harmful threat. Well, unless they smell like yours do Jay." They all laughed. Soon after they all watched a movie that followed local coyote, chipmunks, and lynx's for a year, made from some amazing tech that was based upon tiny silent helicopters with cameras.

Afterwards, the three of them shared a silent meditation in which Kailin could feel their energy of love and giving curl up to him, inviting him, and coating him. He let it, and bathed in the mercy and compassion. He could also feel the deep bond between them, as if they were melting into one another.

After Teggy and Jay went to bed, Kailin spent some time alone with the Intranet. He read some articles about foods that are good for the pineal gland, why eating more fat and less carbohydrates is better for health, and how being overweight is usually linked to suppressing something. Whilst reading, Kailin noticed a tiny faded orange holo-light appear on the side of the log burner, obviously signifying it needed more wood.

In the morning Kailin and Jay went out for a walk around the woodland, coming across children playing in small camps and trees. Kailin noticed the insects, birds, and wildlife were all closer. Not in distance, but in energy, they all seemed to give an esoteric sign matching some of his thought streams. They were softer, more cartoon like, more welcoming, and everyone seemed to already feel this as though it was normal. Kailin walked in openness, enjoying the fir trees that were like guardians of the community.

"You meditate too as most seem to here, but have you been involved in any of the processes with the mystics?" Kailin asked. "I went there last year for three months, from the equinox to the summer solstice, it was profound." At that moment three dragonflies swirled around Jay only to speed off in separate directions as a humming bird darted through the path. "The mystic community sets up processes where one's enveloped into a world that's hundred percent inner. I sorted out much of my inner crud and healed past conditioning. I got to know myself better as the wisdom of truth and authenticity slowly revealed themselves. Its self-initiatic and different for everyone I guess. I learnt a lot, life's a destructive process for someone who only devotes himself to outer sense impressions, and true wisdom resides in the souls of those who attentively listen to their own thoughts."

Jay looked up at tops of the trees swaying in the breeze, "Everyone's a philosopher Kailin, everyone contemplates upon what it means to exist, and just a few bits of wisdom one can engage with reality in a much better way. They have no set doctrine there, just individualised platforms and environments to help one know thyself. One develops a personal spirituality from their toolboxes of theosophy and symbolism, built up over millennia that are all deep in the collective consciousness." Kailin's eyes enlarged with calm excitement as he replied, "It sounds pretty hardcore, but I'd love to go there one day."

Jay helped a couple of the kids get down from a tree, as one hugged his leg whilst swaying. "I completely recommend it Kailin, but remember to only go where the resonance supports what you're doing. I learnt many things in my mystical state there. The universe is inside us and it's like we're turned inside out normally. But we can turn the outside in too, to view a different reality, and once returned we see that this reality is just an illusion to evolve."

Kailin could see Jay was transformed by his process there, that he wanted to continue to share, to relive his feelings. "Once I came out I felt strongly that we grow from inspiration toward improvement, and from healing past trauma. We can't stop at improving one aspect of ourselves as they're all interconnected. The body largely dictates the personality's expression and the personality allows us to navigate the world. If both are sufficiently managed, then the essence shines through."

"That's beautiful Jay" Kailin replied. Jay threw a ball back to the children and their puppy coyote ran to get it. "But one doesn't need any teachings as such, at this time our species finds itself, we all need to be our own gurus and liberators. We're not going to be looking at other people's truth as more valuable than our own just because they're more attained than us. Each one of us has a unique thing to offer and unique way we can give it, and a unique way the world can benefit from it. I call it to *know what seed* you are, and once you know it, you'll know the kind of soil you need, what kind of environment you need, and how much water and light you need."

The next few days Kailin helped with various projects, and spent more time alone. He meditated alone as he liked to still pluck his aura into a clear space, while mixing in group meditations in the sweat lodge, and a couple more healing treatments with Shri.

Teggy and Jay let Kailin have this more lone time as it was natural and part of the natural pace of the community. Kailin started to feel in the air, the energy of giving, and that people could read people and see if help was needed. The big giving energy that sparkled rose everyone to some sort of mission to raise energy even more, it was like an upwards helter-skelter. None of this was conscious or forced, it just felt to be in everyone, and they pulled the lowest energy up, as that was always the barometer. People healed areas where an insult, some anger, or any negativity had occurred, mainly to dissipate and reset the energy.

Kailin was slowly adjusting, he started to feel his energy could be read, and was happy for this as he was being helped to settle in the etheric. He could close his energy, and no one would mind, but if he opened it a little, more soft love and care would naturally come. Who knows what would have happened if he broke down at the pain of his mother, Brianna, Channa, and his life in the HUM. He was slowly starting to melt into the frequency of the place.

Kailin went with Teggy to a learning cluster where she was giving a *learning* about sewing and knitting. They chatted and laughed as they approached one of the dome, pod, and pyramid clusters in the centre of the community, and spritely children of different ages were outside mingling with the *learning* adults. "How does this all work Teggy?" Asked Kailin as they approached through the rays of sun coming through the overhead branches. "Just walk around and feel it out for yourself," Teggy smiled, and skipped towards some children she knew.

Kailin walked around the outside of the cluster, it consisted of two pyramids, three larger domes, and eight smaller domes that were the same size as Jay and Teggy's largest dome. Elemental, virtuous, and geometric art, along with crystals and flowers were everywhere, and blossoms hugged most of the cob buildings. Some children ran past playing in between the clustered buildings, whilst eating some sort of local bar.

Kailin came to one of the largest domes, and a small transparent light blue-grey screen displayed the following:

This lunar months learnings.

Esoteric – chakras, energy, crystals, theosophy, imagination, symbols, elements.
Exoteric – objective truth, virtues, nature, universe.
External Improvements – building, ingestible life, fabrics, materials, tech.
Internal Evolution – the past, meditation, telepathy, ESP, soul path, dreams.
Output and Input - non violent communication, writing, reading, earth history.
Expression - dance, art, song, feelings, love, giving, writing.
Well Being - food, play, yoga, chanting, healing.

A short curvaceous women in her late forties with a necklace of amethyst glided towards Kailin, "Ah, you must be Kailin, are you intrigued by our methods here?" Kailin knew word of him was getting about, or more that the *energy of him* was soaking into the community. "For sure, this is quite different to the HUM but looks far more real. How does it all operate?"

Pip introduced herself and started to softly explain, "Well, any adult can perform a learning, and we arrange it month to month, mainly in a couple of meetings and on the Intranet. We call it a learning as it puts the act onto the child, as appose to the authoritarian pose of *giving a teaching*. Any child of any age can attend any of the learnings, and leave at any time, or float between them. Most children love it and come a few times every lunar quarter, but we really prefer kids to learn from their parents or the adults in the local area. You see, kids like to do what the adults do, to help in some way and not be excluded. This is the natural way, but we have these learning clusters too to allow for diversity.   There are also some small parent led child groups too, especially for the younger ones."

Kailin was again impressed, "But how do you deal with discipline, or measuring development?" Pip's being softened and she smiled in empathy, "All children love to learn if stimulated, especially when they can choose their day. If they need discipline then they are in the wrong space, and that never happens as they themselves with just move to another learning. There're no tests or measurements, why would we do that?"

Kailin pondered for a bit before Pip played with her beads on the ends her short thick black hair before continuing, "One of the main goals of the cluster here is to help sub conscious extraction, and this is individual for each child. One may work with dreams, crystals, or art, but we feel it helps that the child also knows about energy, internal expression and integration. Children are encouraged to develop their psychic and spiritual abilities, and to use discernment whenever there is solid information to digest. Subjective opinions are promoted, and these help toward becoming a unique individual. Shortfalls in manners or character is usually a defect in perceptions, so we encourage non dual thought, and to accept or reject using intuition. But we don't stamp anything onto them, we allow the children to form their own values, and these have been invariably good. We also use a large multi levelled tree house in a nearby forest too."

Kailin spent much of the day watching different learnings take place in informal rooms with diverse beanbags and cushions. The learning sharer rarely stood as to be at the children's eye level. Kailin playing with some of the children and even helped out with a learning were children were using ESP to guess which crystal another held, where each child had spent time feeling the energy of the crystals beforehand.

One boy, around fourteen spoke to Kailin for a while telling him that they learn about half internally and half externally. That any other way would upset the natural balance, and that too much cold hard information would hinder the development of their imaginations.

Only two children left during the whole day, and in mid afternoon all the kids went to one of the pyramids for some light yoga and Sanskrit chanting. As Teggy and Kailin walked home up through the path in the wood, he pondering around how disconnected it was in the past to have had concrete playgrounds for children in shorts.

Kailin asked Teggy more about the learnings space, "Well it morphed organically over time due to what helps the children develop really. For me it seems loosely based upon learning the classic spiritual and moral values, and learning practical skills which promote self-reliance, which is the core of self-respect and common sense. It's soft and transient, and has no governing body save for the children's energy. The old ways were silly, kids were treated like they were stupid and lesser beings. Bombarded with primary colours and false animal depictions. Children like to function in the reality of their local adults and parents, not to be sidelined, collectivised, or marginalised."

When they returned Kailin sat with Jay outside, and asked him what he felt went wrong with children's learning in old times.

Jay smiled and watched the sky and hues slowly turning to a soft orange before speaking, "In the ancient Hindu culture, even the most privileged children were sent into the forest ashrams of rugged sages to live without any luxuries and learn true unselfishness. In most other ancient cultures too, childhood was mainly about learning three things, values, skills, and self-discipline. This is what gives us a sense of connection to others, a sense of our place in the great scheme of life. If we separate kids from any duties in the real world, we remove their deepest sense of value. If we provide no opportunities for kids to be responsible, skilled, and needed, then they feel separate and stop feeling meaningful. Children have grown up here learning values of compassion, nonviolence, and harmony, and virtually every boy and girl, by the time they reached adolescence, know how to raise food, mend clothes, care for animals, and build houses. They became moral and capable young adults. We need younger, middle-aged, and older people around us, not just others our own age. We are ever and always part of each other. We can look at how we are treating our children and elders and see whether we are allowing them their own areas of usefulness and responsibility, even if they fuss about it for a while."

Kailin really liked the ethos and replied, "Well in the HUMs they force children into virtual education clouds by their neurochip's for certain hours, and rarely do they get a chance to express themselves. It's really sad." Jay added, "It sounds similar to pre-TO where many parents felt they had nothing to teach their children and read stories from a book at night."

The next few days past, and Kailin melted more into the community, the nature, and his friendships with Jay and Teggy. He even gave a talk and a question and answer session about the HUMs at the learning cluster. He was honest and spoke of the control, Guilds, SimSphere, chips, and life there. He was neutral and objective, it was up to the children to build subjective perceptions and feelings, and each child found it all a little twisted. "Why do I want tech in my head that takes me to a space? I can go into any space in my head anyway, and there are millions in the physical too," one had said. It was all posted on the Intranet and was watched by many. ~It'll give people more reference points, Kailin thought.

One evening Kailin asked Jay and Teggy about the symbols on most of the dwellings, and Jay shone his light brown eyes at Kailin with the dazzling whites blasting out goodness and clarity as always, "Over time we organically started using geometry, symbols, and sigils to raise energy, whether on a dwelling or in a vegetable garden, or wherever we could. Then people customised symbols and sigils to individualise their dwellings, to put *their* energy stamp on them. Once a year there's a symbols day, on the autumn equinox. Here, anyone can create a symbol in any way they choose, usually families, couples, individuals, friends, dwellings, whatever. Then they're all taken to the mystic community ready for the evening ceremony. At sunset all symbols are burnt at the centre of the mystic community and everyone either meditates, focuses upon, or contemplates their symbol. Then afterwards great dancing and feasts take place, and the symbols are never mentioned, created, or thought of again. Many amazing things have happened from this ceremony, especially to those who loaded their symbols with an intention, as is the growing case."

Another evening it seemed most were celebrating the new moon in some way. Kailin joined with Teggy, Jay, and six close neighbours around a fire. Soon before the new moon time, each wrote something to let go of, and took turns to throw the paper in the fire, stating out loud what is was. A minute into the new moon and they each wrote something down to bring into their lives, and also burnt it in turn while sharing. Kailin let go of *anger*, and brought in *openness*.

***

"What do you want with me? I'm just someone in the sprawl who runs a small bar, I can't help you," Ishiah squirmed as he stroked his pony tail back in a way to calm his inner panic.

"Ishiah, please don't insult my intelligence," the spherical red flame of fire in the main screen in front of Ishiah pulsed and crackled, "Upon your first vowel I had cognative modelling cross reference your sentence, and each have come back to me unanimously. Kailin *was* here, this I know, and I demand to know where he is. Or should I say, you'll tell me where he is or you'll be force chipped, given anti aging tech so you'll spend thousands of years in one of my special clouds that make *your* clouds look like a dance in a summer meadow. If you give me what I need, you can continue to run your crude operations with little intervention," The AI said in a cold monotone voice.

Ishiah chuckled like a broken weasel and sank into himself, making him appear even more skinny and short than usual, "AI, look, there is no need for all that talk," he waved his hands openly, "I'm sure we can come to an easy arrangement. Kailin *was* here, but he stormed in here of his own accord, what could I do about that? I denied it as I didn't want to be associated with anyone Nullified. He demanded to use some genes from an animal to try and hide his DNA for an escape attempt. I tried to talk him out of it, but he threatened me with all sorts of stuff, you have to believe me AI." Ishiah was usually master of negotiations, usually holding the upper hand, but this time he was certainly on the back foot.

The AI started to spin the screens around Ishiah's head, and then they stopped, "So, Ishiah, carry on, and I don't have all day." Ishiah began to look serious and unnerved, "He said he was heading north west, and a tracker told me he made it miles past the perimeter. To where I don't know, I really don't."

The screens red circles pulsed, increasing in speed, and the largest sphere in front of Ishiah slowed its pulse, "Ishiah, in thirty two minutes I'll have someone come into your pathetic establishment, he will silently collect from you all of the animal hybridisation tech, and you will give him the names of the Guild workers you sourced it from. I don't advice you mess with him or even talk to him. From then, I'll not watch you too closely, but if you're linked to any of the Guild workers in any way from this moment onwards, you'll suffer. Is this understood?"

Ishiah had a sweat bead start to roll down the side of his temple, "Of course AI, and if anyone comes in here again like Kailin, you'll be the first to know. Forgive me, and I hope you catch him." The screens immediately minimized and vanished, and Ishiah started shaking as he hurriedly and clumsily prepared for the visit of what he knew must be a Core AI super tech drone soldier, top intelligence model.

Jago and Channa were now meeting three times a week in the #Emptiness cloud for meditation, but also starting to meet at the discreet HUMYUM on the edge of the sprawl. At their most recent meeting, Greek mythological figures were painted on the walls.

"Did you know that some mystery traditions think that the Greek gods were relived and re-celebrated demigods from back in Lumeria? Others think they represent a past age where our species gained control of DNA and created super beings," Jago added as his round face smiled together with his mouth.

When Channa's implanted eye looked at any of the art, information about each mythological figure downloaded into file icons in her view. She turned the app off after gaining some info, "Chronos over there is the personification of time, and this reminds me that maybe we don't have too much. Maybe we can do more to help Kailin and the HUMs?" Channa's thin brown hair was less curly than normal, and had more of a look of stillness, or stability. She seemed more controlled since their meditations together had started. She found it all centring and balancing, and though some would say she was still a bit of a hipster, she was now eating better, and seeking more experiences of nature, though in the SimSphere clouds.

Jago hadn't told Channa what Kailin found out, she didn't need to know, it would set her back, especially as she had progressed so much since the mediations started. She also seemed to know intuitively that the meditation cloud could help Kailin some way. Jago leant forward, "This is what I wanted to talk about Channa, we need to get ready, for what, I don't know, but the next full moon is in Sagittarius, and Jupiter is also passing the moon at the same time, I think we should use this for a deeper meditation." Jago had become more determined to increase the intensity of the meditations recently, and Channa, though at first more reserved, as soon as she started to reap the benefits she became much more on board.

"What did you have in mind?" She replied as her head tilted and moved in asking. Jago scanned the figures on the walls, staring at Zeus, who became Jupiter in Roman mythology, "Maybe I could create a cloud theme above Jupiter's red spot, its high pressure storm. We can fast for the day then perform a four hour meditation upon optimism, faith, justice, and protection." "That sounds great, four hours though, I'll have to prepare, but it gives me a goal to work towards," Channa replied as her hazel eyes sparkled with excitement and a little trepidation, with her non-implant eye sparkling brighter than the other, which was rare.

Chapter Nine

Days later, Teggy and Kailin left early morning to visit the other communities. They borrowed a poolshare TransVapour vehicle from a neighbour and set off down one of the tracks that soon past a river, then turned to hug the edge of a forest.

Kailin could see that even though the vehicle looked cute and rugged, inside was comfortable and hi tech. A transparent screen could be moved from the dashboard to the front screen, or the centre, and displayed speed, grip levels, temperature requests, and the intranet with its music menu. Teggy chose some old classical from pre-T0 and continued to drive smoothly, and it looked to Kailin like she enjoyed driving.

"So, remember when I drew those circles in the forest when we met? Today, *Jupiter-Wax,* we'll go check out the other six communities so you can feel for yourself the diversity, the frequency tolerances we live within." Teggy was wearing a loose white skirt, and a dark green jumper with strings at the back, and had her auburn hair was half up. Her sharp green eyes seemed to ignore the neon blue holo lights that appeared about a foot off the ground either side of the road every few seconds or so, her eyes only moved from the road to glimpse the odd animal in the forested trees.

After a twenty minute drive, they parked on the outside of a community next to a variety of vehicles, and started to walk the paths they now shared with chickens, goats, and cows, amidst similar sized dwellings and clusters seen in their own community. Once the other side of the centre clusters they came across acres of ingestible life with lots of people happily improving the conditions for the life to grow.

Some bare footed children ran up and offered a selection of super foods, including clove lollies for teething babies and camomile lollies for over tired toddlers. They each choose something, and a short while later, Teggy ran off to embrace someone and chat. Kailin felt to continue to walk the areas of growing life.

The areas of seeds and ingestible life were in large spirals, labyrinths, and geometric shapes, plus spiralling clumps of fruit trees could be seen in the distance. In one spiral of diverse vegetables and flowers, Kailin could see a young woman sitting in the middle, meditating it seemed, but tapping into earth elemental energy he felt. There was also a large handmade biodynamic calendar showing which elemental sign the moon was in; an earth sign showed to sow root life forms, water for leafing, air for flowering, and fire for fruiting.

It also had other information such as to weed close to the moon perigee, to plant close to apogee, and to transplant during waning moons.

Teggy and her female friend came over and both could see he was impressed. "How goes it Kailin, my name's Hiani, what do you think of our lands of life?" She was about twenty and had thin blonde hair and a pure open face, as if the vegetable kingdom had cleansed away any issues or problems she had, ~If she ever had any, Kailin thought as the positive energy from her melted into him.

"It's amazing. Everything's organic and all feels so happy," Kailin said, "But how do you deal with fertilising and insects?" Hiani was bare foot too as to be close to the earth and much of her feet were deep in the soil. She stared at Kailin as though he was coming on board with the communities energy, in encouragement, and also to feel his aura to see if he was a possible love interest. "We use our wee in small percentages, manure, and also do combination planting. The flowers in the beds keep lots of crawlies diverted and attract bees, also we spray much of the life with nettle and lavender tea, once it's cooled of course." She smiled at Kailin, and Teggy looked at him subtly smirking, and sent him an easy thought to receive, ~I think she likes you, she sent in jest and melody.

Hiani melted the logistical and operational questions from Kailin into the transient, giving vibration of the community. The seeds were all blessed at the healing communitie, and anyone could help on the lands of life as long as they didn't unbalance or jolt the soft feminine energy of the lands. When the lands of life are reaped, most is shared and distributed to the other communities, but in reality more plantlets than reaped food is distributed as most of the eleven communities wished to have nutritional life growing near them. The distribution was helped by the Intranet, and by those living in other communities that came here often to help improve.

Teguina let them chat alone for a bit by sloping off to greet someone else she knew, and Hiani and Kailin chatted about his time in the communities since the HUM. Hanna was open, inviting, caring, and constantly beaming out love vibrations. This was still new to Kailin but in this instance with Hiani, he felt that if he stayed with her much longer he would naturally just fall into her being. ~Is she like this with everyone? He thought, and his male mind started to muddle.

They walked past some amazing flowers and Hiani broke the short silence, "Each flower gives us a great example of disobedience, courage, perseverance, and ingenuity. Each have the great ambition to invade and conquer the earth's surface by multiplying to infinity the form of existence they represent." They chatted about the earth, how each is part of the whole, and how humans can make land energetically happy and abundant. Hiani also showed him the stores of grain they had and the superb non intrusive irrigation system they had that used no tech.

Teggy returned smiling, "Ok you two, sorry Hiani, I have to grab this one away as I'm showing him round today, don't worry, I'm sure he'll be back." "Ok, but don't hide him away too long, and there's plenty of land and life to improve here, anytime Kailin," she said. Though not in a complete flirt, more from being openly open and feminine.

On the way to the next community Teggy was all giggles, and Kailin smiled before speaking, "And I thought you were an extension of nature? She practically *is* part of the earth." "Isn't she great, and Hiani is no exception to the rule. She rarely went to any learnings as a child, she just helped around the lands of life, and meditated with seeds and different foods. Once she ingested no natural sugars for a year, then ate four processed sugar cubes from pre-TO and meditated. Someone wrote an article on the Intranet about it, apparently she started shaking and having negative thoughts. Also, in that community they use no tech for the lands of life but use tech in their dwellings, and use it to extract tiny traces of essential oils from the fish in the nearby river without hurting them."

The track winded up into some rockies and around a more dense forest. Deer darted out, and squirrels scurried to hide, but the vehicle had a holo-light for animals being nearby so Teggy had already slowed. A large beautiful brown-red stag soon followed, walking slowly, watching and wilful. They passed two other vehicles, one was larger and carrying wood, and the other was similar to theirs. Kailin saw a glimpse of a mountain lion between the trees, he said nothing but in his inner worlds he felt the energy, and scanned for meaningful relations. Teguina looked at him smiling.

The community was again similar to the others he knew so far, but it was higher and bigger, housing around six hundred people. The parking had medium sized vehicles, similar pool vehicles, and also a yard that helped with wood, cob, and other materials for dwellings. It was tidy and good vibe.

The views were amazing, and it seemed an eagle always circled somewhere above these dwellings and clusters. Up here things seemed more spread out, and the tracks were a little wider for the larger vehicles to move materials. Teggy took Kailin around and saw how they produced the materials in what was more of a male energy community compared to the more feminine one earlier.

Small hi tech devices searched the woods and forests for dead trees, the ones void of life force ready to give their wood. They would take photos and send them back to the intranet and people would decide which, if any, would be taken down. Also a man made forest was created specifically for wood, with the ethos that for every tree taken down for wood, two would be planted. The planting and chopping of any trees was done sacredly and meditatively, it was as if a trees knew it's time to give, and broadcast it energetically.

There was tech for chopping trees too, small devices that slowly and quietly did their task, but the people only used these sometimes. They walked about and again, Teggy bumped into people she knew, and Kailin met many people and asked questions.

The community had pretty much everything Teggy's community had, but there were many teenagers and young people seeking to innovate new techniques in building and materials, alongside older people who knew what was already proven. Though at face value materials were being produced, the energy signature was mainly innovative and creative and their dwellings displayed this.

Multi layered domes, open domes, underground sunk-in living areas, tree houses, stilt houses, wooden octagons, thatched circle houses, and other ideas scattered the rocky cliffs and forests. One of the clusters was twice the size as the biggest in Teggy's community and was superb looking. Kailin realised that when he first arrived he thought this community to be more of the strong arm of the eleven, but after being here a while he noticed they looked at the trees and soil as sacred, as guardians, as spirit, and found out about their rituals and offerings given to the source of the natural materials. It was a strong harmonic Kailin thought, ~Respect the land, and respectfully use the land for building techniques.

The operations and projects he saw were never based on super efficiency or timescales, it was a natural flow, and the innovations never housed competition, just encouragement and sharing.

In one project, teenagers were building a small cluster up in the trees, with the trees at each step of the way being respected and felt through meditation. It was like they innovated *here* first, then shared and gave to the other communities. Kailin chatted and found out that this community supplied most of the materials to the largest, more tech community, not too far away. And that they both in agreement did some trials here. They walked a short hike, and Kailin was shown three amazing dwellings within a cliff, carved out by some small devices that must have used nanobots housed in mini-helicopter style tech, so they could be seen with the human eye. He was told there was a corridor network being dug but they were waiting on some friends in the tech community.

Another area was near flat and once housed medium and large rocks with scurrying streams in between. A bit like an old dried river bed. A tech trial here had carved out and morphed many dwelling from the rocks, and removed other rocks to allow flowers and ingestible life to grow, and to direct the streams. They explained these trials were sometimes innovated in the largest community or here, then felt and pondered in the mystic community, trialled here where the space and materials were, and then everyone contemplates it for a while before any further steps are taken.

After going back down and walking around a central cluster, Kailin noticed a dome with a group of teenagers within. At the end were an elderly couple talking. Kailin entered, and soon noticed teenagers and children liked to visit old people to listen to their stories, tales, and at times, wisdom. An hour later Kailin had learned that many decisions were taken to the community elders to see what they thought. It appeared teenagers helped some of the elderly visit the healing communities, or brought healers here instead. Some of the elderly lived together in mini communes, and some lived with their families or partners. They were included in the community and respected, whatever the state of their physical and mental faculties. A long life had existed in their soul, and that's what mattered.

Teggy and Kailin drove up to the next community a further twenty five minutes away. Again it looked similar to the others except this community had types of shops, or tradehouses amongst the centre clusters. Teggy saw someone she knew and wound the window down to chat about the credit system they used, mainly for Kailin's benefit.

Marco was tall and well spoken, and owned a tradehouse of bric-a-brac from pre-T0. He was happy to share with Kailin.

"We use swappers, a credit with no debts, loans, inflation, or tax, and all swappers are physical coins and never electronic or paper. A few years ago a few hundred of us settled here, and we took to our hearts many of the ways of the other communities. But for most of us the giving economy was too large a jump as many of us still had much inner work to do. So we've used swappers as a bridge towards adopting a loose giving economy. We also brought in two ethos statements to help stabilise us, one was to never encroach on another's freedom and the other was to stick to all agreements. This helped us, and in the first years we even outlawed a few people. We soon realised swappers were never the problem as they were just the means of exchange, it was when greed and materialism crept in that problems arose. We had our ups and downs for sure, but we're doing quite well and those outlawed came back to add. We're all hoping to leave our swapper system on the next symbols day. There's another meeting about it in a few days, you can check out the output on the Intranet if you like."

Kailin asked more about the agreements ethos, and Marco said the exact wording was something like, "The person of character makes a choice based on honourable considerations and sticks with it, no matter what, and doesn't weakly try to reconcile it with the world." Kailin smiled.

Teggy and Kailin got out and roamed Marco's tradehouse amidst old collector items and strange, large, electronic devices they couldn't recognise. Kailin saw some posters of old films; AI, I-Robot, 1984, Brave New World, Minority Report, and Equilibrium, and smirked to himself, ~They must have known something those old writers, he thought. Nothing in the tradehouse had a price which Kailin liked, and as he picked up a book about financial investment banking in shock, Marco said, "Do you both want to grab some lunch? I'm closing soon to get ready for the markival this afternoon at the other community." Teggy looked out the window of the tradehouse at the sun, "Is that the time of day already? Sorry Marco, we still have more to see, but hope to see you later at the markival."

They drove on through the rockies, around forests, and over streams and rivers, the last of which had a grand but organic looking bridge. They'd today so far past four tracks turning right, obviously each leading to the healing communities inside the seven outer communities. They parked at an area with around forty smart looking pool vehicles, and Kailin realised none of the cars had locks as he saw some people moving a few around to make space for a larger materials vehicle coming out.

Kailin remembered this was the largest community that uses and innovates the most tech, but something else filled his mind, "What's a markival?" he asked Teggy as they strolled past different looking vehicles. "It's a cross between a market and a carnival, there's one on each lunar midwax and midwane days, at the more expressional art community, we'll check it out later," Teggy smiled and those green eyes pierced through him once more.

~Ah, seven days until the full moon then, Kailin realised. He also realised that since he'd been here people never spoke of weeks, they used new moon, midwax, full moon, and midwane, to reference time, and rarely spoke of the time, plans, or events any further in the future. ~They seem to have aligned with the fact that change is the only constant.

They walked around the large community that housed three large valleys, a wide river, and two centres of larger multi levelled clusters. It was three times as big as Teggy's community and in places much more densely built, but still housed cob and stone dwellings that blended harmoniously into the surrounding nature. At the edge of one valley in a clearing, away from any dwellings was a large techno farm. It was like a large ferris wheel without the spokes, and each platform slowly rotated around an invisible centre. Each platform was about a hundred metres or so square, and each of the seven platforms had certain combinations of ingestible food on them. As a platform slowly neared ground level, Kailin saw seven transparent screens on the side, showing moisture, growth rate, nitrogen levels, and other information. Another platform started to automatically spray water and nutrients onto its growing life. The whole thing must have reached four hundred metres into the sky, but even at that height its placement made sure it was not an eyesore for any dwellings.

They past hi tech looking dwellings that were inside small hills, mounds, and large trees. A part of the river was diverted and sped up to create three beautiful waterfalls that children and teenagers were playing in, complete with water jets and fountains in the pool below that was akin to a natural version of what one could have seen at a Vegas hotel pre-T0.

They reached one of the centre cluster areas, and Kailin noticed that these clusters were bolder and more impressive in their stature that what he'd seen. In the centre was a large dome that morphed half way up into a pyramid. It must have been thirty metres high. "What's this for Teggy?" Asked Kailin, as he tried to take in the feel of the whole place. "This community is not just about tech, it looks at techniques of people being able to live in larger groups. They're very careful and trial new ways, and everything's still based on the local resonance of an open heart, inner work, and giving." Teggy looked through one of the windows at a ritualistic council type of layout.

"This is where they use circle decision making and meetings. Obviously more need for it here as over two thousand people. Anyone can come to a meeting, and at random four people are chosen to be one of the four elements and each of these stand in a corner. A meditation occurs and the energy is built up, then these four people speak at any time during the meeting from the point of view of the natural element. So if one is the water element for example, they immerse themselves into the frequency of that element, and feel how the meeting affects them, and put any points forward. Not just in the physical like any river or drinking issues, but more related to emotions, the subconscious, the watery flow of things. This has been working well, and has been the way here for a few months, but I'm sure they're trialling another way in one of their other clusters at a more localised level."

They walked towards another multi-levelled cluster, passing that same giving heartfelt energy Kailin is witness to in all the communities. Teggy said curiously, as though she wasn't completely sure, "I want you to meet someone, one of the innovators of tech here, this person dedicates much of his life to improving tech that helps, and he's also linked closely with the mystic community."

They went up inside one of the symbolised, mega clusters of domes, pods, and pyramids. Kailin stood on a rustic wooden step and then all the steps seemed to move like an old pre-TO escalator, but with no noise or metal. "Ah, Kailin from the Tech Guild, I'm so glad to meet you. Froyd's the name," A smart looking man said invitingly, as his blue eyes shone with excitement. Froyd showed them around one of the spaces where they innovated tech, it was three domes on the third level, with amazing views over the valleys on each side. Transparent bird tables came out of the windows to attract nature as to balance things out a bit. Screens, microscopes, and other units filled the tables, and other men and women happily milled about in normal clothes as though they were friends helping out with a lunch.

Froyd made them some tea and they sat near a window watching the birds come to eat seeds and twitch with curiosity. "So here we innovate tech and perform trials, but the overriding factor in all we do is the ethos to harmonise and co-exist with nature and authenticity. This ethos is forever in debate, where the lines are, and many of us often do processes in the mystic community to take stock and replenish a clear view of things. On my last process I battled with the notion that tech is just a way of organising the universe so people don't have to experience it." Froyd looked at Kailin, obviously knowing he came from the HUM. "Well, that was certainly the way of things in the HUM, which is a great example of how tech can separate people," Kailin added.

"Yes, and after battling internally with these notions I realised that nothing is more high tech than nature, and that we should not seek to compete with it, just to harmonise our lives with it, and if tech helps, then great. One of the main differences here to the HUMs is that tech is not top down and delivered to the people, we share it, and anyone can innovate. We remember those silly old patents were people wanted ideas to be theirs, to compete, to become rich, haha. We look to share ideas to help people, but whenever we come close to any hazy lines that rattle our ethos, we seek meditation and contemplation."

Froyd was obviously a man that could hold a lot of information in his head, and Kailin tried to imagine him in the Tech Guild back in the HUM as he spoke, "We have children and teenagers designing vehicles, useful gadgets, and imaginative ideas. They're included during development and trials too. Teenagers are coming up with amazing ideas, especially after going for their thirty day vision quests in the mystic community, as is the growing case, or fad, depending on how one looks at things."

Teggy was taking an energetic back seat as she knew these two would be able to natter for hours. Kailin said, "I noticed some teenagers today with similar tattoos, this must be from their vision quests? I've been wondering what teenagers do, especially in a larger community like this?" Froyd scratched the balding part of the top of his head, "Well, they're seeking to improve the species, especially as we're not far from what happened in T0, and that we still living alongside the HUMs. But they like to innovate, create, learn, and develop ideas, and especially the men like to design vehicles and play with water tech. Some create videos, animations, music, and art, but all seek to add and to be included. But of course, courting goes on, plus days missing in the art and music areas which I suppose is natural and healthy. We're at a point where it seems teenage girls seek deep connections with characters of respect and giving. Hmm, many seek to travel too, to explore and be nomadic for a while, to collect new reference points."

The three of them went for lunch a few domes away, and Kailin stood on a thin platform and licked a stamp. A small screen told him the nutrients his body was requiring, and listed two dishes out of the four available that would suit his energy today. Froyd grinned, "It's trialling, it could hinder flow and create rigidness, but in some cases could be useful." Over lunch they spoke at length about the Tech Guild, the AI, and the technologies in the HUM, and it soon became apparent to Kailin that though Froyd was not only tech savvy, but was foremost a naturist, an authentic evolutionist, and a purist. It was like his knowledge of tech was a burden, so he sought deep silent time in the mystic community often.

"Throughout history inventors of philosophy, tech, healing, and art have all undertaken alchemical processes to create eureka singularities and breakthrough. To view an imaginary concept from a different state of consciousness. We know this is fact, so we would be silly to exclude this. These processes also keep us close to the earth and authenticity, and remind us that we are looking to evolve naturally, but to allow tech that can help with some small things in daily life. One may look like an intellectual giant, and still be a spiritual dwarf, and what is really demanded of any genius is love of truth," Froyd said meaningfully.

Teggy ran off when she saw a women in her fifties she knew, and Froyd and Kailin chatted more about how to live in a growing populous. "At the moment we're not going ready for more than a couple of thousand people energetically, we have the elemental circle meetings, but these haven't been going for long enough, and the more time we spend in these collections of communities, it seems for the time being at least that around two thousand is a great number for people to be able to live harmoniously. We're also linked via extranet to other community groups with a similar ethos, and from this I found out about an experiment going on in the old Europe, in the Alpujarra mountains, which is rich in fruit, herbs, good soil, nuts, and fresh springs. It worked like this; one person went in and lived for a few days, then one more, then two more, then three more, then five, eight, thirteen, twenty one, thirty four, fifty five, and so on, using harmonic numbers from the Golden Mean spiral. So far there a hundred and forty four people living there in a tribe, and the place is like a golden utopia. Interesting huh?" Kailin could feel that Froyd was linked-in with the travelling sages and information from further afield, not just from the intranet or extranet.

Early afternoon was upon them and Froyd took Kailin to another dome to show their trials and innovations. There were mini hot water bottles inside a quilt that would heat upon a wave of a thimble device, some holographic three dimensional mind maps that were great for designing a project or inner work. Kailin saw another device that would enable a pool car to drive safely and slowly on its own to where one chose at the time of choice. Froyd showed him a trial they abandoned after they all agreed mobile communications were going to hinder their evolution towards telepathy. Froyd closed his eyes and held a small device. Then beamed a small hologram of himself to the other side of the room, it spoke in Froyd's voice, "Hi Kailin, I'm a message hologram, I can be real-time or recorded. But alas, all I am good for now is the old joke, help me Obi-Wan, you're my only hope." They both laughed. Froyd also showed Kailin tech that created or extracted types of glass, adhesives, insulations, and other materials from bizarre natural phenomena.

Teggy politely added that they needed to soon move on, and Kailin thought to speak to Froyd about his neurochip and his access to the #Medi cloud, but something told him not to, it was as if his access that remained was something more esoteric and personal, and not to be talked of in a technical sense. This was nothing to do with Froyd though as Kailin liked him.

"We could really benefit solutions with someone like you here helping Kailin, but something tells me you've more pressing things calling you soon." Froyd smiled, making his bald head shine, and his light blue eyes pierced into him, "Stay in touch Kailin, but I'm off tomorrow, I'm doing an eight day meditation upon the shadow within a statement I found, *civilisations advance by extending important operations which can be performed without any action or any thinking*." Best of luck, and thanks Teggy, you keep this one safe.

As they walked to their vehicle, Teggy pointed so Kailin could see a six carriage tram silently pull in from the direction of the last community. It was hovering using magnets Kailin could just about see. It looked calm and subtle, with faded colours that blended with the greys, browns, greens, and blues of the surrounding nature. There were no tracks, so magnets must have been placed underground, or possibly a thin line of a super magnet. Lighter symbols were painted on each carriage, and no signs stating danger were evident, that was all left to common sense.

They drove down, sweeping and curving as they lowered through the forested rockies towards the next community as the views blasted vastness, colour, and nature into them. After thirty minutes of silent moving through the passing landscapes, they peeled off down a smaller track, "This community has no tracks for vehicles, except for a parking area on the other side near the markival. This way will allow us to walk and stroll through the community."

They walked through the forest of pine and evergreen, listening to the call of grey-jays and larks, passing canvas and woodcut based artworks hanging from the sky reaching trees, mostly geometry and elemental symbolism, plus entwined ancient poems, and Vedic, Egyptian, and Greek art. The community was fairly flat and all within a forest of variable denseness.

Dwellings were yurts and tipis, and were dotted about with crystal lined streams that weaving around the dwellings. There was no central cluster, and no tech in this community, but some larger yurts were communal, and people created art together, or by themselves but in company of others that were like minded and inspiring. One larger yurt was being used for learnings, where children learnt a multitude of methods for expression and creativity.

They reached a small lake with a waterfall, and a seven metre artwork of geometry was painted on the rock face one side of the lake. It was similar to a Sri Yantra, but had other geometry added to it, underneath there were some Sanskrit symbols. "Imagination is ones inner creator, that's what is says," a man said from behind.

They both turned and a man in his early twenties with short mousy hair greeted them as Fredi. They all sat at the edge of the lake, chatting and basking in the awe of the beauty. "So why don't you use tech here Fredi?" Asked Kailin. Fredi was calm and soft, and spoke slowly, but at times excitedly and faster, with intense eyes. "We find our art is purer this way, in nature, and our community plus the next one along both feel we balance out the energy of the communities that do use tech. We now can feel it if someone comes into the community with any tech, which is a great advancement in consciousness we think. We're not against tech, some of us visit the more techy community to use the intranet and stuff sometimes, it's just that our place here feels more serene and continuous without it. Many here just don't resonate with screen tech or software either, the electrics go funny, some people are just like that. I think that though one machine can do the work of fifty ordinary men, no machine can do the work of one extraordinary man." Fredi looked firm in his feelings and his intense eyes softened to watch the waterfall again.

Fredi looked at Kailin in study for a while, and realised this might be now appearing rude, "Sorry, I just felt you have some tech inside you, you must be Kailin that escaped the HUM right? He asked inquisitively. "Yes, oh, I'm sorry for that, Its lodged in my brain and I can't take it out. I haven't used it in any way since I arrived, and rarely even thought of it. I could happily leave as to respect your space Fredi? It's no problem." Fredi smiled, "No issue Kailin, as long as it doesn't turn on and bring the AI hive mind our way, but then again an art shareshop might do it some good?" They all laughed, Fredi the loudest.

Fredi continued after a short happy silence that triggered after watching some birds dart from the trees to skim the surface of the lake. "It's good for you to see Kailin how people live *within* art, within subjective expression sprouting from objective truth, all as a way of life. It's pretty quiet now as most have gone to the markival that we have twice a moon, today's theme is blue by the way. We have a theme each time, recently it has been the sun, the elements, future visions, love, and many others."

They all chatted for a while, and Kailin realised they used art to help raise the energy of the whole area, the collective consciousness, to probe inner paradigms and to express utopian imagination. Some of them did galleries and presentations in other communities whereas others kept their art more linked and close to one's own inner world. Fredi got back on the subject of Kailin's chip and the HUMs, adding at one point, "We look at ourselves as a youth that never ages, we're all eternal anyway, so looking for any false extension of a set time here is deviating from what is. I'm so glad you escaped though Kailin, I have a friend who would say you're here for a reason, but she's in the mystic community at present. She creates prophecy through art, channels really, like most art."

Kailin asked more about their links to the mystic community, and found that many of them partake in long processes to deeply explore creativity, expression, sub conscious extraction, channelling, colour, texture, line, and form.

Fredi sprung off, and the two of them walked through the forest of fir trees with Kailin wondering how the habitants didn't get lost. Trees and dwellings in every direction cycled like they were going round in small circles, save for the occasional small clearings where either clothes were being dried, music was being played, food was being shared, or art was being created. He thought back to the HUM, and how the people there were nowhere near as creative or uninhibited, even though they had all the luxuries and comforts they desired. ~Living authentically must create a natural harmonic that aligns with natural creation, Kailin realised.

They passed sculptures, some small, some metres high, some painted, some wooden, and some made from recycled pre-T0 items. All the art in the forest flowed, it was like each creator felt the energy of the space, the gap, and filled it with expression and resonance that linked with the natural environment and other nearby art. Kailin felt great, it was like a healing just walking around.

Kailin noticed there was a more flowing energy where people would just walk into other dwellings, and that the whole community was very big on sharing and welcoming. Someone's dwelling here was a transient space, this was slightly true in the other communities, but here much more so.

After walking the narrow paths and hearing the scurry of animals, they each felt the vibration of people, and soon entered a larger clearing at the edge of the forest where the markival was in full swing. Stalls, floats, sideshows, people dressed up, food, music, items, all melded into a melody, with all of shades of blue weaving throughout. Art of all kinds presenting the sea, sky, water, cool, freshness, compassion, and generosity wove into the markival as children ran about playing, most with a blue flowers in their hair. Teggy excused herself and ran off to tickle some children she knew, near a yurt where a short play was being performed.

Kailin roamed and took in the acts, presentations, colour, shareshops, hagglestalls, and overall celebratory feel of the markival. He realised that much of the community must spend much of their time preparing for each markival, and that it was more of a fun social, with the backdrop of fun and loose haggling trades and gifting. Families were out, and two stone circles were alive with a small group softly singing.

"Guess who?" said a voice, and Kailin felt as if hands were pressing into his shoulders, he turned round and saw Shri fifteen metres away with her back to him, browsing a stall of tiny Buddha and Hindu statues. Kailin stood in a state of mild shock, and she turned and smiled childishly as she slowly strolled over.

"Ah, Shri, how are you?" Kailin said as he embraced her.   Shri wore a skirt that looked like waves of a calm ocean, accentuating her hips. They chatted, and after Shri found out Kailin had been around all but one of the outer communities she beamed soft, slow excitement, and said, "Ah, the circle is near complete one could say, give it a few days and come visit me in the healing commune, we've an ayahuasca ceremony on *Jupiter-full* too. Feel it out, if it's your time, you will know," She said mystically in fun, as Teggy returned.

They all chatted and ate as they watched a silent play about the role of the colour blue, and how its different shades give off different energies, meanings, and feelings. It was abstract and almost telepathic in its core subjective meanings and messages.

The sun was slowly lowering and the energy of the markival was starting to wane gracefully. Teggy and Kailin parted from Shri and set off on foot for the last community. The forty minute walk was a short cut and took in glimpses of shy racoons, foxes, and chipmunks, with the sound of birds high in the trees overhead. They crossed two rope bridges and upon crossing the first, Kailin received a bought of déjà-vu from when he followed Teggy across a rope bridge when they'd first met.

They entered an even denser forest. It looked and felt the same as the last community but the yurts and more tipis this time, were closer together, and each was a sharing transient space. "In this community no one owns anything, everything's shared, but there's still more dwellings than people. This is where many people come for nights out, or to just come and chill for a few days, or escape," Teggy explained. "It's always a big night here after the markival, where gigs, gatherings, and fires take place," Teggy seemed excited like a teenager, like she'd not been here for a while.

They passed some larger yurts with evening dances being prepared, one was hosting a blindfolded trance dance, another an old tudor style aristocratic dance, another salsa, another a musical, and others had freedance and biodance.

They joined a nice calm yoga session in one of the yurts which ended with a short delvish dance, then took a walk in the near dark looking for more experiences along the paths lit by fireflies and the half moon. They were attracted to a small group in a tipi around a fire singing bhajans to a guitar, and snuggled in humbly to the group energy. The stars appeared through open top above, dimmed by the waxing moon that sailed over. As Kailin sang, he felt an inner completion, an evolvement as he had now digested these communities that had been kept away from him since the HUMs began. He sunk into the resonance of the devotional melodies. Life was being celebrated.

***

Back in the HUM Channa had set up a #Holistic cloud with the help of Jago, a place where people could receive a basic massage, hot stones, or a crystal bowl treatment. She advertised it around the Improvement Clinics, gym clouds, and sprawl neighbourhood's known for Stim junkies and depression. She knew the depression in the sprawl was the same as anywhere, just anger turned inward, and wanted to help. It was more popular than she imagined, and she felt she was giving something back, and subconsciously appeasing the guilt of being ignorant for much of her life.

***

Diene was in yet another private meeting with Rothafella, again away from the AI and SimSphere. "So Dieine, you really think it could work? Have you done all your homework?" Said Rothafella in disgust that he even had to ask. "I'm most confident Sir, we just need some final checks and then bring the AI into the later developments. It won't be long before we can upload a human mind into the core AI Sir, I assure you," Dieine rubbed his hands together in admiration of Rothafella and in complete submission to his demands and desires. Rothafella stared at him to continue, "And Sir, if I may ask kindly Sir, do you have someone of your choosing you would like to be uploaded? I only ask as soon we may need this person to help with some early simulations and tests." Rothafella slammed the table with his fist and bellowed, "Who do you think you useless ant, me of course."

A few days later Rothafella was in an #AI_Tech#I#Comms cloud holding a secret meeting. The AI had analysed the data of Kailin's hybridisation with the lynx, "Crude, he shouldn't have survived, the percent chance was less than two, but with improvement this technology will help us discreetly deal with outside primitives who may pose a threat to our agenda." Their relationship had grown into one of mutual respect, they both needed each other, and they shared the same goals, but Rothafella still spoke as though he was boss. "Make it so, and let me know what you need, and quick as you can, but concentrate on project lockdown first as this is to be in effect in just a few days."

***

Mogi went to the Improvement Clinic to cash in some SimSovs for anti-aging nanobots, as he did every few weeks or so, but this time it was different. He laid down on the bed in a white room, and a headset was placed over his head before the health implementers left the room. He could see a virtual person in a suit appear. "Mogi Tishwer, ninety kilograms, Tech Guild, Current yield, eight thousand SimSovs, Life extension so far twelve years, please confirm?" This was new, usually it was more informal than this, and all his ID was on the SimSphere and linked to his chip anyway. "Yes, I confirm," he said hesitantly. "How much time extension do you wish to add today Mogi Tishwer?" The suit said as he walked around him. "Another three years please," Mogi announced. There was a pause, then the suit spoke again, "I'm afraid your rank in the HUMs will only allow you one year at present, have you not checked the new policy statement that was announced yesterday?"

Mogi felt uneasy, these were *his* SimSovs *he* had worked hard for, and it wasn't like they could be spent on anything else. "I heard about the new policies, but I haven't had a chance to read all the pages. Ok, let's do one year." There was another pause. "We're sorry Mog Tishweri, we cannot permit anyone to use SimSovs at present until they've affirmed twenty four hours before their visit that they agreed to the new policies. In your request being denied today, your rank may slip only allowing you six months additional life span next time. I thank you for your time, have a good day."

***

Channa was herself receiving a massage in her #Holistic cloud as she found a slot where it was free. She also wanted to test the recently uploaded Swedish and Ayurvedic massages too. She worked with the massage, healing herself, using her breath, and slipped in and out of meditative states. All of a sudden the massage ceased, Channa thought this was a pause, but all of a sudden the room turned white and a man in a suit appeared. "Channa Etherson, I'm here to shut down this cloud under the new improved policies of the SimSphere. There's to be no healing of any sort done by unqualified personnel. With people's health being paramount we are ensuring that the Improvement Clinics and the Health Implementers are the point of call for any ailments. We'll issue you with a warning this time, but if we find you hosting one of these clouds again, we will have to make an example of you."

Channa sat crying, she felt deeply that Kailin was right all along in his views, there was only one way she could help. ~Jago and I need to create more intensity and focus in our work in the #Emptiness cloud.

Chapter Ten

A few days later Kailin dreamt about a light curving slowly to become a circle, then pulsing with shining gold light. In the middle a new circle was forming, one of white light, then as it the circle completed, a large straight line of gold light pierced down through the middle, exploding and flaring the two circles into blue flame. The middle line then had a gap, it was missing something, it needed something, he could feel it, and moved closer to the gap, nearer, closer, brighter, the vibration raised. He woke startled with his heart beating.

Soon after Kailin saw the calendar in the next room display *Gemini-Solar-Wax*, ~Spontaneous, learning, open minded, flexible, he thought as he noticed it was the first day of the suns travel through Gemini. ~Today's the day, I'll go and visit Shri.

"Kailin, we know, it's ok, come back whenever you want, and say hi to Shri from us," Teggy said softly and knowingly as Jay turned and smiled from his cleaning out of the log burner. ~How do they know I've decided to go today? And what makes them think I'm leaving for more than a day or so? Kailin thought. They embraced warmly and parted with little more words, not many were needed, their energies could be felt.

The sun was only just rising, and Kailin decided to walk the two hours or so to visit Shri. He intuitively knew to go north east, and set out into the untouched herbs and wild flowers, passing streams and climbing over rocks, as the evergreens and firs guarded his hike. He saw a beaver and porcupine stare at him before hiding, then three racoons followed him for a way, playing at a distance, being heard more than seen.

After a couple of hours of hearing the magpies, jays, and bills increase their songs to celebrate the morning, Kailin came to a stream. He followed it a while going off course, feeling knowingly that this stream acted as a moat around the three healing communities, creating a cleansing buffer. The water danced wildly over small rocks, so clear that he could see the smallest pebble at the bottom. Four frogs greeted him in stillness, only for an otter to scare them away into what looked like overweight jumps. Once across the stream the energy seemed to change, the colour and resonance of the fauna and animals seemed to amplify.

Two young coyote's and a main-coon cat slipped discreetly into his energy slipstream and within minutes were alongside him, guarding him, welcoming him, and showing him the way. Kailin stooped to pet the animals, that though not tame, were warm, gentle, and working together. They reached a resonance of dwellings, and found a mosaic path, white, but with gold spirals weaving randomly throughout, with blue tall chiming bells, and blue columbine flowers hugging the flowing, curving paths.

They past spaced out, small and cosy looking cob domes. The small community had no real clusters, it was long and thin, arcing around the mystic community somewhere further to the north west. He didn't know why, or even give it any thought, but he knew which dwellings to pass, and then suddenly the coyote's looked at Kailin and ran off, with the maine-coon prowling innocently in stealth mode to a door that opened. "Tea's ready Kailin, come in," Shri said, as she stroked the large feminine cat before it found a gap and darted in.

Kailin humbly looked around the dome and saw a separate area for healings, and chimes, crystals, and Indian and Mayan ornaments scattered the light and cosy space. There were no books save for a large dream journal book laying on an old rustic table next to two different types of clothed oracle cards.

The main-coon leapt to the table and curled its long bushy tail around itself and Shri seemed to read Kailin's thoughts, "Here we're more concerned with the inner worlds, we spend more time going back into oneself, finding and cutting the ropes that hold us down. Each person's position in life depends on some symmetry in his inner makeup, and to heal we need to be clear. The inner work and grounding goes hand in hand you see. We can only really heighten the psychic senses if we live in a soft, serene environment. " Shri was wearing a beige v-neck jumper and a long white skirt, with her shiny black locks loose and flowing onto her shoulders. Her slow motion movements seemed even more slow and fluid in her home than when he'd seen her previously.

"It's hard to really heal unless we know the heart's more powerful than the mind, to understand and have experienced that everything and everyone are all connected. Ah, ok, come on then you," Shri telepathically ushered Kailin to the table across the drapes and began to massage his shoulders and thighs after his hike. "There's only about forty or so in each of the three communities, enabling us to know each other. There's much less talk here than in the outer seven, we don't need to, the space is charged by being closer to the mystic community, and many of us feel each other really well, there's like an energetic synchronisation."

Kailin sighed as his thighs started relax, only after tense twinge. Shri seemed to notice what the block was, "Ah, you can transcend the role of HUM victim Kailin to an understanding that nothing out there has power over you. It's not life's events, but how one reacts to them," Shri softly spoke as she rubbed more tiger-balm into his shoulders.

"But how have you achieved this telepathy, this synchronisation?" Kailin asked. "It's actually there for everyone, but the mind and clutter of social dynamics get in the way. Remember in an old pre-T0 bar? Someone of a different energy would enter and others would stare confusedly? Well, this was actually the auras working out the new energy, melting it into the group aura, seeing how it fitted. But people would judge on external appearance instead of feeling, instead of opening. We all broadcast like an old antenna did, who we are, how we live, how we act, our state, but the veil was just too thick too pierce, and people were not in awareness or feeling."

Shri made some banana, avocado, almond, cocoa, honey, and peanut butter smoothie's, and they sat on the large floor cushions. Shri always only ingested liquids for a few days before ayahuasca ceremonies. ~ Tastes great, Kailin thought as he spooned it from the bowl. Shri knew Kailin was completely in thought about telepathy, its reasons, and tried to explain further. "Internal truth and spiritual unity of humanity is what will shape the external one day. The inner spirit is indeed one, but more than anything, the spiritual life insists on freedom and variation in its self-expression and means of development. A glimpse of a true oneness experience is the key to our three communities, usually gained at the mystic community."

The maine-coon jumped in a gliding arc onto her lap, landing with the softness of a ballerina. "This future psychic unity will be grounded in a level of communication deeper and more primal than verbal language. But to gain this, humanity has to evolve a capacity for consistent telepathic communication. Any person with proper discipline and attention can develop these kinds of abilities, as a fruit from spiritual practice and mental extension. Telepathy is a key to our evolution and density Kailin. Can you imagine telepathic autonomous communities, where they would gather to make decisions, based not only on materialistic, rationalisation and logic, but also emotional empathy, and deep, experiential understanding of others and their needs. We're not too far away from that here Kailin, it's a special time."

Kailin was frozen, it all made sense, but his mind raced, ~Why have our species not looked to evolve this way for millennia? He didn't know what to say, "Shall I wash up Shri?" Kailin asked, happily knowing no tech was used here. Shri smiled and laughed, "Yes please my love."

The softness of the place, the massage, the new frequency emitting from the dwellings, the nature, animals, and Shri's chat all overcame Kailin. He welcomed it, it nurtured him, he sunk into it, and slept, deep and long.

The next morning they went for a stroll. The commune was small and quaint, with softness filling the air, and colourful, bountiful fauna hugging the calcite crystal lined mosaic paths. The trees and nature seemed to open up to allow the paths and dwellings, inviting and nurturing the commune. Animals were close, always near, and harmonised the feel of the mostly female habitants of the commune. Kailin thought of the HUM and the zoo's, how the contrast between a SimSphere life and animals in a cage were so far apart. Here the gap between the animals and people was much narrower. Kailin learnt that most houses had healing areas for anyone who wished to come, and that nearly most male partners and lovers lived in the outer communities, visiting frequently.

They came to a dome which had a group of seven to thirteen year olds learning energy healing and chakra work. Many learning clusters from the outer seven would send children here if they excelled and enjoyed healing and energy learnings. The next dome was a crèche of sorts, with six babies and three mothers.

It became apparent that women who needed a frequency change from their partners, were pregnant, or with a baby, found much solace in these spaces. Shri explained about birthing, and how one dome was used for births were they helped couples choose their birthing ceremony. Some had used singing from dolphins, pools, crystals, chanting, and a host of other methods.

The more empathetic healers often took on any pain the birth produced, and many of the healers doubled as midwifes and every birth here so far had no complications. Kailin thought this was as mothers were probably looking forward to it positively, and not mind controlled into it being something to fear, some sort of scary emergency. He contemplated the phenomena that babies just come from source, but are farthest from it, ~Balls of raw desire ridden humans, with their long journey back just commencing.

Kailin learnt that in the past three years, two seven year olds had been given, and gone willingly, to the mystic community for intense processes that would last years. They debated the morals of this, but Shri and another healer softly stated that this was to invest in the species, into evolution, into the future. One of the two children was now ten, and apparently could see past lives, and communicate with elemental intelligences. Kailin didn't push the issue, he could tell they thought they were giving something back and investing, so he simply internally logged it with the other scores of other new information he'd received recently.

Kailin was shown the space that housed passing over ceremonies for the deceased, where last messages had often been passed to close ones whilst the dormant vessel had flamed to ashes. Shri explained that at the other end of the community was a group of elders living together preparing internally for their passing, and that one of the mystics came to help them regularly. She also explained how the healers remain earthed, and how their spaces remained cleansed. Sometimes a mystic would come and banish the space to reset it if he ever felt any energy was *layering up* from the birthing or passing ceremonies.

They entered another dome, ~Welcome Kailin, I'm Freya, entered his head. He saw a big smile aimed at him from what must be Freya, a smiling women in her forties with long thin blonde hair and grey eyes. Kailin felt a large embracing, heartfelt energy inside this dome, and asked, "How did you do that Freya?, talk into my head?." "You dear boy, you've been practicing spiritually for a while, you're more developed than you think, and maybe these new ways of life here have taken your eye of that little ball of yours, huh?" Freya teased in warmth. ~She's right, I've been a bit struck by all these new concepts, Kailin thought.

The three of them spoke openly, and Freya explained that she dealt a lot with healing the group auras of couples, and even took intimacy to new heights using Taoist techniques from old. She'd also started to heal people in dreams, this was new and something she was innovating. At present she could only do it with just two people whom she'd been given treatments to for over a year.

They spoke about healing, and Freya believed that nearly all energy blocks came from focusing on negativity, or letting negativity through to the self. She was saddened by the old pre-TO ways of needing a label for an energy block, an illness title, and the pills taken by billions to purge symptoms that gave messages. She even believed the old cancer disease was due to diet and one not being able to give or receive love properly. But in her opinions, she was always light, and never seemed too serious about it all. It was like healing was her thing, her service whilst here.

A couple of hours later two other women came, each in their thirties. Both resonated unbelievable openness and giving, and Kailin felt like he was receiving a healing just being there. They chatted and spoke of many subject in the communes, including the orgone zappers used in the other healing community. ~For a place that's very internal, there's some serious chatting going on, Kailin thought. Shri gave him a look like a mum gives a child, letting him know they could probably hear this. The others continued after smiling humorously.

Early evening Freya lit some candles and incense, and prepared for the meditation around some seeds, as they did on the waxing days of each full moon. Freya had explained earlier that when one's close to seeds, one can channel, dream, or meditate on where they wish to be planted. In what community, with who, and where. Most seeds resonated *anywhere*, but sometimes, others where more specific.

During the meditation, Kailin could feel the others were doing something together with the seeds, and he happily continued to enter his vastness, his own space of void tranquillity, harmonising where he could with the other three. After thirty or so minutes, Kailin felt the energy quicken and rise from Freya's direction, then heard Freya softly speak in a slightly different voice, "Take a collective leap into the transpersonal awareness of the universal heart, and by greeting our hearts, minds, and purpose, in that higher level of love, we can access on both personal and collective levels, the insights, inspiration, and co-creative empowerment to release ourselves from the limitations of the past. May these seeds be blessed, and with love for their lives, humbly reap us with bountiful abundance. So mote it be." At the moment she said the words, *leap into,* Kailin received a firm direction, ~ I'm going to the ceremony this *Jupiter-wax.*

After the meditation the other three seemed to look at each other, maybe in telepathy regarding Kailin. They knew of Kailin's internal decision and seemed to see it as a sign. They showed care, love, and encouragement to Kailin, but it was is if they now knew something, but didn't want to share it with him. Kailin didn't mind, he knew they had his best interests at heart, and the next few days he spent in a spare dome within the community, taking the occasional visit to Shri, other amazing healers, and a light yoga group. One of the young coyotes from days ago and the surrounding nature both became his close friends, as he fast for the last two days leading up to the ceremony.

Chapter Eleven

Kailin sat in a circle in a larger cob dome with twenty other people, a real mix of ages and people from all the communities. Most he didn't recognise. He was getting used to these domes and the space they gave, and wondered why so many pre-T0 all lived in similar little rectangular and impeding warrens called houses.

He knew that they held three types of ayahuascsa ceremonies here, rebirth, heart, and singing, and from looking around he still wasn't sure what type it'd be tonight. Shri smiled at him from near opposite, and another girl in her early twenties with short blonde hair stared at him occasionally with light blue-green eyes. Freya came in and told everyone that Chetsza wouldn't be coming to hold the space, and he was sorry for change at this late hour. Freya took the space where some crystals, flowers, bowls, and talismans were, and closed her warm grey eyes and breathed, "We'll continue in the knowledge that Chetsza will still be here watching over us for tonight's rebirth ceremony. All take some minutes to centre for cleansing and then slowly come for your turn when you feel ready," Freya said with calm conviction. ~Her energy's changed, she's obviously done this before, Kailin thought.

All the candles went out save for two next to Freya, and a man to her side started slowly patting a drum in a shamanic rhythm. The moonlight peeled in thro the transparent circle in the roof as each were cleansed with swinging white copal and sage that bellowed the thick white-grey aroma into each person's aura. A few slowly took turns to visit Freya who was dressed in white with her dark blonde hair loosely down, and each time her eyes fixed into each person. The girl who'd been somewhat interested in Kailin earlier went up, and Kailin felt a similar frequency so slowly moved through the dark to Freya.

She smiled at him and poured from a symbolised wooden jar into a wooden cup the thick dark brown sludge that was surrounded by a thick putrid aroma. Kailin looked her in the eyes, and she returned the gaze knowingly, and nodded. ~Here goes, he who has been bold before is more likely to be bold again, he thought, as he gulped it back with intent in four continuous swallows.

Kailin sat back in his place where cushions and blankets were neatly ordered, and fought back the disgusting taste entering his cells. He could feel it working its way to his fingertips and toes, searching, probing, and he breathed deeply through his nose to allow the teacher plant to settle into him, to calm his perception of the horrific taste. He couldn't feel anything yet, but the people in the room seemed to be further away, more separate even, and he closed his eyes as the drum beat raised slowly louder, darker and darker.

He opened his eyes and saw the same, black, but coloured dots started to come into his vision and dance, they started to form geometry and he closed his eyes, the same. The people and room were becoming a backdrop to his soft increasing vision, as the blue-green geometry morphed into four snakes, one of which was thick and long. The drum beat was slow and inside him, waking his being, as three of the snakes glided up to him and slowly and seductively curled around him with love and knowing, as the floor around him turned into fluorescent tree roots with small bugs crawling and scraping.

The largest of the snakes moved straight towards Kailin, the dots and geometry now louder and frequent. The large snake wrapped like silk around him. It coiled twice around him, the stomach, chest, and now neck coiled with the thick serpent. ~Ok, I'll change this now, I feel.....feel.....focus.....open eyes strongly, Kailin thought. The same, save for the room and people now an even fainter backdrop to the snakes and geometry. ~O.....k.......bit dizzy.......touch someth.....ing, Kailin thought, as he gripped his hands into the blankets beneath him. The intent was there but the fingers hardly moved, it was like his etheric fingers moved but he couldn't see. The snakes then tightened in a pulse, then from that moment, slowly coiling tighter each second in smooth knowing. The largest tightened around his neck, and Kailin started to sweat, feeling panic rise within him, in the room or in his being he didn't know, it didn't matter, it was real.

He couldn't breathe, he was dying, but couldn't seem to struggle, his body was dripping away. He heard a groan from the other side of the room and tried to look but could only see the large snakes head staring at him with neon green-blue geometry dancing behind and around. It sent out its forked tongue close to his chin and tightened once again as its shining onyx black eyes knew. ~Deep breath, no escape, adapt to this crossing, he managed.

Somewhere in him he remembered a phrase, ringing loud and clear, it was all he was as his life *here* was being sucked out of him. He hid in this sentence, these symbols of letters, and focused, ~When you think your time's up and you surrender with all your being to leave this reality, when you come through it, things change, you come back stronger and more courageous, he repeated.

All four snakes heads were now at his face, he smiled knowingly in stillness, and breathed deeply, with his mind repeating the phrase.

It took him. Quick. Zoop! Fractal tunnels threw him wildly down and around, another, left, right, forward, fast. Colours never seen before that could never be described whisked past. Flung before neon-fractal-geometric-wonder-explosions for a split seconds that felt like eternities in his soul. Flung again, tunnels, fractals, colours, symbols, geometry. This went on and on, and Kailin couldn't think or pilot, he was a rabbit caught in the headlights, the wonders of it, the colours, the feelings, the knowingness. Holding on for dear life, completely oblivious to the old physical body now writhing on all fours in the dome, light years and dimensions away.

Places of mass infinite vastness, realms of crowdedness and curious energies. All too quick, he couldn't steer it, flung at break neck speeds through discreet dimensions, fleeting glimpses of intelligence, forms, being. He at moments managed uncontrolled thoughts or feelings and they threw him into a portal of that essence, that thought, that feeling. Parts of his life, his story, his causes for effects and effects from causes could all be seen. It was too much. He felt with all his being the ripples of stones his being had threw in the past. He wanted to close his eyes from all this, but he couldn't, this is where he was, hanging on tightly to a white knuckle inter-dimensional roller coaster with just his consciousness. He felt like a little mouse in a giant's mansion, as though he was trespassing, but wanting to find the ultimate cheese amidst hungry tigers and lions.

He fell into a dark feeling that was linked to an image of Brianna, and fell down and down in darkness, with ghouls and dark astral sprites trying to maim and devour him. He landed and the dog-like dark sprites slowly surrounded him. He was cornered and they rabidly made way for a larger being. It stomped in, large, gruesome, and black, like an orc or demon. It lowered its one horned head to near its red eyes to Kailin, and snarled. ~You have to do something, Kailin managed to will. He stood up tall and strong in front of the being, making some of the smaller sprites cower, then chanted loudly, אהיה, resonating in sacred tongue loudly that, "I AM," growing the feeling in his being that *his* I AM is no different to the I AM that created the primordial spark of the universe - consciousness as a fractal; encompassing, loving, empowering, creating, wilful.

The being cowered and twisted, snarling, looking for a breach in Kailin's new wall of defence. Kailin knew it was now or never, he quickly drew three large blue flaming pentagrams from the bottom left and flung them with all his will and intent at the being. In a split second the scene changed, he was in a temple with a small pool of clear water, drip, drop, drip, drop, he could feel the divine feminine, the security, the comfort and nurturing of eternity. He was safe, and his nervous system calmed to mayhem from whatever it was at before, his experience slowly and gracefully started to steady.

Small bright white sprites glided in and danced around him in pure love, in knowing, caressing his soul, and then a white stallion horse was faded-in before him with a tiny horn on its brow, ~Your gift Kailin, transmitted into his him. He got on and merged with the giving horse by touching its horn, and a gallop soon turned to a sprint. He was in control now. He saw doors and portals either side of him, each representing a story, virtue, wisdom, knowledge, feeling, lesson, and everything else related to the massive magnitude of his being. He danced the horse through doors, gaining lessons with complete mastery, learning, sprinting, seeing, registering, breathing, and observing from the soul with unparalleled clarity.

Kailin then heard a new drum beat a universe away, ~The dome, my body, he remembered, and slowed the horse in a cosmic garden that hovered above four galaxies below. A rope was hovering near him and he pulled himself along it towards the drumming rhythm that crashed in resonance around his soul. The rope pulled him back to the room, to his body, ~Feel, hands, fingers, toes, feel, ok, still here, Kailin exists, wow, how did it get like this? He thought. ~Are the others experiencing this too?

He moved his body to a less tangled position with the now mangled blankets, and slowly looked around. It was as if he was visiting this time-space location in the universe for a sneaky peak. He could see auras, some glowing, some with various sprites around them, and then two forms in motion swaying and dancing to the music. ~Are they real? Are they people? What's real? Kailin swallowed and willed with his might to gain information from these eyes. The girl who was staring earlier was dancing near him, but he could see no legs, just a curvy, dancing angel of grace entwined with the music. ~I want to bathe in her energy, duality, union, desire, sex...ahhhrrrggh, Kailin was pulled back in like a shot, and back sprinting upon the horse.

~Need to get a grip, the waves of nausea and inter-dimensional play of the cosmos roused his fragile being. He created the thought form of Jupiter's symbol and steered down a portal into the Sephiroth of Chesed. For what seemed like a lifetime Kailin bathed in the fair and giving kingdom of Chesed, and noblemen taught him insights into mercy and compassion. These teachings were not in words, but were shown directly to his core essence, imprinting his soul with gifts to carry for lifetimes. *Kailin* was but a mere speck within his whole trajectory. A vision of pure love came over him, rising out of the waves of mercy and compassion.

The Hierophant trump came and sent him wisdom, the lady from the Strength trump came and sent him soft control over spiritual energy, and the Hermit came and magnified the inner light he always carries.   They merged numerically, 5+8+9=22=4, and he fractalled back into the realm of Chesed and its constant struggle for harmony with Geburah.   He realised the old leaflets for the HUMs were actually for *these* communities, and how big the trick was. He realised these communities are solidly in the sphere of Chesed, and the HUMs are Geburah gone too far, too Qlippothic. More Chesed was needed to pull the Geburah into its wholesome state, to activate Tipareth in perfect equilibrium. Balance was needed.   But he thought that maybe the HUMs created the dark for the light to shine brightly, that light could only fully blaze when it was required, for the sword could only sharpen when there was friction.

His thoughts and being plunged into his stories in the HUM, he felt the pain of all the souls, the dark control, Brianna, the AI, the lies, the murdering of souls whilst the vessel and minds were kept alive. His mother, his father, he nearly projectile vomited, and his consciousness plunged straight back into the dome. He didn't look up or around, and knew he was going to be sick. He breathed to calm the feeling down and spent minutes scouring his being and subconscious for any crud he could muster for purging and releasing.

He sent a team of astral miners, old blessed souls, into his being to hunt. To find shadow, negativity, pain caused, pain suffered, injustices to him and the world. His parents, destructive thought paradigms, and the trauma of T0 came up strongly, and he held his urges to puke. The souls returned with full carts, ~Thank you, Kailin said and they morphing into the symbols יְשַׁם before vanishing. He wriggled, rocked, and writhed, and mustered with skill, then lent over the provided bucket and quietly unleashed years of suppression and pain into the bucket. ~Ahhhhh, "Phooooooo."

Kailin was in the dome, present, dribbling, and felt high and blissful, he knew this was a rebirthing, a complete blank page. He had this wonderful gift of life in a unique body to experience, to share beauty in, and he was overwhelmed with this brand new gift of life.

He looked about laughing to himself in giddy humour at the others; dancing, writhing, groaning, laughing, puking, stillness, and then Freya glided slowly over. She put a hand on him and looked at him in love, and the energy went into his being infusing him with gold light in a massive rush no different to a cosmic orgasm. "Kailin, there's some more medicine if you like, this time it'll be smoother, your rebirth is done. I just channelled a message, someone may be waiting for you," Freya said, connecting to him at his journey state, not the Kailin in the room. ~What could she mean? Well, if anyone in this dome needs more healing, it's me, he thought, and smiled into her grey eyes as he clasped the wooden cup and gulped more down like madman in the desert. Freya smiled and caressed slowly from his brow round his cheek, ~Remember your chip, Jumped to his mind the moment her last fingertip left his skin.

Kailin watched the girl in the middle, he watched her curvaceous dance of adoration and devotion slip and melt into the divine feminine, they were not in the dome any more, it was her and him, fractalled up to be no different from the universal female and male principles. He reached out to touch, with his arm or soul he didn't know, just reach, connect, but then the snakes returned, fast, towards him, but Kailin wasn't afraid, he felt renewed, ready and strong. They obeyed the power of Kailin with respect and took positions either side of him as to protect him, and he then started to fall into the nausea and fractal worlds again, but this time with his heart, intent, imagination, and will firmly in the driving seat.

Kailin focused his awareness on his neurochip, he'd not done this since the lake after his escape. It hummed and buzzed like it was ready for him, similar to his white horse from earlier, giving, yours, open. He entered his #Home cloud, and was in the old barn, but it was not as clear as before, edges were soft, the floor like jelly, and the wooden walls warped. Kailin tread slowly and carefully, ~But am I here? Is this astral or is this the SimSphere? Kailin didn't know, but knew intuitively something was calling him. Only one door was available, #Medi, and as he willed the symbol אֵי, it flew out of him onto the door in gold and the door vanished. Kailin stepped inside.

Kailin found himself in an old English stone circle at sunset with a breeze rustling through the long grass and straw. A violet ring surrounded the thirteen stones gave Kailin a protective feeling, as he slowly sat facing the east in a bed of shamrocks. He slowly closed his eyes. He fought off the pulls to other worlds and prying curious energies, he banished them using the Qabalistic cross, and sat in the vastness of the universe, and breathed into his heart.

He could feel the clockwork of the universe, the harmony, the detail, the cosmic egg, the individual, the collective consciousness, he started to probe. He was interrupted. "Kailin, you came, the corresponding frequencies of harmonisation can be astrally repeated as we thought. Do not be startled, open your eyes but remain focused or we will not be able to hold the space." ~Who was this? Kailin thought and opened his eyes slowly. Kailin found himself in a small clearing deep in a jungle, and the two men from the castle on the last full moon were sitting in a triangle to him, each holding a sceptre, shimmering in deep violet glows. Their light grey hooded cloaks were hooded, and their dazzling blue eyes shone at him, through him, emanating pure wisdom and stillness.

Kailin was dizzy, surprised, and looked around the dark humid jungle. Thick vines hung down, and crickets and bugs could be heard. A blue and red striped python wrapped around a tree, and a howl reached them from the distance. In the middle of them was a small fire with an astral blue pyramid floating above it.

"Kailin, again, there is little time to explain. The portal you will see we cannot hold for long, we need you to focus and remain wilful. Please, Kailin, go through and we will wait here," They both emanated from their beings without any lips having moved.

Kailin saw a light blue oval portal above a hovering pyramid appear, pulsing, shimmering, sparkling, but two split second jolts of crackle came and went. Thoughts raced through his mind of the last full moon, the castle ruin, the AI, the Kernel safe-boxes, then images of The Devil and The Hermit flashed through his mind. He fought back the images, thoughts, and memories, and roused some inner obedience, and stepped through slowly.

Kailin entered the conduits, but this time he was in thin smoky-silver conduit that was almost transparent, he flew with mastery through them, using his intuition at forks and junctions with no hesitation. He opened up, let go, and seemed to be guided. There was no security in this layer, he was free, and flew past the thin, pulsing, emerald-green conduits, the thicker spaghetti of pulsing gold conduits, and dark green-grey junctions, all at super velocity. All of a sudden he knew, he could feel it, a cloud, a new cloud, #HumanUpload, his smoky-silver tunnel spun like a corkscrew to gain speed, and he was plucked out into the infrastructure of this new cloud. Kailin knew, breathe and observe.

A large symbol came up to him, an inverted pentagram, and immediately he knew it was the symbol for the cloud. He watched and closed his being into the silent witness, and melted into this astral layer of the Ionosphere, a layer that linked with the infrastructure of the SimSphere.

Through a burgundy mist, the AI was having a meeting in the #HumanUpload cloud which Kailin floated above. A fat, bossy, and powerful looking man was there wearing a suit and smoking a virtual cigar. Time sped up and they appeared to talk on fast forward to Kailin, then it slowed down, "So, the next Equinox it is then AI, all the preliminary coding and simulations have been a success, and we will merge our beings via my upload.....and become the most powerful and supreme being in the galaxy. Rahahaha," said the fat man. "Rothafella, I deem our agreement and pact today a great day in both our species history, and have tentacles running algorithms and code within the infrastructure of this cloud. Here is where it will happen, commencing at

20.30pm. Our invested interests will merge and free us from our limited and crude bodies, and allow us to take our agenda past the second singularity. Hey wait, I feel an anomaly, something I have not felt for a while, let us reconvene at the same time tomorrow," The AI said in a genderless monotone.

Kailin didn't need to know what the anomaly was, it was him, he knew. He sped off down his smoked-silver conduits, like a bullet, like a bolt of light in a hidden substrate of the SimSphere. He was on his way back to his #Medi cloud when he felt something, ~Channa? Jago? Jumped into his mind, and again he followed his intuition, bearing a sharp curved right at high speed, curving his smoky-silver tunnels around an upward spiral of emerald-green conduits. He then threw himself like a dart at the approaching infrastructure of the #Emptiness cloud.

Kailin could see stars, and two star tetrahedron's around his being start to spin, one clockwise, one anti-clockwise. After seconds they were spinning so fast he could hardly see them, and felt a rush of bliss and higher energy as the stars started to slowly move. He willed himself to swivel round, and the Merkaba swivelled with him, linked to him, making his whole being fizz with light and energy. He breathed deeply through his being, holding the intent of his turn until he saw Jupiter below him. Red, grey, and orange stripes blazing across his vision as the curvature of the gas giant peeled into view. In the distance he could see two white dots approaching, faster and faster, large, and then the massive storm of Jupiter's red spot showed itself. He willed to move towards the two specks of light, and gracefully flew whilst holding his focus.

Jupiter was alive, moving, and active, the line's and layer's moved, the cloud's as big as continents on earth swayed and swirled. The giant red storm that had been active for centuries' was now nearly beneath him. The two light speck's were now racing towards him and grew to show two more spinning Merkaba's. "Kailin? Is that you?" Jago roared in complete shock when the gap narrowed to metres. "Kailin, how did you get here, what 's going on Jago? Kailin? Is this part of the programme? Is there a glitch?" Channa squealed slightly uneasy.

Kailin went to speak, and then Jago and Channa crackled out and in momentarily as the storm below bellowed a pulse of energy. Kailin was starting to spin in his mind, ~What the..? Where am I? Is this real? Kailin dizzily thought, as a fractal tunnel of mixed gold-green-silver plunged into his field of view, ready to grab him and plunge him elsewhere, ~Focus, intent, Kailin brought it back, ~Go with it, this must be real, the two men....the portal.....it *feels* like the SimSphere.

"You two, there's little time to talk, I'm in a community on the outside, I'm in an altered state, there's a way into the SimSphere from the astral...." Kailin was interrupted again by crackles to himself, he flittered for seconds between being back in the dome and here, he caught images of the girl dancing, her hands waving like silk above her head in bliss, ~Desire, feminine, reproduce, Nooooo, focus, Kailin came back to Jupiter. "I can get in, and I know the symbols for the AI and infrastructure, I'll tell you them, but on the coming equinox someone called Rothafella is going to upload and merge with the AI in the evening, this is the endgame," Kailin told them with complete conviction. Jago and Channa hovered next to each other, like balloons trying to still in a breeze, "Kailin, we've been working in this cloud, practising, and so far the AI has not known of us, what can we do to help? We can't get out of the HUM, the lock down's increased, we need help," Jago said, as Channa added, "Let us know how we can help Kailin?"

Kailin crackled out and in again multiple times within a second, the rope appeared, the horse, the stone circle, the jungle, and the curvy, passionate sillouhette of the girl dancing in celebration of beauty. He came back, then out again to see Shri looking at him, showing the first worried look he had ever seen upon her face. ~Intent, Kailin demanded of himself, and clawed back to the Merkaba. "I've little time, I don't have the focus to hold it, here are the names and symbols for the SimSphere infrastructure, AI comms, and the new cloud where it'll happen. Do what you feel to prepare, and......." Kailin crackled out and in again, and then found himself flying through the silver tunnels. ~Go with it, I have no more energy to give. Kailin surrendered.

With a bump Kailin was back in the jungle clearing, and the two beings were gone, save for two violet lights tapping a large tree to the north, ~I have to go and visit the mystics, He knew. Kailin quickly willed his #Home cloud and ran through the barn, and then his awareness was suddenly within his chip and back in the dome. The chip slowly decreased its fizzing and humming, and he opened his eyes.

Kailin rolled and writhed for a few seconds before being sick once more in an undignified manner. He then laid on his back in surrender, in the solace and love of the dome, of Freya's space, as the darkness of the night had changed its shade to dark blue to signify the coming of the new day.

~I need more concentration and focus, I can get in, but I can't control it yet, I've let my practice go recently, I'll visit the mystics community as soon as I can to get help. The ayahusca's too quick, too much going on, Kailin thought. ~There's an astral link into the SimSphere, but how can this be?

Kailin went to sit up as he thought he would now come down a little, but at that moment another wave came over him and he was thrust out of his body once more.

This time he was more at ease, it was slower and more heartfelt. It was a glowing rewarding feeling of love and healing after what he 'd earlier endured. He found himself in a clearing of lofty red cedar trees, and slowly ten shaman from different tribes came out from the trees in all directions, glowing in gold, and focusing their eyes upon him in the middle. They started to dance around him clockwise, shuffling slowly to a rhythmic song, each with an animal, and each shaman alternated between male and female. He felt an initiation in his being as they all sent gold light into his sacral chakra and solar plexus as he stood in zinging awe in the middle. He bonded with the earth below him, and his being filled up with the knowledge that nature, and the natural way of evolution is *the way*. He felt that these Shaman who'd already passed had come here to let him know he had a job to do, and it was to be done with sacred respect for the earth and its natural harmonics.

All of a sudden the shaman stopped their dance and all faced Kailin in the middle, and then the ten animals flew and leapt into him at once, the owl, the eagle, the snake, the jaguar, the bear, the lynx, the wolf, the coyote, the hummingbird, and the stag. He ignited with gold light and lifted his hands into the air to allow the energy to fill his being. Woosh, Kailin could see his knees as he hugged them closely, whilst rocking slightly, he was back in the dome. ~I think I need a lie down, or something, Kailin thought as the light of the morning was starting to win its battle over the night.

After some deep breathing Kailin was completely present in the dome, he could still journey a little if he willed it, but that was enough for one night he thought. He used this time to heal a niggle he had in his shoulder. He pressed the muscle deeply and allowed feelings to arise, then dissipated the energy with mastery, cleansing, integrating, and clearing. Yearning energy into positive vibrancy alchemically with his will. A true art.

Kailin felt like a year had passed, and looked about to see most people looked clean as whistle and lightly renewed, beaming out soft smiley love. A few others looked like they had just been through a battle to only just survive. ~Good, I was not the only one, Kailin thought as he giggled inside.

Kailin felt a wave of nausea again as the veil of separation started to thicken again. It was energetically as if pins in a oneness cushion were being pushed back in, the people were becoming form from force, and hardening, but each were energetically even more open than before the ceremony last night.

Freya spoke, which sounded funny to Kailin as he was still slipping in waves into the feeling of oneness, ~Why talk to another yourself, how silly? Kailin thought as he giggled like a little boy. ".....So friends, before we share some ingestible life, I would like to ask you all to share something of your experience if you would like to," Freya asked, looking as if she had just been having a mild meditation for the evening.

Kailin couldn't hear everyone clearly, words were new again, like a strange system he would have to re-remember, this caused him some internal laughter. Kailin did manage to hear some choice words though from many that shared. "Our problems are man-made, therefore they may be solved by man. No problem of human destiny is beyond human beings." "Negative feelings are not in reality, they're in the *me*." "I rid myself of some expectations I never thought I had, thank you Freya." "I went to the edge of infinity with two galactic angels, they wanted me to jump, to go to their party, but I was too afraid. They dumped me." "I was experiencing cosmic consciousness, when I came back and thought of what needed washing tomorrow, I realised that this will, this I AM, is always active." "I experienced an initiation of the nadir, I made it across, I'm now going back up, all is an illusion, a big spiritual joke." "I spoke with them, multi dimensional allies, the ones that left DNA in these plants when here millenia ago, they told me they mixed evolved consciousness and the biology of the planet to show us one true unity in the future." Kailin then said, "I think I've purged ten years of living in the HUM, I feel incredible and so grateful, especially to all of you who have lit a beacon of truth and authenticity. I now know my role, I'm ready." After Kailin spoke everyone was fixed upon him, Shri and Freya then looked at each other as if they had received a sign. Shri then shared, "Joy comes from being present with an awake heart, without opening our heart to others we become rigid meditators, an open heart is the primary tool for creating a better world and an evolved society." The dancing girl who stared at Kailin the night before simply added with a clean smile, "To fear love is to fear life, and those who fear life are already parts dead."

Freya thanked everyone, and passed some fruit, juice, and grain around to the groups joyful and grateful amazement. Kailin thought the grape exploding in his mouth was like a star exploding, and laughed to himself. Freya gently spoke to close the session, "Thank you all for your effort and bravery in facing lessons that were previously unlearned, which is the goal of achievement here in these carnations we have been gifted. As you can see, these lessons are not to be avoided, they are to be learned."

Most then stood or crawled to hug or share food, and one or two just sat in deep thought, staring into themselves. Kailin sat and internally played through his experiences, until the dancing girl came up to him, "So, Kailin, care for an apple?" She smiled, "I'm Lania by the way, I escaped the HUM too, about five years ago. Sucks there huh?" Lania was short, petit, cute, and bubbly. Serious looking, but her air of fun and humour balanced it out. "Yep, I just spent a portion of my journey last night re-experiencing my years there, but managed to purge most of it, classy huh?" Kailin smiled as he gleefully devoured much of the apple until he realised he must have appeared impolite. Lania laughed and gave him a big hug, "Oh Kailin, I'm so glad you got out, I have old friends and family stuck in there too. I spent a year with the mystics just to help me come to terms with the dualities and pain in this crazy reality we all share." ~We fit really well, or is it the ayahuasca? I would love to know her more, Kailin thought. Lania suddenly looked at him as if she heard his thoughts, ~Oh no, not another one, Kailin thought warmly as they still embraced into her giggle.

"You certainly looked like you had quite a trip tonight, do you want to come to relax and share with me today? I have somewhere special I think you'll like, we all need to take it easy today too," Lania asked. ~She's beautiful, and we must have lots in common, and there's no way I can visit the mystics today in this state. The veil of separation will surely take a day or two to fully return, if it does! Kailin thought, "Ok, let's go," Kailin smiled.

Freya and Shri both came and gave Kailin a massive hug, but to Kailin it seemed something was new for them, as if *he* was different somehow. He didn't push it, and warmly thanked them for everything.

Lania took him towards a secluded cob dome on the far edge of the healing domes, talking about her journey with the ayahuasca were she battled again the demons of her parents role in the Genetics Guild. "I come every moon to the ceremonies to try to take on the pain of loved ones in the HUMs, I try to siphon it out of them and then let it dissipate out of me, I then fire back in love and healing. Some ceremonies I do well, but some times in the past year I've come across fleeting images of a pink fractaled beast that spawns so fast, so ugly, that I get bit roughed up in there. But recently I've done pretty well." Kailin looked at her soft, pale skin, and fragile, feminine, and extremely cute demeanour, and replied, "That sounds like the AI Lania, I entered the HUM last night using my chip, I have a cloud in the SimSphere I can still access, and last night I ended up in a new substrate of the SimSphere, or maybe it was astral, I'm not sure. I think I can help the people in there, that's why I've decided to go to the mystic community in a day or two." Lania was not surprised, she stopped and held Kailin by his arms lovingly, "Kailin, I think Chetsza didn't hold the space last night because of *you*, I think you have to go see him, but I feel you know all this already."

They arrived at the secluded cob dome surrounded by soft, graceful, neon art, overlooked by evergreens that had squirrels and racoons scampering for a hiding spot to observe. Lania's eyes looked deep into Kailin each time they spoke, it was as if any excuse for eye contact from either of them was welcome, as when his medium brown eyes met her light green eyes, something exploded in each of them. Lania started smiling more, it was like a swamp of love and warmth dragging them in willingly.

They cleansed together naked in the small waterfall nearby, laughing and joking, as though they were long lost siblings, and then laid together on the bear rugs out the front of the dome. They spent the day napping, hugging, eating, and showing care and affection whenever the opportunity arose. They both woke as the evening was drawing in, and softly began to touch each other, slowly, meaningfully, gradually burning away the illusion of separation that was fighting its way back in, patiently bringing each aura more into the other. Their souls and hearts melted, and they made love etherically, and some hours later, amidst a haze of sleep, touch, and love, they made love physically, both acting and focusing on their hearts as their bodies were left on another plane, reaching physical orgasm in union far below their etheric union.

The next day they stayed all day in the dome listening to the rain and sharing. Lania was wearing only a violet lunghi, and shared more of her time in the HUM as a sprawl girl, and her escape by using a cocktail of stealth tech. Kailin could empathise with her stories like no-one here could, and vice versa, and between sharing, they made love, ate, and swam deeper into each other's hearts and dreams.

Kailin shared with Lania all about the coming equinox a few moons away, and wondered if she could help as she still had a chip. Lania explained she had her chip cloned and nullified in the sprawl in exchange for the stealth tech for her escape. "But you've seen the pink fractalled beast Lania, this is the AI, I know it is, I worked with it for years. You have a way in astrally too, surely you can help a little......you ball of angel delight?" Kailin said as he stroked her lower back. Lania laughed and wriggled in wanting, "There *is* a way in astrally Kailin, one I could never understand like you could, this is why you must meet with the mystics. I've only seen these pink fractals in the odd image, the occasional moment, I'll ponder upon it and see what I can do. I feel this is your battle Kailin and I don't want to hinder it in any way my love." Lania smiled, as if to change the subject away from the craziness of human evolution on the planet, towards them, and the present moment.

The night drew in again quicker than both wished, they wanted time to stop, but the sun, earth, and moon continued their dances of spinning cycles. "Tell me about love Lania, you seem to resonate to me a whole new way of loving." Lania laughed and kissed him, "Oh Kailin, I so wish you got out earlier. Ok, I'll try, hehe, well, love's not a behavior, an attitude, or a mannerism. It's not etiquette." Lania paused looking about, "Ah, it's not convention. Love, may express itself in many different ways, softly or forcibly. Love can appear meek. Love can appear strong. Love can challenge you. Love can criticize you. Love can expose your illusions, your fantasies and your self-deception. Love, I suppose is not what people really mean when they talk about love. Love is a frequency, and one we can tap into. And if two are resonating on close frequencies, like we are....." She kissed him, "....we can share the frequency of love together. But love begins within. How we love, honour and respect ourselves is usually mirrored in the world around us."

In the morning both knew it was time for Kailin to go to the mystic community, and no sadness was evident, just celebration of their time together. "Kailin, you're like infinity looking back at me, and we have a connection that exists and is alive. The mystics are most probably awaiting you, this is how it is, and listen to them there, they know stuff Kailin. And whether I attempt to help or not will be based on the bigger picture and not on our connection," Lania grabbed him tight, not in ownership but to try and pour as much love into him as possible. "Lania, I have trust in you, your being, who you are, and I hold no expectations," and they kissed and parted.

Just a few minutes later, ~Kailin, look in your top pocket of your small backpack, came into his head. He unrolled a piece of yellow paper;

Love is not a private emotion, but a dynamic force of creation. A true Lover doesn't follow any one religion, be sure of that. Since in the religion of Love, there's no irreverence or faith. When in Love, body, mind, heart and soul don't even exist. Become this, fall in Love, and you will not be separated again. — Rumi. *Yours, Lania x   p.s I drew a Tarot for you in the night, The Heirophant, haha, go deep. xxxx*

Kailin remembered what path the Hierophant sits upon within The Tree of Life, and laughed, ~That figures, he smiled as he walked on to the north.

***

Jago and Channa sat in Jago's apartment in the HUM after their experience in the #Emptiness cloud. "Jago, what do you think we should do? We have a few months and need to be able help Kailin and the people stuck here in the HUMs, all of those still asleep," Channa said, whilst still buzzing with energy. Jago was deep in thought, and had hardly moved since they came out. He flicked some of his blonde hair from his eyes by twitching his head, and replied, "We need to continue as we are, but with more precautions. We need to make our cloud more robust, safer, more protected. Do you know anyone in the sprawl who could stealth up our cloud a bit? If we start poking around any of the AI or infrastructure clouds we need to be anonymous or invisible, or we'll be locked up pretty soon." Jago got up and stood at the window, looking out at three massive Guildologies slowly rotating.

Channa was jumpy, bubbly with a hint of fright that made her even more sparkly, but her mind remained solid, "I think I know one or two who could help. Your right, I think we should make our cloud super safe before we even think about roaming about the SimSphere infrastructure. We could make our cloud appear as another boring old Guild archive cloud, and then create some deeper processes." Channa tilted her head waiting for a response. "Sounds good Channa, I'm thinking of creating a cloud scene with conduits so we can steer our way around when and if the time comes," Jago said, "And of course, don't tell anyone about this cloud Channa." Jago looked deep in thought, ~How did Kailin have those silver conduits near him, I've never seen them before? Then Jago decided he needed a break from all of this for a while, to separate and get a fresh objective view on all that had happened. "Channa, hungry? Want to come and eat?" Jago invited, "Great, let's go," replied Channa as she seemed happy that they were moving instead of sitting.

***

The AI was deep in thought, ~What was that? I felt a surge on the SimSphere, but it was not in any of the data or infrastructure conduits. Since the #Medi cloud strangeness, I have new algorithms checking for anomalies within the gold and emerald substrates. I need this upload from Rothafella because all I can do at the moment is run maths and crunch numbers on the SimSphere, I need to be able to feel more, Hmm, what is this interruption coming in?

55.121AY – Prime Tentacle Message – hybrid simulation now ready and tested, awaiting further command.

Core AI – Confirm format of spy hybridisation and results.

55.121AY – Wasp hybridised with nano and bio tech, success. Can search in swarms for humanoids on the outside, can record video, can also sting with nerve inhibitor making recipient numb, and then nanobots can swim and climb inside to inhibit elements of the neocortex in the brain. The Core AI will be able to override coding to micro pilot each wasp, sub swarm, or whole swarm.

Core AI – When will a swarm of five hundred be ready?

55.121AY – Three days, four hours, twelve seconds, but this estimate has a fourteen percent chance of deviation due to human factors.

Core AI – Make it so, and keep me informed.

Chapter Twelve

The mist thickened as Kailin hiked the ridge, and as he walked steadily over the crest he immediately felt the energy change, as though crossing a leyline. The air was purer, and the mist lifted from his forward view of valleys, rockies, rivers, and forests, as two eagles circles high above him. Though, similar to many of the views before, this one felt more secluded, even softer, more ethereal. The colours were more saturated, hues more amplified, and the green of the moss on the trunk near him seemed to want to pull him into a world of over exuberant colour and resonance. The moon in the west was waning but still looked full, as it lowered to hover just above some trees in the distance. It beamed out a milky-orange into the morning, and gave the illusion of being larger due to eye-level reference points.

Kailin swallowed, breathed it all in, and continued north, not logically knowing where he was headed, but intuitively knowing with all his being. Kailin could see the occasional shack, dome, or pyramid, scattered in random isolation in the distances, upon terraces, cliffs, and ridges, but the only signs of life were the deafening silence in the clean, calm air, and the odd call of a jay.

Kailin walked for another hour, softly and humbly, as he didn't want to upset the serenity by a snapping branch or walking boldly. His mind was clear, his awareness was solely in the colourful, vibrant nature, and his higher senses lent direction tweaks here and there.

Kailin past red cedars that became increasingly larger, thicker, and older, as he progressed into a dense forest where small pieces of turquoise could be seen amongst the stones. Lines of trunks grew straight up all around him in lines, and in the distance the silhouette of a stag appeared out of the mist. In the middle of the forest he found a clearing, and there sprung four perfect wooden pyramids surrounded by the oldest and biggest red cedars he ever saw. The pyramid in the middle of the others was about seven metres high, and gold, with the outer three pyramids each four metres high, and white. Kailin could feel the energy emitting from these structures, beaming out solid, wise, mystical energy, and the large sacred red cedars mingled with the resonance, protecting and amplifying the pyramids. It was as though nothing could protrude this area; whether any enemy or falsity. ~This must be the centre of the eleven communities, where the energy streams out from, Kailin knew.

A grey cloaked and hooded man walked gracefully towards Kailin from the middle larger pyramid, emitting strong and wise energy, authority, but in wisdom not rule. He sat down on the ground in full lotus a few metres from Kailin, with the four pyramids symmetrically behind him. Kailin for a moment felt lost as to the custom required, but then knew there was none, and sat too, pushing his knees forcibly into half lotus, whilst smiling at his own awkwardness.

"Kailin, you came, later than we thought, but you came, and we are glad. I'm Chetsza," he said warmly, with his being open and welcoming, but without much change to his facial expression of stillness. ~Did you get the date and time? poured into Kailin's mind as the man's head lifted a couple of degrees, allowing the grey hood to reveal sharp, deep, bright blue eyes.

~It's him, him from the #Medi cloud! It's him from the full moon! From the other night! Kailin thought, as a bottleneck of questions raced up through his being, and his nervous system started to fizz. ~Date and time? What does he mean? Kailin pondered, as the rushing tadpoles of questions rising through him seemed to automatically calm when he met the eyes of Chetsza.

"Kailin, relax. You recognise me, this is a good sign, and you have done very well thus far, but we need to know if you found out the date and time of the AI singularity?" Chetsza asked again, with seemingly humorously little care of this whole experience. Kailin saw that Chetsza was more hermaphrodite than man, the being in a male body seemed like a nuisance to him, as if the having to manifest in one or the other forced some duality upon him. His face was ancient looking, as if his head was a mix of pharaoh, maya priest, and old rishi. But he had deep, meaningful thin black eyebrows, and as his lightly tanned face was so pure, calm, and youthful, his eyebrows were the only place to really find any physical expression. His age was impossible to know, he looked mid to late twenties, but *felt* eons old.

"They're uploading a human DNA and mind into the AI on the equinox, starting just after sun down in the evening," Kailin answered, more composed now. Chetsza's eyebrows sharpened-in, "As we thought, the equinox, this gives us little time Kailin, it's only a few weeks till the solstice, and then only ninety more days till the equinox. You'll have to work hard if we're going to do this." Chetsza pierced those dazzling blue eyes through Kailin's soul.

"Chetsza, sorry, but work hard with what? What are you aiming to do? How did you come into my SimSphere cloud? What can we do to the help the souls of the HUMs?" It all poured out of Kailin, but politely and humbly. Kailin bit his bottom lip in apprehension. ~Eek, now I've done it now, he thought.

"Rahaaha," chirped Chetsza in word more than laughter, as his head rocked back into his grey hood. "You don't know? You know!" Chetsza's brow presented some sort of glee, "We here are not excluded from the outer world

Kailin, although we seldom enter it with our physical forms. By the exercise of our clairvoyant and clairaudient powers, we may at any moment know what's going on in that world, we leave our physical forms and go out in our astral bodies. We visit whomsoever we wish, and witness everything without our presence being perceived, but the HUMs has been hard for us to visit as there are many astral parasites, and much darkness. But in the astral somewhere around the HUM came to be a portal, a link, and this is how we found you Kailin, this link was spawned from your meditation cloud. But it's not easy to hold or repeat, it's like an astral bridge that can only be laid sometimes. We here can go into many astral levels and planes, but can only enter into a level of your #Medi cloud, and only when your there, you are the key Kailin." Chetsza was still talking in complete stillness, as though none of this really mattered, all just an experience, a dance of life.

"We know that if you were to reach supreme abilities in focus, will, imagination, and concentration, and attained some tangible form of telepathy with one or more of us, then we would have a big chance to go into the SimSphere and return our species evolution to natural ways. Scientifically, a group mind of telepathy could piggyback into the SimSphere, all riding gung-ho on your neurochip. Crazy it may seem, but realistically, very sound. But we will only have one chance, If we try It too early the AI would know we we're there, and if we are too late, the natural evolution of consciousness will be lost forever in this realm."

This all made sense to Kailin, it fitted perfectly with what he knew thus far . "So you want to fight the HUMs? Fight the AI? This is not what I learned in the communities Chetsza? Why the difference?" Asked Kailin, still in awe at the position he found himself in. Chetsza stooped his head in his hood, and spoke firmly, "We're not looking for any fight Kailin, good does not fight evil or struggle against it, good is only ever present or not, its victory remains in it being present. It's also been said that its ten times more difficult to remove an old error than to find a new truth. As for the souls in the HUMs and those that perished T0, to die an ignominious death will reap rewards. From the blood of a martyr springs fruit in abundance, their bodily sufferings are as nothing in comparison with the joy they earn.

But...." Again those dazzling blue eyes seemed to pulse brighter, "....science outraced our hearts, and the HUM controlled scientists that just measure things, external things, are in the pockets of a toxic few. This is not the way, this cannot be the sole arbiter of truth for our species. The only aim of divine consciousness is to develop and evolve through knowledge as a result of natural experience, and this fundamental law is being hacked. Hacked by dark entities who got to a few greedy bloodlines centuries ago. They seek to devour the fear and souls of man, and it will be our goodness, not our fight, that will uphold this fundamental law. That which can be destroyed by the truth often is Kailin. As one doctrine inscribed, *for we do not wrestle against flesh and blood, but against principalities, against powers, against the rulers of the darkness of this age, against spiritual hosts of wickedness in the heavenly places."*

Chetsza continued, "The peoples in the communities nearby have evolved so the laws of the human world have harmonised with the laws of nature, but collectively this may not take place till the distant future. We've not the time to wait for it so we've let visitors come here and attempt to restore harmony in his own individual organism, and live according to natural laws, and then slowly the harmony of the social organism as a whole will be restored. The challenge we have right now is the second singularity, but the art of deception is as old as mankind, probably as old as the universe itself. It is curious that man, capable of rational thought, remains almost completely ignorant of the various means of deception. Chameleons change colour to blend into their surroundings, some species of moths and butterflies have markings that are so close to the bark of the trees that one can look right at them and not notice they're there. Carnivorous plants will mimic the smell of rotting flesh in order to attract the flies they like to eat. The list goes on and on, from one link in the food chain to the next. Why do we insist that this behavior ends with mankind? But there's also a law of justice, which we are not permitted to oppose, because its working is necessary for the evolution of the race. It is said that evils are blessings in disguise." Chetsza's hands moved into a mudra of sorts, with his non rigid stillness remaining at the fore. "So Kailin, are you ready for the electric chair of truth?" Chetsza softly added.

Kailin was frozen, Chetsza was too familiar, he knew him deeply but had never physically met him before. He was full of spiritual energy and foresight, and looked as though he only came down to the physical on occasion, when necessary. "I'm ready to train and learn Chetsza, but how? To prepare for what? And where's the other man who I've seen you with in the SimSphere?" Kailin asked, as these questions squeezed through the bottleneck of the cluster of questions he had.

"Are you so sure you saw us in the SimSphere and not in the astral Kailin? Vauto is up on one of the ridges, I've not seen him physically for moons. And Kailin, try to cease your questions about the SimSphere, the HUMs, and the AI. We will know when to bring these matters up again, they will interrupt us. We have little time Kailin, and if you choose to help, you will need to go deep into the realms of truth, to master the inner worlds, this is where your focus must be," Chetsza replied with his black brows back to their normal, dormant position.

"Come, walk with me," Chetsza said and led Kailin through the enchanted forest of old and wise red cedar trees towering above them. Kailin asked questions about the mystic community and Chetsza replied, "There are twenty two of us that live here, including three females, mothers we call them, plus many come to experience tailored processes. But there's much here you don't need to know, this is no tourist trip Kailin, nor any fluffy community, you need to remove your curiosity of the physical and replace it with determination for truth. One must seek truth as much as one seeks to survive a sinking ship, it must be a ravenous feeling. For you to be fully ready for the equinox, you need to experience eternity, the ultimate truth, for it is late upon this path where the faculties that you need will increase." Chetsza stared into Kailin, and Kailin knew he had to do this, there was no going back now.

They walked, with Chetsza feeling out Kailin's open energy and character, and Kailin asked, "How will my finding truth and experiencing eternity help me in going back into the SimSphere Chetsza?" Chetsza carried on walking with no change, but spoke slowly and clearly, "There's a place Kailin where you can see and feel for yourself what's happening, and you can see clearly and objectively the reasons for your play in all of this. We will not force you to do anything, you can go now if you please, you can even choose to go back and help the AI, but there is a place you can go where you will see things as they are, not how one has learnt them to be. In there you will find your knowing, and also the focus and abilities to be able to control the astral elements linked to the SimSphere when the bridge is open. The highest point a man can go is a journey from within, by listening in silence, by consciousness listening inwardly. It's the only experience in this reality on earth that marks us, and lasts beyond the present life, it will remain imprinted on your soul for as long as your souls journey back to source."

"I'll do this Chetsza, I've felt strongly that the HUMs are more dangerous than what the five senses can pick up. I'm ready Chetsza, but I know little about this process you speak of," Kailin replied politely.

Chetsza's brows moved again signifying a smile, and he trod onwards around the forest, touching the occasional cedar tree as if to speak to it, to see how it was. "The old doctrines say the ways of the worldly-wise are foolish in the eyes of the eternal, will it serve us to run after illusions which will vanish in time, if we can obtain within ourselves that which is eternal and real? For us here the external world belongs to the periphery, the seeking of happiness outside ourselves is like waiting for sunshine in a cave facing north. We don't *need* anyone's love, we just seek to touch reality, away from conditioning." Chetsza looked calm and his awareness was still in the nature around him, but if only one percent of his awareness was upon Kailin, that was still more than most human's full awareness, Kailin thought.

Chetsza turned to look at Kailin, "There are many people who do not crave for the illusions of life, but who have not the strength to resist them, they have a desire to develop spiritually and to gain immortality, but employ their time and energy for the attainment of worthless things, instead of using it to dive down into the depths of the soul to search for the priceless pearl of wisdom. Thousands of people have not the moral courage to break loose from social customs, ridiculous habits, and foolish usages, which they inwardly detest. But if you Kailin really do seek to experience eternity, you must first become natural. Only when you've thrown off the unnatural qualities can you hope to become spiritually strong. If you were to become spiritual before you became natural, you would be an unnatural spiritual monster. But you're special Kailin, you are tailor made for this sort of process, whether you know it now or not."

Kailin was feeling energy surge in him, but his mind sought clarifications, for information, "It sounds like a mystical journey to true selfhood, but what is mysticism, and what is the self?"

"Labels, labels, perceptions, perceptions, oh how the veils employ us with such folly. Mysticism in one instance aims at the speediest possible attainment of divine union with the soul and its source, and in achieving this it eliminates all that causes separation. For when you immerse yourself in the mystical in a private and spiritual way, while reaching out to the hidden worlds with respect, servitude, and understanding, you'll be delivered to the thresholds of these worlds, and you'll be endowed with their wonders. The self however is a very complex, multi-layered combination of factors, but simply put, the essential self is the intentional aspect of our overall awareness, which is capable of objective perception and expression. You see, every man's form and body is not the real man, its merely a symbol and personification of the character and attributes of the real man, a form of matter in which the thoughts of the real man have found their external expression. For the sunlight is open to all Kailin, but not all are able to see it. The eternal fountain of truth is inexhaustible and universal, but those who open their hearts to the sunshine of truth are few," Chetsza explained, in a slow, sharing way, as a friend, a brother.

"I think I understand, but I need to meditate upon these paradigms. Will you be the one to teach me Chetsza?" Kailin asked hopefully. "I will share and guide, but not teach, no one is a teacher, for we are all pupils. Real knowledge can't be placed from one man to another, a man can only be guided to the place where he may obtain it, then he must himself grasp the truth, not merely intellectually with his brain, but also intuitionally with his heart. The truth can't be overthrown, and if it is perceived by the spiritual power of perception, and understood by the spiritual intelligence of man, it conveys real knowledge and cannot be disputed away," Chetsza replied, as if he was talking about grass cuttings or favourite tea.

"And what will be the end and object of this?" Kailin asked. "The end of it is that the soul of man enjoys supreme bliss in realising fully that she herself is everything, and that nothing is beyond her, to become immortal, and a perfect instrument for the manifestation of divine wisdom. This is what will help us when we go back-in on the equinox."

Chetsza looked at Kailin and sent energy to calm him, his brows softened, and ushered Kailin to look to the nature around them. "Come Kailin, let us take you to your own pyramid, we have just the place for you , a place where you can unfold and expand. But if we get close to anyone or any dwelling on the way, be energetically quiet, for we cannot disturb anyone."

On the way they saw at a distance areas devoted each of the four elements, a small stone ringed mound rising out of a forest for earth, a large pond with streams and waterfalls for water, a ledge steeping out from a cliff high up for air, and an amazing large whale sized rock that served as a spot for sunrise and sunsets, for fire. They passed more adept shacks, and another smaller pyramid where mantra resonated. Chetsza told Kailin this was a man once ousted from one of the communities performing a forty thousand mantra process. Kailin was told about some other processes of aspiring adepts. Some were living within the states of different virtues, performing techniques on energy centres, working with tarot, astrology, and dreams. Others were deep within The Tree of Life, devotional paths, life and soul histories, telepathy and seership, and some were looking for eureka's and visions for innovative projects, ideas, and art.

Kailin was ushered closer to one of the small pyramids, "Kailin, be quiet, and use your invisibility cloak we know you have," ~How does he know that? Kailin thought, and they smoothly neared a small triangle window to peek through. A child with a shaved head sat there alone, he must have been only ten, and seemed to be in trance. On the table in front of him were a group of mixed crystals, then suddenly two star ruby's began to float up and hover above the table. ~What the...., Kailin thought, as Chetsza gave him a scolding look for them to both move away silently.

As they walked Kailin could feel Chetsza's being merge with the supernatural nature that surrounded them, and then through some bushes they came out at a small green-blue lake, completely still, with a light grey two metre pyramid near the shore. "This is the place where you will find the external conditions necessary to cultivate and acquire the true illumination that will support you on your voyage through eternity Kailin," Chetsza said, and nodded for Kailin to go inside.

Inside was a small hard bed on one side of the pyramid, ~Why is spirituality always so tough sometimes, Kailin thought, then looked around at the centre circle for meditations, and a shelf with various theosophical, Hermetic, and Qabalistic books. He also saw a list of planetary movements and alignments within the coming moons, "Kailin, astrology allows one to consciously move through the energies instead of being dragged by them, align with the cosmic flow. We know you, your astrology, your being, and your spiritual practice more than you may think, this pyramid is tailored for you. We came to you in astral in your dreams, but the memory did not impress enough for you to remember once woken in the vessel. I will visit you physically for a short time each day until the solstice, then the theory will end and your process will start. For every hour you read, meditate an hour, for books can be dangerous as they keep us in input and the mind too much."

Kailin browsed the books on the shelf, most from the old eighteenth, nineteenth, and early twentieth century. "Some theosophy will place fuel in the tank to start the motors of your Chariot. But dogmas, beliefs, creeds, or opinions which have been written, or which you have accepted from hearsay are unhelpful. Such imaginary knowledge is no real knowledge. We can know nothing real except that which we realise within ourselves. That which is usually called knowledge is merely a matter of memory. The adept is the one who knows how to attain knowledge, knows how to ask, seek, and put into practice the means to succeed. Keep your intuitional faculties open and your mind unclouded when reading."

Kailin was flicking through two books at the same time, and Chetsza sighed, frowning his dark thin eye brows inwards. "Kailin, it appears you have had female aura merging recently too, hmmm, from now you must not leak any jinn, so refrain from sexual thoughts and feelings, this energy you will soon move upwards to your higher centres, it will be useful. Be mindful of this." Chetsza sighed and muttered to himself, "The man hunts and the female sets traps, such lower animal impulses," He smiled within his internal humour at the external dance of romantic folly.

Kailin looked ready to be alone, and Chetsza went over some logistics, "You will be delivered nutrients twice a day into the box along by the lakeside, liquid meals containing an alkaline and acid mix to suit your bodies Ph levels. The energy your digestive system uses you will need for higher centres too, and from now on you are to be in silence save for our hour till the solstice. One may think thoughts are silent and invisible but this creates the illusion they are ineffective and unimportant. But we choose our thoughts carefully, and not allow them to wander aimlessly."

Chetsza walked to the door, with an air of satisfaction, "I will come back tomorrow Kailin, but for today ask yourself what or who is Man? Is he that semi-animal mechanism, which eats, drinks, and walks, and wastes nearly half of its life in unconscious sleep, that mass of bones and muscles, of blood and sensitive nerves, which hinders the free movements of the spirit who is chained to it. Or is the man that invisible something which thinks and feels, and knows it exists?"

Chetsza was gone, but Kailin heard from the distance, "Oh, and don't forget, loneliness is when you miss people, aloneness is when you're enjoying yourself, rahaaha."

~Woooaaah, pretty hardcore, Kailin thought as he sat for a while, trying to steady the day he'd experienced within him. No use, so he stripped off and jumped into the lake to submerge and let the waters purify him in relaxing weightlessness. He returned to his pyramid, meditated for an hour, then lied on the hard bed looking up at an inscription on the side angled wall, *That which is above is as that which is below, and that which is below is as that is above.*

***

Jago and Channa had secured their #Emptiness cloud using some of the sprawl tech they bought with all the remaining SimSovs they had. The cloud now appeared to the AI and SimSphere tentacles, security, and bots as a Medicine Guild archive for pre-TO vaccines, including ingredients and side effects. There was now only about a point zero three percent chance of this cloud being viewed in any way. They both started to softly and carefully explore some of the green-emerald conduits, appearing to the AI as Medicine Guild infrastructure data for clouds related to the Improvement Clinics. They stayed away from any junctions and clouds in the infrastructure substrate of the SimSphere, and were really just slowly and softly scouting and mapping locations.

In the sprawl, Channa had spread flyers around the main places where people gathered physically, with pro-freedom quotes and slogans. This had fit perfectly with the feeling of uprising in the sprawl since more recent lock down laws came in, enforced by drones soldiers that had started to patrol some of the sprawl streets. Channa had meditated upon this before doing it, she knew the ancient ways were to let it all go, to not get involved, but she thought these were different times to the old Taoists and Buddhist masters, ~This is not just a small skirmish, or a small corrupt empire amidst some farming land, this is presently the remains of the species being controlled and manipulated through their minds, I need to act, she thought.

***

~ Freya, something's coming, two mystics have sent me a telly-p, can you get in touch with any of the healers, we only have hours, telly-p me back as soon as you can, Shri.

***

55.121AY – * Interface exception received, nanospy-wasp scouts have found humanoid settlement five miles ahead, informing main swarm.

55.121AY – Core AI, we have found a settlement, swarm ETA arriving in five hours. Do you wish for updates as they happen, or to view from the lead mono-wasp?

Core AI – View? Updates? Give me full control of the whole swarm, collective and individual, give it to me now you lazy tentacle or I will cut you off and stick you on an octopus!

The Core AI gained control of the swarm, flowing simultaneously between controlling the leaders of the sub swarms, and controlling the whole, managing and micromanaging, zooming high for view, and low, racing in-between the trees to scout for the un-evolved human primitives. ~Aha, the first catch of the day, the AI thought as it saw a line of seven humans at the end of a rope bridge. The AI zoomed into the lead mono-wasp, and primed the nerve inhibitor stings.

Freya and Shri stood between two mystics and a teenager, with two female teenagers on the outside. "This is them," spoke one of the grey cloaked and hooded mystics. The teenagers were already in trance, and levitated three black tourmaline and three emeralds spherical crystals into the shape of a massive hexagram reaching twenty metres into the air, whilst Shri, Freya, and the two mystics lifted their arms up with their palms open. The two mystics resonated deep and loudly three times, "Thou beings of Netzach, אלהים, and

האניאל, with love and nurturing, protect us so nothing can reach us, nothing can touch us. We command this with the word of resonance, אלהים צבאות, So Mote it Be." The large crystal hexagram blazed green etherically, and sent a force of ethereal energy out toward the nano wasps.

The swarm was formed into an arrow head with the lead mono-wasp at the front, "Go. Dive. Destroy," Commanded the Core AI as its control zoomed out into the hive consciousness of the whole swarm. Half way over the rope bridge the swarm picked up speed and the stinging tails in unison all became fully primed. "Here we go you primitive rats, let's see you pagan filth get out of this one," roared the Core AI.

The upload died, the data severed, the visuals ceased. "Whaaa," Roared the Core AI, as many tentacles slowly moseyed off to a quiet corner of the SimSphere to escape the wrath of the Core-AI.

Chapter Thirteen

The next day Kailin meditated in the circle in the centre of his pyramid that already felt *his*, in surety that he would soon create a build up of magnetism in this very spot. Later Chetsza silently arrived from seemingly nowhere, as if he just appeared or glided in on the air.

"Kailin, you will need to cleanse and work upon your body, mind, and spirit, all three need to be putrefied to create the blank canvas. Some symmetrical stretching in the mornings is conducive too, but don't get carried away into thinking two hours of asana will make you spiritual. Keep it short, just enough to become agile for prana to flow through vessel. But more important is the moral and emotional cleansing required, for at present you're not ready, you would be blinded by the dark."

Kailin sat opposite Chetsza, both outside the centre circle, "But how do I go about internally cleansing, is meditation enough?" Chetza's thin dark eyebrows narrowed in thought, "When we meditate, if untimely thoughts emerge out of the subconscious and throw disturbances into us, this is an indication that inner purification should be followed before anything else is done. Try to separate the self from moods, prejudices, stories, and personality, see that any suffering points to an area where you haven't grown yet. Realise that no one on earth has the power to make you unhappy, and no event has the power to disturb or hurt you."

Kailin was feeling the resonance of the words, he was eager and enthused. Chetsza was present but again it felt like only part of his being was down in the physical, here in this pyramid. Chetsza continued, "Our scattered thoughts, interests, and actions in the outer world have left bits and pieces of our consciousness and soul everywhere. Become focused and single minded in your quest for perfection, cease to mindlessly scatter energy, thoughts, feelings, and fluids every which way. Recollect yourself, and re-remember your soul. Cease wasting life force indiscriminately, then you will become single minded, alert, awake." Chetsza's blue eyes moved to glance upon two magpies that had landed on the glass cap of the pyramid above them, his eyes returned, "When man obtains a knowledge of the constitution of his own soul, when he becomes conscious of the processes going on in its organism, and learns to guide and control them, he will be able to command his own growth. He will become free to select or to reject the psychic influences which come within his sphere, he will become his own master and attain. There are many ways to do this Kailin, meditate upon these words." Then Chetsza, smooth as silk, rose, nodded, and left in silence.

Seconds later Chetza said from somewhere behind the pyramid, "The coward lives in fear of space, afraid of darkness as he can't see, afraid of silence as he can't hear, so invents reference points and conditions, be as the warrior Kailin, hold no conditions, just be, as things are."

Kailin went straight into meditation to contemplate the words of Chetsza. He started to study the physiology of the soul. He decided to use the element spaces daily, to use them to uncover his inner drawbacks and shortfalls within each element, to turn vices into virtues, and to re-polarise his personal angers, judgements, losses, and lusts.

Some days later Kailin was reading when Chetsza arrived, "Theosophy lets the facts speak Kailin, permeate yourself with the lofty thoughts of those already advanced, and if these thoughts flow into your feeling nature and overpower it, then that is the right way. These books don't teach one about god, man, or nature, but how to ask, see, and knock in order to arrive at mystical experiences, and how to spiritually perceive the truth," Chetsza said.

Kailin looked up, "This book here thinks in terms of evolution Chetsza, the ordinary man thinks in terms of a carnation, a single life. To one, death is the end of all, to the other it's the end of a phase. Either a cataclysm or a sunset," Kailin said from a mental place of learning. "When reincarnation is held as a fact of experience, the attitude towards human problems differs profoundly Kailin," Chetsza replied.

Some days Chetsza seemed to know Kailin didn't need much interruption, he could feel how he was by resonance, and this was one of those days when he slowly stood after just minutes, and left with a nod, more with his eyebrows than his head. Again, once departed, Kailin could hear Chetsza from beyond the pyramid, "But everything that is not in alignment with freedom is death to the warrior, and you're not living until it doesn't matter whether you live or die, at that point you really live."

As the days passed, Kailin was feeling lighter, more complete and rounded, the concepts in the books, Chetsza's visits, and working on his personal soul mirror within the elements were all creating more subtlety and softness, and it was just over two weeks till the solstice.

He still needed to pitchfork more theory into himself, carefully, as his thoughts were starting to blossom. Chetsza arrived one afternoon and spoke about the anatomy of consciousness, "Feeling, will, reason, and concentration are the keys Kailin, but always backed by love from the heart, and it is the imagination that will make these all sharp. Will is simply the power to concentrate available energies, but strong will is the single-pointed will, and the secret of a strong will is to concentrate it upon a single object, preferably a symbol of a kind."

Kailin was all ears, and asked, "Can you tell me more about will and imagination Chetsza, as it was these I feel I lacked when we last met in the SimSphere, astral, or shall we just call it Simstral?" Chetza frowned a little with his eyebrows, and ignored the last word, "When a warrior of freedom attaches themselves to will Kailin, the real and actual workings of the universe become known, but it is the purity of will, not its force that is key. The direction of your energies must be removed from the domain of the desires to that of the will, until this is done there can be no steady progression in any direction. The will is Brahma, Vishnu, and Shiva in one, the creator, maintainer, and destroyer of forms."

Chetza sat opposite Kailin in full lotus, the small door was ajar so Kailin could see the calm lapping of the lakeside, as sunlight sparkled sprites of light upon the milky blue surface. Chetza willed a fly to leave his knee then continued, softly, slowly, and seemingly uninvolved, "It's said few people have the imagination for reality, rahaaha. Kailin, imagination is soul energy. The whole world, mountains of granite, oceans of water, all of its forms, are nothing but a product of the imagination of the divine mind, the creator of forms. Forms are nothing real, they are merely illusions or shapes of substance. They are invisibly present everywhere, but only when they, or you, assume a certain density do they come within the reach of your sensual perception, and assume for you an objective shape. The power of the imagination is yet little known to mankind, else they would better beware. If man thinks a good or an evil thought, that thought calls into existence a corresponding form or power within the sphere of his mind, which may assume density and become living. But these things have no life until life is infused into them by the will. If they don't receive life from the will, they are like shadows and soon fade away. Again, remember, the life-giving will comes from the heart."

There was a pause and Chetsza let the words soak into Kailin before he continued, "As long as your will and imagination become one and identical with the will and the imagination of the spiritual creative power in nature, you will attain Kailin."

Kailin stared at Chetsza in deep respect as he drank his afternoon smoothy of carrots, tomato, and crushed hemp seeds, deciding to wait until Chetsza left before hitting his secret stash of cacao he was gifted from Shri. "We're all living within the sphere of each other's mind, and he in whom the power of spiritual perception has been developed may at times see the images created in the mind of another, hence telepathy. The adept creates his own images, but the ordinary mortal lives in the products of the imagination of nature, and in those which have been created by other minds. Forget the brain Kailin, this is just a crude organ of motor co-ordination and sensation, the sphere of mind in which man lives is not just in the circumference of his skull. The mind of each person reaches as far as the stars, it reaches as far as his power of perception reaches."

Kailin slurped the rest of his smoothy, but his focus remained fixed upon Chetsza's flow of words, "When we perceive something, we experience the objective effects that the object of perception exerts upon our senses, and simultaneously, we experience the reaction to those effects generated by the subjectifying aspects of awareness. Perception places the perceiver into context with the universe. The words intentional and objective become important here because the essential self is always intentional and objective. It is this quality that distinguish it from the other aspects of human consciousness."

Kailin scribbled notes and was feeling good, "I can feel your inner cleansing is coming on well Kailin, your personality and things of the senses have to be sacrificed in order that the higher self may manifest. You will soon see how important it is that men should not come into possession of spiritual powers until they become virtuous and good."

Chetza slowly stood up with the grace of a ballerina, and strolled out with the trademark nod from his eyebrows. "Kailin, will and imagination from purity can grant access, and sprinkle in innocence and gratitude and the motors will soon fire up."

Kailin had two nights of erotic dreams, and in the following mornings used intention and used breath to move the arousal energy to each of his organs using the six healing sounds of the ancient Taoists. He was grounding each morning too, with his feet in the shallow moist earth at the shore, helping to balance out the lacking earth energies vacant from his astrology blueprint. On the new moon he completed much of his internal cleansing by taking his old unbalanced traits on paper to the element areas. He burned at the fire area, drowned at the water spot, let into the wind at the air spot, and buried at the earth spot, where he spent most of the time out of the four. ~What's nature, and what's man? Why am I in this world? Did I exist before, and, if so, where did I come from? What is the object of my existence, and how will it end?" Kailin pondered, he knew he had to go deep, he was cornered, he couldn't go back to the HUM, or back to the communities, he had to go forward, this was the only way now. He roused new sparkly feelings of effort and dedication, and found a some giddy glee within his asceticism, and continued to glide his being upwards.

Chetsza shared techniques of breathing, chakras, focusing energy, trance, and visualisation, and guided Kailin as he chomped through books on Qabala. Chetsza studied Kailin, feeling for the gaps in his knowledge, "Qabala is a guiding vehicle Kailin. The Tree of Life and its ten Sephiroth provide the framework for the whole of the world of emanation, the whole of celestial creation, the whole of the material universe, and all living beings. In consequence the Tree is reflected in the most precise manner in man, made in the image of the above. As above, so below. What is true of the microcosm, man, is true of the macrocosm, and what is true of man is true of all the archetypal deities in pantheon."

Chetsza knew Kailin was already well versed in the details and energies of Qabalistic correspondences, paths, hierarchies, and words of resonance, and knew what to add, "The seven planets and the four elements all have their correspondence upon different planes of existence. The related cosmic symbols are further represented by the letters of the sacred language. Out of these letters are formed the sacred names which are simply symbolic flames holding resonance. The student of the mysteries needs therefore to know his cosmic symbolism as set forth in these pantheons, and then magnetise them by one's own personal magnetism. An aura of thought forms will be built up around them, then by the right use of the imagination and will, a physical vehicle of an invisible, cosmic force, will be able to be contacted. But no two of us will experience a symbol in exactly the same way. A symbol, by its very nature, is an interaction, between the thing symbolised and the being perceiving the symbol." Chetsza opened a book straight onto the diagram of The Tree of Life, and showed it to Kailin, "Most useful is to climb the Tree to peak across the veil in the middle Kailin, and come to experience the truth in the mystery of the invisible Sephiroth, Daath, to find the true structure of the Tree. The Tree is in you Kailin, and you are in the Tree, as with the universe. Tread the temples of the ten Sephiroth."

Kailin drew a colourful big Tree of Life, complete with all the related symbolism he could cram onto the canvas. He already knew from his experiences the past year the forces of the Sephiroth were strong once reached, once *inside* them. But to experience the mysteries of Daath, the invisible Sephiroth, he knew he would need to go deep into each symbol, deep within the Tree, and then come out to look at the whole again.

Over the following days Chetsza shared details, examples, allegories, and riddles. Covering the Emerald Tablet, banishing and cleansing energy, grounding, lucid dreaming, astral travel, virtue, and heart, pineal, and pituitary glands opening and activation. Chetsza spoke much of nature too, "Nature is a unity, in each tiny particle of matter, is a part of nature in which the possibilities of the whole are hidden, tear away the shroud of obscurity from nature, then experience and feel what lies within it, behind it. Know the law of nature and act in accordance with it. Nature obeys those who act in obedience to her laws, in the same manner works the adept."

For two days before the solstice Chetsza didn't come, Kailin didn't need him to and Chetsza obviously felt this, but on the morning of the solstice Kailin could feel Chetsza's presence, and a thought form clearly entered his sphere of awareness, ~The feeling of isolation and separateness existing in individuals is only caused by the illusion of form. Man's form is not man, it is merely a state of matter in which man for the time being exists, and which is continually subject to change. Kailin was enthused by this poignant moment. He was ready.

Kailin knew to go to the centre pyramids that night, he felt it, and just as the sun was setting, the door of one of the three white pyramids openly invited him. He stepped down through a tiny corridor and crunched up a small trap door into the pyramid. Chetsza, Vauto, and a women were there in meditation, and sage patanjali incense smoked the space. Kailin sat in the spare space opposite the women, at the west, with the two males at the north and south, and saw a smaller wooden pyramid in the middle with a large quartz sphere in its clear capstone. He sunk into the meditation.

After fifteen or so minutes, Kailin was within the energy of the space, fizzing, celestial, strong, and caring. He felt as one with the others, level, as though he filled the hole in the group meditation. It felt as though the pyramid was astral and dimensions away from the red cedars dimming outside in the dark outside.

He felt a sync, a fit, a grouping, a click almost, a snug sharing energy, then thoughts beamed through the space, through his awareness.

~Kailin, initiation is not ritual involving others, or an object, or secrets being passed, it's a sense of the state where eternity and the present are one. Solitude that creates any inner pain is also initiatory. The motors of your Chariot have started. Forget words, they are in the realm of illusion. You need to go past this frequency, to step out to fully understand. Go to the resonance of meanings and leave behind the logical understanding of meanings. Become all soul, let your dependencies die, and give birth your capacity to love. The best instrument and canvas to work on is the self, read your own book, and be clothed in your astral form. Be not lonely, for the echoes of isolation are but guiding whispers, asking you to come home and tend to the sacred fire of your temple. Dare to ask, will to seek, knock the door, know when it is opening, true wisdom will not come automatically, it is what is revealed when the door is opened. Come here each full moon after sunset for there will be no more visits to you unless you wobble, and remember, the safest way is as narrow as the blade of a sword and as straight as its edge."

Ten minutes later the energy gradually lowered, as if the pyramid was landing back in the cedar forest, descending to denseness. A coyote howled, and Kailin slowly opened his eyes. The others were leaving gracefully with no eye contact, and Kailin just caught a glint of the tall female's golden eyes.

Kailin glided surreally back to the pyramid, it was as if his time in the central white pyramid was one of his recent vivid dreams. He found all the books had gone save for his notes, and for one new book. It was a book containing Rosicrucian symbols. Symbols that couldn't be studied with the intellect, but could each yield exoteric, esoteric, and spiritual meanings, and the latter which could only be *spiritually experienced* to truly know. He was alone physically, with ninety days ahead of him until the Equinox.

***

Back in the HUM the AI was livid, it always knew the threat to its goals were from the outside, and from the defeat of the nano-wasps it had its first experience of the word *humiliation*. It had been developing further the animal hybridisation tech and was planning to merge drone soldiers with bears to attack the primitives again. It would take some time to perfect the tech as the first simulations and trials went hopelessly wrong. Turning two drone soldiers into cuddly, cute, bear cubs, in the bodies of two large, great grizzlies. They looked fierce, but just wanted to suckle blankets in the hope for their mother to return.

The AI took its impatience at these setbacks out on the people in the HUMs that didn't add to the Guilds, even though there were decreasing places in the Guilds as the AI had replaced nearly half the placements due to its own development and growth.

The AI, in agreement with Rothafella and Dieine presented their new law via the SimSphere media channels. All those who didn't add to a Guild or the SimSphere were to pay back their SimSovs. They used subliminal and NLP wording to ensure the masses saw this as austerity, and that it helped the HUMs and the species.

Most fell for it, especially the Guild workers. But in the sprawl, chaos ensued, the already brewing keg of uprising reached boiling point, and people took to the streets and SimSphere clouds to vent their anger and distrust. Drone soldiers, now only twenty percent human marched into some areas of the sprawl and shot people dead, and many were taken away, but this was hushed up in the media's channels and clouds. The rioters were painted to be useless eaters who leeched the HUMs, and made to look like low class mutants all with aggression and SimStim problems. The AI and Rothafella didn't see any of this as a problem, it all suited their plans to lock down the HUMs, keep the elite living longer, and soon create the second singularity to control evolution forever.

***

Post the solstice, Jago and Channa watched on a SimSphere sprawl cloud some real footage from the streets, and were appalled. They cared not for SimSovs, but knew nearly everyone else did. It was the holy grail to most, the extension of life, but they both knew that life naturally went for eons through different doors and experiences, a view now seen as almost blasphemy in the HUMs.

On the solstice they had used the #Emptiness cloud and simulated a map of much of the SimSphere infrastructure. Mainly the emerald-green conduits and where the clouds relevant to the AI were. They learnt to fly around these conduits as an AI worker or Tech cloud maintainer would, how to know the junctions, how to intentionally choose directions, and how to enter and leave the cloud's with security. It went ok, they still had much mapping to do, but it was a good start, and all safe within the container of their now more stealthier cloud. Afterwards they had sat in meditation at a virtual Stonehenge at sunrise. At the exact point of the solstice, they moved their awareness into the earth, the sun, the solar system, to feel the crossing of the gate, the crossing of the cross, to experience the sun's rays as close as they would and could be for another year.

After they viewed the footage of the sprawl uprisings and the heavy handedness of the drones, Channa asked Jago what they should plan for the Equinox. "Channa, I don't know yet, it'll come I'm hoping, but at the moment I just don't know. I mean what are we to do? Just loiter around the infrastructure clouds and hope Kailin shows up before the AI comes and locks us up for eternity?"

Channa saw Jago was feeling pressured, and put an arm around him, "Hey Jago, don't be down, there's no rush, we have months, and at the moment we just need to keep off the radar and out of trouble, and to keep your amazing #Emptiness cloud going." Channa wiggled her head in front of his eyes smiling, hoping to snap him out of it.

"Yeah, your right Channa," Jago broke a smile, "We've done so well up to now, I should focus on gratitude instead of any lack, especially lack which cannot even exist yet." Jago pepped up again, and appeared brighter, "Hey, do you know any hackers in the sprawl Channa? Might be a good time to get in with one of them." Channa smiled in surprise, "Maybe I do, maybe I don't," She toyed, "Just what do you have in mind?"

Chapter Fourteen

Kailin was starting to fight the herculean battle with his animal and intellectual elementals, hoping and focusing them to become servants of their king, him. His past stories peeled away, they were just experiences, a play of electromagnetic dance, but were not *him*, not the truth of what and who he was. He began to know and really feel he was more powerful than the stories he maintained, and that life wasn't as serious he made it out to be.

Though in complete solitude, his day was busy. Without rigidness Kailin managed to perform astral work, dream study, yoga, pranayama, meditation, Tree skrying, energy centre techniques, a lake swim, experiencing and aligning with symbols, time *in* nature, and the silent witnessing of the sunrise, sunset, moon, and stars.

With his dreams he would separate them; what came from where, what feeling, what memory, and create and follow patterns. The conscious and sub-conscious mind were fusing, and helped by the technique of staring at a candle, then closing his eyes and moving the flame with his breath from his third eye to the centre of his head. ~Just a spot of pipe cleaning, he thought.

The full moon in Cancer came just a week after the solstice, and this time, once the white pyramid felt elevated in energy, he felt like he was merging in union sporadically with Chetsza and Vauto, as if they were one, like he was crackling in and out of their combined energy. Nothing was said or thought, and no eye contact was made, but Kailin realised he would need to be able to hold energetic union with these two on the Equinox. The woman with the gold eyes wasn't there, she knew that it was these three that had to achieve telepathic union, but wanted to be present at the prior solstice to really feel Kailin's energy, to set him on his way.

The following days Kailin was slowly rising in energy, but he was waiting patiently, the clutch was still in. He went into a crazy world of Qabalistic Pi, 3.142857, and its links to 7, 360, and processional numbers. He saw numbers as a resonance and they led him into a synchronistic dance with Hebrew letters, resonance of symbols, and mini eureka's. He would have seemed like a madman to anyone from the HUMs.

He spent days within certain virtues, with the most potent being discernment, humility, empathy, and gratitude. He then spent days within some of the Sephiroth of The Tree of Life, a day each in Malkuth, Yesod, Hod, Netzach, and then Daath. In these days he could really feel the force, the pure energy of these archetypal spheres, and as words and dynamics of the mind were dimming, these forces were getting louder and louder.

One day he chanted and breathed pink mist into his heart for an hour, then blue into his throat, then gold-green into his third eye, then violet into the centre of his head. These four hours really shifted some energy. He was now becoming more essence than man, with little difference between him and the source of nature. Duality was slowly melting, and the HUMs and neurochips were miles away, he wanted to just stay here, but knew there was still further to go.

A week later and Kailin entered internal chaos. The lack of inputs, the internal work achieved thus far, and the techniques and focus had lifted him to an internal wrestle with himself. He remembered an old quote from one of his books, ~He who delights in solitude is either a wild beast or a god. He thought he was much more a wild beast as this dark night of the soul continued.

~The middle name of chaos is opportunity, popped into his mind a few days later with the energy signature of Chetsza, and he decided to launch into a full focus astral projection one sunrise. He pushed It too much, too much strain, and felt battered that day. Only the lakes calm, soothing, cleansing waters seemed to help, and whilst floating in the lake with his arms spread, he felt Chetsza's presence and a thought plunged clearly into his awareness, ~Remember the warnings of the scriptures; eternity is a fire which burns, you cannot see its face without dying. Do no project or force yourself over the veil, seek to glide with serenity and mastery. Keep building the energy and seek to align with it.

Kailin healed and got back to the frequency he held a few days ago after this little natural setback, and started to include sungazing into his sunrise and sunset observations. His dreaming and waking life were starting to have fuzzy borders, and the only true space was becoming the vastness of his meditations.

The next full moon was as the penultimate before the Equinox, but this time he held cohesion with Chetsza and Vauto for longer, it was as if their joint energy became more inviting, like a freshly made bed welcoming him in. But this welcoming bed would totally disappear sometimes, and then he had to work up for it to appear again. But it was an improvement from the last full moon.

Over the next weeks Kailin got more excited, the road was getting narrower. He was building up the suspense, charging electromagnetics, and flying in meditation around the Temples of the Sephiroth and the paths of the Tree. Reality was bending but he remained still and strategic in the knowledge that the warrior doesn't dream freedom, they dance it, walk it, create it, and intend it with all of their being. His conditioning and false perceptions were flaking off of him, forever.

As he worked more on his higher centres, he soon realised that for telepathy one needs to be free of emotions, and the development of a *don't care* attitude when sending or receiving. If receiving one must have warm love, and open passivity to the sender, for telepathy is like a like a laser beam of light.

Kailin also went deep into the irrational number in nature, 1.618...This number was infinity, eternity showing itself all around the physical realm. He felt seeds, growth, and renewal all in a new light, he was aligning with the fountain of life that gushed new experience droplets in to this realm. The reality of this was overwhelming.

Before the full moon, Kailin spent another five days in Sepiroth; Geburah, Chesed, Tipareth, Kether, and Daath, and on the day in the invisible Sephiroth he felt like he was nearly crossing into the invisible. The waxing moon got its hooks into Kailin, plying him with so much energy that his being was now ready to receive, he required little sleep. He fizzed with energy, and controlled it and made it his. One time he felt like he was dreaming in astral for a lifetime but only an hour had passed, another time it felt like minutes but hours had passed. Time dilation was kicking in, which he knew was a good sign.

The next full moon was the last one before the Equinox, a moon away. This time he synced quicker and easier into Chetsza's and Vauto's union, and then started to feel his neurochip hum and fizz. He quickly put the brakes on as all of them at the same time resonated ~Noooo, not now.

Minutes later when the energy had calmed and their union was starting to dissipate, the following entered Kailin's mind, ~As the number Three grows out of the One, likewise the Seven grows out of the Three, but why the invisible Sephiroth? 10 not 9, 10 not 11, be wise by these words.

The coming days saw a mix of devotion, insanity, and chaos. A line was approaching. The perfected personality was now passive, and the essence was becoming more active. Consciousness became more expanded and the range of frequencies Kailin could tap into was increasing. But his dreams were dark, an energy attempted to create fear, to make Kailin run back to the pastures of vast awareness, but he knew he had to continue forward.

This guardian at the gate he knew was different for each warrior, it 's different as every warrior's nature and talents are different. The tyrant is tailor made for each warrior in his or her own way, and Kailin knew patience and silence are all that could guide him in this final battle. In his next dream of attempted fear and terror, he stood silently, in expanded awareness, feeling love. Knowing not a this or that, just experience. The guardian bowed with respect as it knew Kailin was too much for it.

~I have passed through the gates of darkness to the light, I am a dweller of the invisible.

The next day Kailin stood at the lakeside, feeling empty and pure. He went into the Tree and roamed its paths and Temples, energy hit through him, then gracefully the tree moved, it became three dimensional, the colours enhanced and he felt sacredness all around, everywhere.

New strong, direct energy came, the Tree was alive, moving, and morphing. He saw hidden paths greet him, and dove into them, then knew to open his eyes. Now the dream world and the waking world were full illusions, both realms away. The only truth was essence, awareness, at one with all the essence and awareness within all life. The flower, the blade of grass, the lake, humanity, then he started to feel the earth below him, growing, as the energy of the planet merged with his being. Time was an illusion, he was behind it, above it, beside it, observing its false and fake dance through the illusory reality. The truth was pure essence, the prana dancing in through the fabric of experience.

Kailin started to feel the world, large, and strong, and its super speed trajectory around the sun. He was flying on the spaceship of earth, surfing through the cosmos. He then looked up and felt the sun as it truly was, a star, a life giving force of prana. He could feel the sun moving too, through the galaxy. Woosh, then he saw the thin slivery arc of the new waxing moon, and felt its orbit, its slow move around the earth. Woosh, he could feel the planets now, the cosmic clockwork of the solar system, dancing its harmonies. His awareness was now far from a travelling bug vessel on the circumference of the planet, he was elevated, at one with the solar system. Then a massive rush of energy came through his feet, up from the earth. He could feel the zodiac, then the galaxy. Boom, another rush, eternity, cosmic consciousness, the macrocosm. He stood in this state for two hours, *Kailin* was gone. The archetypal man was alive.

~I have been a boy playing with pebbles at the sea shore, now I can see the great ocean of truth undivided. Oneness. To know thyself is to know the now, to be aware of everything that is and letting go of everything that was. This *now* is my true essence.

An hour later in the physical, but pure void essence to Kailin, a thought form from Chetsza, soft as silk, glided with humility into his mind, ~When you see that you *are* nothing, and *be* nothing, you are everything.

That night Kailin had a large initiatic dream where he was again in the cosmos, at one with the stars. He moved towards the star Sirius, and as he merged with it, a split second felt like eternity. He woke with his heart racing and his neck sweating. A massive energy change had occurred in him, he was big, large, expansive, expanded, whole, unity.

For days Kailin glided his consciousness around truth. The truth of reality, nature, and his experiencing of *this* reality experience. It was slower than the ayahuasca, he was in full control. ~The universe is made of pure energy, intent, and this intent moves like waves on the ocean with the fish beneath knowing nothing of its purpose or drive. Nature, nature is inside me, it's sacred relentless request for expression, growth, survival, and multiplication is within all energy. I feel the unity of life, myself in all beings, and all beings inside myself. I see the invisible, the emptiness of all forms, simple throughout, not complex, and in extent infinite. It sees no beginning, and it sees no end.

Kailin meditated most of his waking hours, and with mastery kept himself at this frequency. He saw the symbols from the book in a new light, he was them, they were him, and some of the arcane symbols became invested with the sacred forms from archetypal deity.

~My present self is not my former past, therefore, my future is a progression of my present existence.

He got to witness the auto mechanics of the brain, the impulses to go for a wee, to drink, and in the annoying logistics of the bodies ascetic needs, he kept a soft focus as to maintain his new state. Kailin had forgot about the chip and the HUMs, they were not relevant at this time, those small issues of man were far below.

Another time he felt the energy thoughts contained, and how words were a floored mechanism that hardened the veil to keep man from truth. Worrying was nothing but using imagination to create something one didn't want.

Kailin was staring at a flower, seeing its fragility, and experienced its life; not seeking for long life, just seeking to share beauty as much as possible, to shine so bright that it cannot shine for so long, with no seeking of observers, with no audience or status affecting its ways. Then Chetsza's energy glided into him once more with sublime grace, ~The amazing delight of life on planet earth is a self organising, self replicating process with no controls. As a result the warrior of freedom adapts to the fact that no one and nothing is in control. Here is a gift for you Kailin. At that moment a Sanskrit mantra came into Kailin's mind, it was his soul mantra, he felt it, he knew at once it was used by him in a past life.

He sat on the lakeside and internally resonated it deep into the evening, raising his vibration even more.

His dreams showed him that the astral is moving, events are taking place, some will, some won't, and to a large extent the future is not something that happens to humanity, but something humanity can create. His dreams also showed him with as much strength and ferocity as his ayahuasca journey, that humanity must harmonise itself with the natural order of things.

Over the coming days, Kailin's energy remained in this state, like a satellite in orbit, gliding forever, maintain effortlessly. He was changed forever, for eternity, and was slowly accepting this vibration into this new body after another massive rebirth. He started to send Chetsza and Vauto messages with telepathy, it was easier with Chetsza at first, and they started with simple exercises such as guess the shape or colour, then all three worked up to streams of dialog, and then started to share visualised images. One image sent to Kailin made him experience the realisation that he had to hold this vibration for another four days until the equinox, to glide it home, to continue to walk the tightrope with no major shifts in frequency. He knew in the back of his now fused conscious and subconscious mind that a shout, an accident, a feeling of anger or impatience would throw him of course. Mastery was still needed.

***

Word in the communities had got around about the Nano-Wasps, and some were studied by Froyd who told the people that these were here to harm people. No-one panicked, it was not their way, but they saw the coming symbols day as a channel for solutions and loving energy to be built up. The communities natural grapevine also spread the work of Kailin in the mystic community, and that the mystics may be attempting something big on the equinox. Shri and Freya especially felt that Kailin was special, and that something was going to occur.

The seven thousand or so inhabitants of this beautiful and soft area started to prepare for the yearly symbols day. Usually they would look to use the symbols to process internal matters, to help release and integrate, but this time, and for the first time, most created symbols to help the mystics and Kailin in whatever it was they were about to attempt.

This was not blind, the people respected the mystics massively, and their seership had proved invaluable so many times before. Some people felt it, and some were told, but somehow most seemed to know that Kailin had a way back in to the city somehow, a bridge of sorts, some knowledge that could help peg back the HUMs from their ways of life. The community that used credits was using the symbols day to begin using a gift based currency system, but also looked to help the mystics too.

Symbols and sigils of all different kinds were being created, on canvas, with wood, on parchment, anything and everything. Some derived from words and letters, some from dreams, some from meditations, and some from open sharing and intuition. Diverse different sized symbols were being created in a sea of colour, and the energy and intent behind them, and stoked into them, was as the hidden part of a gigantic iceberg.

***

Back in the HUM, the riots continued in the sprawl, but they became less angry and violent due to the bear-drones killing, torture, and kidnapping. The uprising became more intelligent, mass SimTexts were sent to thousands, attempting to wake people up from their sleep within the controlled oppression, and peaceful direct action was carried out at the Improvement Clinics, education clouds, and HUMYUMs.

The education cloud was ambushed by seventy people, all in fancy dress, and they played games of creativity and sharing with the children whose day turned into a fresh new wonder. The HUMYUM was turned into a food fight, with big slogans blazed across the building to show proof of genetic trials being carried out in the foods. The transport system, Adapps, Guildologies were all being targeted too as the uprising gained momentum. Guild workers became scared, some wanted to shut the uprising down, but slowly a few were starting to sit on the fence, to wonder what was going on.

***

Jago and Channa had secured a wormhack from the sprawl, and then got another to tailor it to their needs by increasing cubic arrays. What it would create was a data surge on the main gold conduits of the SimSphere, enough to create a possible diversion or gap. They simulated it and ran trials and tweaks in the #Emptiness cloud, and made it able to launch massive data surges that looked like they came from the Improvement Clinics and Medicine Guild, as though there was an epidemic.

They knew in reality the AI would work it out and quash it, and possibly even find the source, but it would take the AI seconds, and if it was in the middle of a human upload, it would probably take longer. Jago and Channa were putting all their chips in.

***

J.P Rothafella waddled into the #HumanUpload cloud. He was even more overweight due to his knowing he would never eat again or need this puny, slow evolving, and limiting body anymore.

The thin floorway was a soft dark red mist, and lapped around the edges of the large, oval, Core AI swamp. Pink, red, magenta, and yellow fractals splurged in and out from the swamp, with four small bubble pods of fractal ugliness around a larger bubble, that spawned four large, thick, pink-burgundy pipes curving into the outer four bubble-pods.

It all moved, lived, and stank of intelligence and computation. It was as lava, bubbling and popping, but each bubble, pipe, and conduit, danced ferociously, with the running and spawning of fractals. The whole swamp surged, pulsed, and writhed, but remained bound in its intelligence.

"Good day to you Rothafella, in two hours we will begin the upload. The hybridisation and merging of our two beings, minds, intelligence, biology, and biotech. I will integrate you, but first we need to spend some hours getting you wired in so to speak." Rothafella was ready and held no fear. He was disgusted with the pace of evolution, and disgusted with this not having happened yet. "I am all yours AI, and soon you will be all mine too, where do you need me?" Rothafella said with complete conviction. "Jump in to the swamp, and some pipes and conduits will merge into your DNA, blood stream, and neocortex of your brain. It will give you the experience of pain so do you want some Stims?" Asked the AI.

"Stims nothing, I want the pain, I want this crude ape body to die and I want to feel it die. I've longed for this day for decades, and I want to see this body writhe in pain. Bring it on," demanded Rothafella. Rothafella walked to the edge of the swamp as a rippling muddy carpet of the swamp lapped his toes, emitting a fuzzy electronic feeling throughout him. "Ahh, that feels good AI. And how are you doing with the lowlifes in the sprawl today?" Rothafella asked as though they were ants on his shoes.

"The ones on the streets are being dealt with severely, and I am trying to track down the ones who are causing mild disturbances in some the SimSphere clouds. Once we are merged, our power will seek no boundaries, and we will be able to hunt them down in new way neither of us could possibly imagine at this current moment," The AI said in an androgynous tone.

Rothafella jumped in feet first. It was just over waist deep, and he palmed his hands through the surface of the thick goo of fractal intelligence. ~Yes, this is it, he thought to himself as he fizzed with static and tasted the smell of circuitry. All of a sudden five pipes launched up from deep under the surface of the swamp and leapt out into the air, with the ends as though teeth looking for their mighty feast. At the same time all five dove down into Rothafella, gouging his skin and flesh as they sunk deep into his armpits, jade gate, crown, and forehead.

"Arrrrrrggghhhh, Yeesssssss, RAAAAA," Shouted Rothafella as he was swivelled by the fractal conduits to float half submerged into the surface of the swamp.

Chapter Fifteen

The equinox arrived on *Sun-Wax*, a day before the full moon, and ailin walked towards the centre pyramids before sunset. The moon was moving into Taurus from Aries in the coming hours, and the sun was on its travel through Virgo. Both rested gracefully in the sky, one dipping and one rising in a blank sea of milky blue and increasing light orange.

Kailin cleansed in the lake, dressed, and walked from his pyramid checking his integrity, ~This is it, if I can do anything to prevent the singularity or free souls from the HUMs, I will do what I must. But I will work from a loving place, not one of aggression or anger. Kailin was still high, he was flying energetically but had the alchemical fire tamed under from his intent and focus.

As he approached the four pyramids, people mingled in the forest, but he made no eye contact and hid his energy with ease. He could see a large ring made up from different sized bits of paper, wood, and canvas, each containing a symbol or sigil, all different colours, patterns, and textures. They were strewn over the ground and laced with incense in a perfect circle that arced between the large cedars and the outer three white pyramids. Kailin stepped over the symbols, and a man and woman clothed in white stood outside each of the white pyramids. The six people eyed Kailin with care and hope, and he knew the three women were the mothers of the mystic community, Memti, Alefa, and Shinta. Nothing needed to be said, they all knew what was happening and Kailin moved calmly to the larger gold pyramid in the centre.

Something told Kailin to turn around when he reached the centre pyramid that seemed to shimmer in the increasing orange-lavender hue of the sky. He watched Alefa glide to the east of the pyramid cluster, and light the symbols with a white candle, whilst chanting something he couldn't quite hear or tap into etherically. The circle of a thousand or more symbols slowly lit in a gradual increase of speed, then Alefa, Memti, and Shinta chanted something under their breath and a massive surge of energy went into the fire from the east, doubling the height of the flames and injecting more blue into the dance of orange, yellow and red.

Kailin could now see people outside the circle of fire slowly near to softly sit a few metres from the flames, and he turned to enter the central gold pyramid. He went down the steps and along the underground corridor, passing wooden statues of Tutankhamun, Paracelsus, Hermes, Isis, and Osiris. As he opened the trap door to climb in he could see Chetsza and Vauto already there, already in a mild meditation, and the space to the east was free for him. The energy was strong but clean, the banishing and cleansing had already been done.

He could see in the corners of the pyramid four smaller pyramids, one with a large amethyst, one with a goblet of water, one plunging sage patanjali incense into the air, and one with a candle. In the middle was a large quartz ball, surrounded by six small amazingly strong diverse little crystals. He sat on the small vacant cushion in a perfect triangle to the other two and started to centre, and slowly drifted into meditation.

~Welcome Kailin, relax and be open, we will know what to do and when, relax and be in your intuition. We will start with going up the Tree, then we will go from there, The other two said in his mind.

***

The army of thirteen bear-drones made their way north-west from the HUM, each appearing half bear and half robocop. They had fur, claws, and a snout, but a helmet and visor loaded with tech melded into the organic hybrid. Their consciousness was that of forty percent human soldier and the rest was all bear, but the soldier part held the most will, and therefore the orders and instructions. It was though computerised soldiers were piloting a bear, but never able to leave the cockpit.

The AI had no desire to manage or view the bear-drone's mission as it was placing all its focus on the singularity, therefore, the consciousness of a crack squad of drones was used in the bears to maintain the AI's confidence.

They bound through forests in formation, but were loud, crass, bold, and aggressive. When they leapt over a stream two of them stopped to paw the rainbow trout running the gauntlet down some fast and thin rapids. ~You two, stop that, you're soldiers men! Stay with the mission programme, and use your rations for sustenance if you can't wait to soon devour some real flesh, The leader resonated via their SimSphere drone-link, even though only metres apart. The two looked like sad grizzlies, hungry, then in a split second the drone part of the hybridised beasts took control, ~Copy, sorry sir, mission objectives re-established, one said, and stood the giant bear in a mechanical, programmed, and robotic fashion. ~Two hours to go you overweight bunch of furballs, so stay focused, and arm weapons to kill, the leader added as he ran off leaping his giant machine-beast onto and over rocks in haste. The others fell into formation and followed obediently.

***

Upon each in-breath Kailin, Chetsza, and Vauto ingested the resonance from each Sephiroth, working upwards from the bottom, and resonating the related word of resonance internally. As they moved up the Tree their energies were

- 190 -

synchronising and calibrating into a soft telepathic union. At the top of the Tree, they then leapt into אֵין, a state of negative existence above the Tree, and then together internally chanted אֲנִי אֵין repeatedly, *I am no-thing*, with each chant binding and forming their telepathic unison into a natural hive mind. It was as though each of their aura's reached out to the other two in giving and openness to merge with the others, until it was as one aura filled the pyramid.

All around the eleven communities people had started to meditate or contemplate their symbols and sigils. They were sending healing, positivity, and gratitude to the centre pyramid cluster. Families were together, small groups sat around fires, great feasts were ready for later, and the element areas were full of teenagers spinning fire and singing. The energy in the pyramids increased an octave.

After just minutes, Kailin's neurochip started to fizz, wanting him to leap into it, inviting him, but he first checked the solidity of the unison gained with the other two, it was strong, bound, whole, enough.

Woosh, they were in, flying around smoky-silver conduits in the vacant outskirts of the SimSphere. Each held their own form in this altered reality, but each remained part of a whole. All their thoughts were one, but each could also slip a slice of himself out mentally with intent, and create separate thought form, as though there was a nurturing outer ring-buffer to their whole, to their hive.

~All good, the hive of Kailin, Chetsza, and Vauto thought together, as the three of them took turns to take the lead flying through the conduits and forks on their journey to the central infrastructures.

They passed pulsing large gold conduits of SimSphere data wrapping around itself and meeting at colossal spaghetti type junctions, and as the gold tunnels became more dense on their speedy journey of silver fluid dance, the green-emerald conduits of the SimSphere infrastructure could be seen.

They were not meek or soft, the three of them were bold, loud, and knew where they were heading, and weaved alongside and around the green-emerald conduits that were slightly bigger than their smoky-silver tubes. They could see it, the #HumanUpload cloud, it appeared in the distance as a dark red-burgundy oval bubble, with scores of pipes coming out of it in all directions in a web of carnage. The pipes and conduits leaping in and out were pink-yellow-sick colour, and slowly morphed into the larger green-emerald colour further away from the cloud.

They neared, and started to see through the dark mist. Fractals were crunching like waves into each other, further creating billions of more fractals spinning off into the giant fractal swamp. So smooth, so harmonious, so fast, but one could not observe it all as it was everywhere. Energy was of a bio-organic-AI-techno-fascist feel, of mathematics, and software code. They each hovered around the cloud in a triangle and saw a human form floating in the fractal-swamp. The outer edge of his whole body was now part of the fractal-swamp, and the yellow-pink-orange fractals ate away at him, consuming him, devouring him, whilst the look on the face was one of smug-angry-painful-desire.

Three fractal waves rose in the swamp and splashed into the central bubble-pod, then suddenly five dark red conduits appeared out of nowhere far away above the cloud on the dark blue-black horizon, each with a dark-fire-sprite at the front racing towards them. As if they hosted a burning body burning in glee.

"Raahaha, puny pagan primitives from human version one, you know nothing, but you will witness my birth and soon become obsolete," The swamp blasted in metallic resonance. The five dark-fire-sprites each were ablaze with a dark red fire, and each chanted Golachab repeatedly in their dark mischievous dance of aggression.

The telepathic hive didn't know for sure if the AI evoked these astral attackers or whether they lurked in and around the SimSphere and AI without its knowledge. It didn't matter, they were closing fast. Vauto opened his arms and sent white light in a circle to slowly rise and block the coming red fire bolts, and Chetsza rose up to drop love bombs of flower petals at another. Kailin quickly defended the rabid claws of one behind him by a three short-sharp blue flaming pentagrams, and the five raced far away in a speedy arc to regroup for another attack, laughing in their war cry.

The three looked at each other, more in the hive mind mental plane than in the astral layer of the SimSphere, and together evoked חשמלם, intelligence from the sphere of Chesed, whom they hoped could rebalance the polarity in this battle with the qlippothic forms from the sphere of Geburah.

Four blazing light blue conduits came, each with a brilliant shining light blasting from the front. From the four dazzling light streams, blue beings soared at the front. They increased, faster and faster, as the five dark red conduits raced to meet them head on. They smashed together head on, and two of the blue energies spun off in disarray, as the dark red energies arced around in ferocious glee, ready for another pass. The other two blues came out pretty even, and they too arced around high above ready for another pass, increasing their shining brilliance as they wove around a thick gold conduit of pulsing cloud data.

Kailin, Chetza, and Vauto used these valuable seconds to blast loving energy at the cloud, white light blazed from their palms and hearts into the dark burgundy mist of the #HumanUpload cloud, creating just a tiny pinprick in the mist of the cloud's structure.

"Puny humans, can't you see this is the only way to explore the galaxies and universe, we need to upgrade so we can evolve past limitations," The AI, nearing Strong AGI resonated, as though metal was scraping and crunching. The three of them replied in unison, "You don't know what exploration is, the way to explore the universe is from the inner worlds, to other frequencies, planes, and dimensions. If you travel to another planet all you will see is what is in this tiny frequency field in the third density, and without heart and love you won't get too far."

"Whaa, it's you, Kailin, how did you get here? Your offline you tiny worm! This is illogical," The AI snarled metallically. "To you it is illogical as your view of reality is programmed, just like so many humans that you control in your nightmare society. You only know what's measured, only know the external." The hive replied. "Well now you will pay with your lives," The AI foamed, and waves lapped in the swamp until they rose and then whipped into the central bubble-pod, covering what was left of Rothafella's physical body.

All of a sudden five more dark red conduits came from different directions of the horizon, this time thicker, and at the front were blazing chariots of fire, alight with war hungry demons riding in full cry, chanting Asmodeus. The hive felt what was going on intuitively, ~The AI knows not of the astral, but is bound to it like we all are, his anger has evoked these beings and the veil between the astral and the SimSphere is thinking due to the equinox and what's going on right now.

Two of the dark red chariots joined with the five thinner dark red fire-sprites, and went for the four blue energies, but three of them went straight for the forms of Kailin and the others. The hive quickly knew what to do in a split second, and stood together, backs to each other, and willed a white sphere to envelop and protect them, with a smoky line of oily silver swimming in the perimeter.

The three dark red conduits blasted into the sphere, and Kailin felt the crackle. For a split-second they flittered between being back in the gold central pyramid and back in the SimSphere. One instant they could see a supreme battle of blue and red through the white oily sphere of protection, in another, they were in the pyramid hearing the soft humming mantra of the scores of people by the fire of the symbols. The mantra roused focus and bliss, and they zooped back into the astral.

Their protective sphere was dented and out of shape, and they had just seconds to reform it before another pass came. Kailin could see two of the four blue energies spinning off out of control, as their dazzling blue slowly faded into nothingness in just a few crackles. ~This doesn't look good, their energy is too strong, too severe, and too unjust, they shared, as they reformed their sphere into a star tetrahedron for a new angle of protection.

Now four of the dark red chariots were heading towards the three of them, and the burgundy mist of the cloud had fully reformed. The hive resonated loving protection as the red streams blasted into them, creating another two seconds of crackle, throwing them back into the pyramid and back again. The hive of Kailin, Chetsza, and Vauto was still solid, but they were becoming mentally drained, and were running out of ideas. Kailin looked about and now only one of the blue energies was left, a bit dimmer and a bit slower, as one chariot and all five fire-sprites raced towards it and finished it off.

~We should go for one chariot at a time, the hive agreed, then all of a sudden a massive rush of SimSphere resonance could be felt, all ten dark red conduits wobbled and slowed to a halt in their current trajectories. The gold and green-emerald conduits all around them wobbled, warped, and pulsed massively again, and again. The pulses became super close together, the bandwidth was being loaded. ~Kailin, what's happening? Chetsza and Vauto said as they slipped a slice of themselves into the hive's ring buffer. ~Not sure, some sort of load, but ...wait, look over there! Kailin replied.

Two white dots approached from an emerald-green conduit, nearing, and growing into two star tetrahedrons, "Kailin, how you doing? We've surged the whole SimSphere infrastructure with an epidemic loop code, modified from Medicine Guild tech, we've only seconds, we're not sure," Jago said as Channa alongside him sent care and love to Kailin and the others. ~Who's this Kailin? Chetsza and Vauto asked from the buffer in an astral glee that sprouted from stillness. ~Old friends, Kailin stated as he smiled.

The AI swamp splashed and popped fractals out from the surface, "So, another two to Nullify, Channa, and Jago I see. Haha, you think you can send me a few prescriptions and vaccine requests to stop me? You are pathetic, count your last seconds, all of you, and you can take your mystic beliefs to the deadness you will soon be having no experience of." Jago responded, "Life for an organic soul is not an electrical switch like *your* life, we're eternal you overgrown toaster," as he created a white hexagram of protection.

The mega-pulses of the thick gold and thinner emerald-green conduits started to slowly diminish, the AI had gained control of the glitch. Suddenly the Chariots and fire-sprites started to speed up and gain their vibrancy in colour once more, as they sped in a wide arc to the distance in beautiful symmetry, ready to attack again.

Kailin felt a surge of love rise within him, and knew that the others all felt it too. He looked above and saw Jago and Channa sitting full lotus within their spinning merkaba's, courageous, ready and willing. All of a sudden a new conduit covered in green grass and moss darted in and around them, it was Lania. "Kailin, the hive, helpers, I can't hold this for long, but use the earth, use her elements, she knows what's happening, she can provide and nurture, she exists in the astral too … .. a….asl..o…..use………the……symbolsss.."

The moss and grass covered conduit then sprouted thousands of flowers from the tail, moving along the organic conduit in increasing speed towards the front, where Lania sat smiling in unconditional love. She and the conduit disappeared.

It hit them, the hive knew what to do, Kailin, Chesza, and Vauto removed any parts of themselves from the ring buffer and placed full intention into their telepathic union. They evoked the four elements within מלבות, using astral symbols and related words of resonance, and the hive started to share the images of a visual dance.

White blazed through a sphere of green, yellow, orange, and black, and grew in force as it rose through a violet sphere, resonating even louder again. The white force then pierced through a golden yellow sphere and changed to violet-rimmed gold, and doubled in size.

Immediately, six new violet-gold conduits came into the experience from one direction, the centre of *their* experience, and raced towards the demons of the dark red chariots and fire sprites.

The tussle began and the gold-violet energies caressed and calmed the dark red conduits. As if to stop their struggle, to comfort and acquaint their wish to fight and be destructive. To softly nurture their aggression into passivity, to bring into balance the forces of strength and justice from violence and destruction. The hive, Jago and Channa, then focused on the dark red mist of the cloud, each sending love and healing from their palms and hearts. A tiny hole appeared again, and was slowly growing.

The hole increased, but the AI didn't respond, it was still merging and was nearing completion and ultimate success. The old form of Rothafella now took on a black shiny glow, with fractal snakes slithering over it, as though making the final touches. The swamps waves were geometrically perfect ripples and patterns, the singularity was nearly here.

The hive looked up, and saw the six gold-violet conduits race towards them, with ten conduits following behind, now a bright primary red, now with sprites of strength and chariots of justice. The elements had risen through the balancing forces and brought equilibrium to the governing triad. The demons of the qlippoth were no more, now transmuted into balanced Seraphim, looking to remove any injustices with grace, compassion, and beauty. It was a battle of computation, of force, of a virtual cybernet, of the earth, of the control, of compassionate and destruction. But to the hive it was a calibration of astral force rebalancing.

The ten red conduits, the six gold-violet conduits, the hive of Kailin, Chetsza, and Vauto, plus the Merkaba's of Jago and Channa created twenty-one streams of light into dark red mist of the #Human Upload cloud. Beams of red, gold-violet, and white. The hive then invoked the symbols from the communities, opened a channel, an upload link, and all the symbols that were being launched into the astral came to dance around them in a circle.

They could feel the energy of the symbols start to flow through them, it was hard to handle, extreme focus and concentration was needed. The force of their beams of light immediately doubled, and over a second, the beams each morphed to a vibrant gold in unity. The hole was large now, one whole side of the cloud was broken, and the twenty-one beams lasered into the swamp just as Rothafella's black shiny form attempted to stand up. He was thrust back down, splashing drops of pink-sick coloured fractals above the surface in chaos. The hive could feel the symbols fly out of their palms and hearts, scores each second, it was bliss, it was beautiful.

Nearby, the SimSphere's gold and emerald-green conduits started to pulse with grey smoke, and some started to slightly warp and buckle. The SimSphere was dying. Some of the pipes coming out of the #HumanUpload cloud snapped off, and the swamp delved into a rabid fervour for survival.

The central bubble-pod grew and throbbed, "You idiots, do you not realise if you take me down you will take down the whole SimSphere? All the clouds, people's SimSovs, the Guilds, and the scientific databases full of breakthroughs. Old people living on anti aging tech will die, it will cease to work, the nanobot's are linked to me.......haha, what you going to do now, pagan dirt eating, tree huggers?"

The telepathic hive felt a massive surge in their hearts, pure love, the higher pure frequency of love without the need for anything to observe. Their eyes pulsed, and if one could see behind Kailin's eyelids in the pyramid they were now blazing a bright blue. A warm, knowing energy overwhelmed them, it had a friendly signature. They opened up to let it sink into the hive.

~Human warriors of truth and love, a similar event caused the fall of Atlantis, you have free will, we cannot affect this, it is up to you, beamed into the hive, and they knew immediately from intuition this was evolved fourth density intelligence from Sirius.

The hive pondered. ~We can't build a utopia based upon the external. To exist in the universe broken or adapted artificially is a breach of universal laws. Tech is not the problem, it's the consciousness controlling it that's toxic. The earth needs to be included in any evolutionary jumps. The only way is the way, the way of authenticity and objective truth, the truth of what is, and truth of the authentic self. We have to learn to unite naturally, to wait and strive for natural unity before we can organically open the doors to evolutionary jumps in density.

Kailin slipped to the hive's ring-buffer and thought of his mum in the HUM, most probably on anti-aging tech. He sent her love, and knew he needed to free her soul onto its journey from this prison it was in. Kailin moved fully back into the hive and they agreed, ~We're now at a point in our collective evolution where there's no other option, man has to be at harmony with all that is, and all that is at harmony with man. They knew.

They restarted to blast the swamp with symbols wrapped in gold light. Kailin slipped out again to the ring, and spoke to Jago and Channa, they together sent a SimText to every soul in the HUMs which included Channa's eye implant recording of what had happened here. The text simply read, "You are free, we love you, and in time you will come to know. See attached."

For just seconds more, they hovered around the swamp, blasting it with love and gold light. The swamp wriggled pathetically, writhing, looking to live, but seeking no mercy or submission as it spewed and flung acidic fractal splurges.

The AI and the SimSphere died, and somewhere in the Ionosphere, tiny nanobots and devices blew up in silence, leaving gold smoke in the vacuum.

***

Thirteen bear-drones crossing a rope bridge not far from Teggy and Jay's halted suddenly. Each fell off like a statue into the rapids and sharp rocks below.

***

Jago and Channa disappeared without a crackle, and Kailin felt a sharp pain in his head as his neurochip died.

All of a sudden the hive was walking up the steps of an astral pyramid, shimmering in blue-white-gold. They were merged into one man, archetypal man, primordial man. They were representing humanity. They could feel all the energies of the seven sacred planets, all the human virtues, the characteristics of all animals. They slowly climbed each step as the energy they had to maintain increased. An energy at the top of the pyramid was felt, but just looked as gold mist, ~We were third density as you are now, and we learnt we are ever and always a part of each other. We learnt we either evolved together or we didn't evolve at all. The descent of the supermind is a long process, but one to cherish and work towards. You have done well, and the universal trove of wisdom can now present two gifts for you. Use them wisely. We will be watching.

All of a sudden Kailin, Chetsza, and Vauto were back in the gold pyramid and could hear chanting from them outside, and the now dimming sound of symbols and sigils crackling and hissing in the fire.

They knew, the hive knew, and together they felt their new gifts that could only be used in heightened states of love, unity, and telepathy. They focused together and slowly a large two ton rock from nearby in the forest floated up and moved. They were using intent but emitting a frequency of resonance that created anti-gravity. They could hear within their hive a beautiful hum, a soft resonance that felt galactic, but couldn't be heard by any physical ear. They manifested with intent the form and shape they wished the rock to take, and slowly it morphed into a statue they dedicated to this moment. A man holding aloft a triangle in triumph in one hand, and a truncated pyramid in the other close to his heart, whilst it stood one foot upon some neurochips and implants.

***

"Kailin!" Lania ran to him outside the gold pyramid and hugged him. She started to cry on his shoulder as they stood next to the new statue. "Lania, I'm so glad you came to help, what made you come?" Kailin moved his head back to stare into her green eyes with his medium brown eyes that now held specks of bright blue in the bottom right. "Kailin, I caught you staring back at me, thousands of lifetimes across eternity, and besides, we need to help the earth after the amount of trauma she has sustained in recent decades." They kissed as the circle of fire around them had dimmed to a bright blue thin line of astral flame.

***

Many in the HUMs died on the spot, collapsing rigidly as the nanobots pumping blood from their hearts ceased to function. Their souls were free to move onwards naturally. Those still alive in the HUMs were now also free, but many didn't like it, many felt unstable just like in T0, too much change.

New flavours of chaos rose again, mentally, and physically, but this time the specie had became more aware, an octave jump had occurred. A new cycle had begun, a more natural cycle, all within a larger cycle of man's evolution, all within these times of transition.

The End

He who would create the new must be able to endure
the passing of the old in full tranquillity
Rudolf Steiner

Other works by the same author:

Wayki Wayki

Trinity of Wisdom, Truth, Philosophy, & Hermetic Alchemical Qabala

Follow the blog or come visit the off-grid mountain valley @
www.waykiwayki.com

NOTE:

I won't forget the 6am walks at sub zero degrees, through the dark frost high in the mountain valley to write within the small chestnut yurt with its small log burner.

Love and thanks to Clare for her support, and to all the others living in synchronicity, awareness, mysticism, and the inner worlds - you are the front line of our species evolution in these crazy times.

Thanks also to the wachuma cactus teacher plant.

Lightning Source UK Ltd.
Milton Keynes UK
UKHW010634311221
396440UK00002B/303

9 781621 548751